Beyond the Turnstile

BEYOND THE TURNSTILE
Making the Case for Museums and Sustainable Values

SELMA HOLO
& MARI-TERE ÁLVAREZ

P R E S S

A division of
ROWMAN & LITTLEFIELD PUBLISHERS, INC.
Lanham • New York • Toronto • Plymouth, UK

museo universitario
arte contemporáneo

Published by AltaMira Press
A division of Rowman & Littlefield Publishers, Inc.
A wholly owned subsidary of The Rowman & Littlefield Publishing Group, Inc.
4501 Forbes Boulevard, Suite 200, Lanham, Maryland 20706
http://www.altamirapress.com

Estover Road, Plymouth PL6 7PY, United Kingdom

British Library Cataloguing in Publication Information Available

Library of Congress Cataloging-in-Publication Data

Holo, Selma.
    Beyond the turnstile : making the case for museums and sustainable values / Selma Holo and Mari-Tere Álvarez.
       p. cm.
    Includes bibliographical references and index.
    ISBN 978-0-7591-1221-6 (cloth : alk. paper) —
    ISBN 978-0-7591-1915-4 (electronic : alk. paper)
    1. Museums—Social aspects. 2. Social values. 3. Sustainability. 4. Success. 5. Museums—Management. I. Álvarez, Mari-Tere. II. Title.
AM7.H64 2009
069—dc22
                                                 2009017077

Printed in the United States of America

Table of Contents

Preface

THE INTERNATIONAL MUSEUM INSTITUTE: ORIGIN AND CAUSE

Joseph E. Aoun

 In my ongoing conversations with Dr. Selma Holo, director of the University of Southern California's (USC's) Fisher Museum of Art and for twenty-five years the director of its renowned graduate program in museum studies, we often touched on how the civic role of museums is continually being questioned and reevaluated—as much by the profession itself as by its funders and its increasingly wide range of supporters and critics. It is this constant, shifting inquiry into the value and success of the museum that has given the institution of the museum its historical dynamism and, frankly, forced its relatively recent evolution from mausoleum to lively site for a vast array of cultural experiences.

Over a century ago a critical mass of museums came into existence explicitly dedicated to educating the local citizenry while also instilling and affirming national pride through an accumulation of art and artifacts. Now the contemporary climate brings more complex audience needs to the task of museums. These needs stem from an inevitably more globalized consciousness among consumers and producers of the arts and sciences, along with the persistence of vociferous demands related to issues of local identity. They also emerge from a growing insecurity about financial support, from competition in the cultural spheres, and from a myriad of other challenges ranging, for example, from threats to the public trust, the questioning of the nature of an authentic experience in a museum, and the expectation of relevance to the communities a museum serves.

Challenges and, indeed, opportunities abound. Selma Holo and I wondered together about today's recurring questions, about how attempting to address them might uncover the possibilities and uncertainties that museums all over the world are facing, and how facing those questions head-on in small influential groups might yield some creative answers about how museums might best face the future. We decided to create the International Museum Institute, known as the IMI, to be a think tank specifically dedicated to discussing those challenges and opportunities.

This book, *Beyond the Turnstile: Making the Case for Museums and Sustainable Values,* is the product of the first series of workshops that USC and IMI engaged in with its founding partner, the National Autonomous University of Mexico (UNAM). Mexico was invited to be the Institute's first international partner because it is our closest friend and neighbor in California. It is a country that brings its own distinct, extremely rich, and lengthy museum history to the conversation. Furthermore, as in the United States, Mexican museums find themselves in the process of deeply questioning their institutions' obligations within their own shifting cultural, economic, and political landscapes.

Professor Holo's counterpart, Graciela de la Torre, director general of visual arts of UNAM and director of the University Museum of Art (MUAC), UNAM's recently inaugurated, ambitious contemporary art museum, assumed the role of Mexico's IMI representative and led her country's participation in the Institute partnership. Conceived of as a series of dialogic encounters, the Institute focuses on a specific objective over a given period that has been chosen by the advisory groups to the Institute. The leadership and participation of Graciela de la Torre was central to the success of the first project—to the continuity of the workshops and to the preparation of this book. She mobilized not just UNAM and garnered its institutional backing, but she also encouraged the engagement of the larger academic and museum community of Mexico City. Hence the generous involvement on the IMI advisory committee by Miguel Fernández Félix, director of the National Museum of Art (MUNAL), the national painting museum; Ramiro Martínez, then the director of the Tamayo Museum; and Marco Barerra Bassols, former director of the National Museum of Natural History and now one of the most innovative museum consultants in Mexico. The IMI advisory committee also received the ongoing support of Gerardo Estrada, at that time coordinator for cultural diffusion for UNAM, and before that, director of the National Institute of Fine Arts (INBA).

The established objective of the first partnership with UNAM was the development of a kind of handbook and guide to the perplexed. The goal was to propose a set of sustainable values that any museum could adopt (or adapt) as they deemed appropriate. Those values would allow for a qualitative evaluation of museum success. The handbook, *Beyond the Turnstile: Making the Case for Museums and Sustainable Values,* is meant to propose a framework of values that allows museums to reframe their concepts of success and to travel beyond the repetition of the standard profit-driven statistics surrounding attendance, gift shop sales, and restaurant revenues. This book represents a synthesis of ideas born in our think tank and is enhanced by a range of international writers stimulated by the dialogue originated in the United States and Mexico at USC and at UNAM.

I am proud to have been able to launch this Institute and to see this book published. I know that it will have an influence on the future thinking by and about museums.

Joseph E. Aoun, who received his doctorate in linguistics from Massachusetts Institute of Technology, and is an internationally known scholar. He is the seventh president of Northeastern University. Dr. Aoun holds the Chevalier de l'Ordre des Palmes Academiques from the French government and the degree of Doctor of Humane Letters, *honoris causa*, from Hebrew Union College, Jewish Institute of Religion.

Introduction

A CRISIS IS A TERRIBLE THING TO WASTE

Selma Holo

 By the turn of the twenty-first century, it seemed that most of us had learned our financial management lessons well. These were lessons that we had no choice but to learn as our institutional needs and responsibilities became more complex and our funding less predictable. And by "we," I mean all of us: museum directors and administrators, curators, boards of trustees, ministries and heads of culture internationally, our private and public funding sources, and our associations of museums and museum professionals. Directors of museums large and small, most coming with academic training in their museum's discipline, worked hard both to plan and balance budgets. We attended and led seminars promoting entrepreneurship, producing ever-more-popular exhibitions, more extensive museum restaurants and amenities, more seductive shops, and, of course, those glamorous (expensive) expansions. With the encouragement and guidance of supporters and critics, we entertained and attempted to educate masses of people, exchanged art and staff, and swapped cultural and natural materials with institutions all over the world, all the while dutifully counting every head and every coin generated by these activities.

The long trend has been toward acceptance of the business model: boards of trustees in the United States began demanding sharpened financial skills in the directors they hired; ministries of culture and government heads of culture in Latin America, Europe, and Asia began to encourage some private and creative fundraising. A few museums recruited university administrators as their chief executive officers. The oversight was supposed to be rigorous. At the same time, the calls for inclusivity, access, and relevance (the societal demands emerging from the late 1960s and 1970s); for spectacle and for dynamic, changing programming did come with big price tags: those concepts were translated to mean an unrelenting need for growth—more space, community-based collections, lots of public events, and of course a constant schedule of razzle-dazzle temporary exhibitions.

Certainly the trend toward business-based values may have solved some short-term fiscal problems, but in many cases the traditional values of the museums that bought entirely into this model were being threatened—for the foreseeable long term. There was an evolving contradiction in terms.

By the 1980s and 1990s, ambitious new museums or expansions of old museums, exhausting and expensive temporary exhibition schedules, as well as passionate collecting programs, were proliferating throughout Europe, the United States, Latin America, and parts of Asia. By 2000 the museum mania had spread to China. Given the cycles of prosperity and recession that also accompanied the period, it became apparent that the leadership did need to have some practical management training or experience beyond their academic preparation. This was not illusory. More than a few museums suffered from fiscal irresponsibility and lack of accountability in the fulfillment of their ambitions, and their distress further fueled the demand for transparency, for strategic planning skills, for financial planning skills, and for fundraising ability in the directors of museums. An industry developed to provide museums with the professionals they needed to help them manage themselves responsibly.

Museum studies programs worked to prepare graduate students for the practical side of the museum careers they were pursuing; museum management seminars inculcated the business model into mid-career professionals internationally; an elite program was created in the United States in 2008 specifically for curators who desired to learn the practical business skills now required of directors; and advanced, elite museum summer workshops were held in glamorous international locations for directors who sought to be steeped in the realities of management and the latest theories and practices of leadership.

The sum of this training and subsequent experience of incorporating business practice into the leadership of the institution of the museum was the stunning awareness that if museums did not want to be taken over for the long term by corporate managers or university administrators, they needed to gain management and leadership skills for themselves. The extremely positive result of all of this was that a critical mass of academically trained museum people did gain the ability and the authority to shape their museums by building and maintaining them with a scaffolding of business credibility, while maintaining a core structure of sustainable values. The profession now accepts that business skills are an integral part of running our museums. But it is time now to make the case for the primacy of those museum values, the sustainable values, for which business skills should only be the handmaidens.

Those fundamental business lessons and attendant values that were acquired beginning in the late 1970s are, for the most part, now an inextricable part of the basic literacy of the museum world. They should, can, and are being taught to aspiring museum professionals. Even curators now need to be able to show that they can prepare and adhere to a budget and that they will, if necessary, participate in the fundraising to enable a project of their own. Board members need to be aware of their fiduciary responsibilities and a public demand for transparency. In short, these are the lessons for which the case has been already made. It is time now to move forward, deeper into the twenty-first century and to recognize that museums need, first and foremost, to represent unique and sustainable values. It is the moment to clearly identify those values and to make the case that it is only in fulfilling those values that museums can articulate and claim their indispensability to society and to its continuing betterment. That is the purpose of this book.

Those who did not heed the call to be fiscally alert and responsible, who did not pay attention to those business lessons, inevitably faced financial crises—some sooner, some later, some bigger, some smaller. By 2008 an international financial crisis burst everyone's balloon. But surely those who had led and managed in a more financially sound manner and had lived within their institution's means, raising and responsibly shepherding funds and budgets, suffered less drastic consequences than those who didn't. The financial crisis, it should be stressed, was not due to the fact that principles of sound business practice were flawed. But, rather it was because the world of international finance did not follow those practices themselves.

So, if a crisis is a terrible thing to waste, the first thing we need to do is to relearn the lessons of sound business practice, just as the rest of the world needs to do. That being said, we are left with a nagging sense that this is an opportunity to rethink what museums are about. In *Beyond the Turnstile: Making the Case for Museums and Sustainable Values,* we have gathered together the reflections of forty writers in an attempt to address the questions nagging those of us who are in leadership positions in our museums now or who aspire to be in the future. We know that once we have actually relearned our business lessons (for those of us who forgot them in the frenzy to grow and entertain), we have the opportunity to ask, "Is that all there is?" Need museums once again allow themselves to be vulnerable to every numerically driven inquiry (threat) from every corner of the funding world? Must museum leaders meekly agree to be measured exclusively by the questions "How many?" and "How much?"

We believe that the answer is unequivocally, "No." The purpose of this handbook is to lay out another set of values that can provide indicators of our success. These values, more subjective, but still measurable in nonquantitative ways, will enable a clearer articulation of the unique purposes of museums and why they are so important in our society the world over. These "other" criteria are, we believe, sustainable ones that will help us to advance the conversation about how to measure our successes and how to improve on our weaknesses. Because measure we must. We argue that while museums must, of course, remain accountable for their finances and their figures, they are special and unique societal institutions—in ways that are often venerable and sometimes new. We have to make the case for these values, to identify them as existing "beyond the turnstile," and then we have to find the words to fight for them.

We can no longer take for granted that there is an unchanging and unchallenged agreement about the indispensability of museums today. Thus we need to uncover, clarify, articulate, disclose, and be able to prove the indispensability that we contend characterizes all worthy museums. It is our job to demonstrate how museums contribute to the well being of their communities. *Beyond the Turnstile: Making the Case for Museums and Sustainable Values* proposes that we can aggressively defend what is intrinsic to the success of our own museums in their spheres of influence. By definition, that means that we must also be able to identify our failings. *Beyond the Turnstile* will help us to communicate why the many publics we serve are enriched by being engaged with the cultural, historical, scientific, and natural heritages, which our museums make available to them in uniquely authentic ways.

We need to be open to new ways of engaging the world we serve in what we do—embracing its citizens whether by means of technology or traditionally. We should be able to convince our essential stakeholders that without museums, our shared world would be less interesting, less illuminating, less serious, less joyful, less connected to humanity, less equipped to understand and innovatively cope with the present and survive the future.

Beyond the Turnstile is meant to allow all of us the intellectual room to explain *in our own ways* our *particular museum's* successes with respect to the values we have established as intrinsic to all museums. To find that space in our institutions, we as leaders must be willing to explore methods of evaluation beyond metrics—methods that will require a harmonious blend of integrity, flexibility, and dynamic engagement with our staff, our profession, our patrons, and our publics.

We believe that we can better articulate the case for sustainable values by reminding ourselves that we have spent a lot of time chasing and being bolstered by the unsustainable. To become a museum that is sustainable, leaders on all sides of the conversation will be required to be more transparent, more inclusive, and less protectionist about their operations and policies than we have been in the past. With our heretofore much-guarded opacity in mind, this handbook offers a set of ten values by which we might propose to judge ourselves and actually ask to be judged as we make the case for our museums' performance.

The set of sustainable values and their accompanying essays will prove to be a resource to any museum charged with demonstrating its value to society and to justify continuing support for its survival and prosperity. Unlike other attempts to develop an "alternate metrics," this alternative set of metrics is not limited to one kind of museum. It has been designed to apply to a broad swathe of museums: to art museums, history museums, gardens, archaeology site museums, science museums, and natural history museums. Because we all know by now that knowledge, whether it is in a university or a museum, cannot exist in a silo, we assume that there will be more and more communication among museums and across traditional boundaries. Art is commissioned for gardens; gardens are built as a part of art museums; science and art museums share programs, as do natural history museums and art museums; history museums incorporate techniques developed for the theater. And so on. Beyond the breaking of a strict typology of knowledge and its presentation, this *set of sustainable values* applies to museums of all sizes, with all types of governance. But be forewarned: the values that we propose both recognize and accept that we live in a time that takes no institution's survival for granted simply "because it exists." The reality is that in each museum's self-examination it will be found that there is need for improvement; that creative thinking about the future is required; that new alliances need to be forged in order to survive. Indeed, there is no assumption of indispensability in this book!

The set of sustainable values has also been shaped so as to be applicable to museums in an international context. We have learned in our IMI workshops that museums in all countries share many but not all of the same ideals. Nor do they necessarily share the same solutions or sometimes even the same problems. There are different assumptions of funding, for example, in Latin America than in the United States or in China. Former colonizing countries have different attitudes that they may wish to overcome through display and programming than those countries that were once colonies. Justice can mean apparently incompatible things for a country reclaiming a work of art and for one refusing to relinquish what it considers to be a crucial bit of its own history and patrimony. The purpose of museums can also shift from the notion of an art museum contributing to the creation of a more educated citizenry to a desire to promote "art for art's sake." Nevertheless, the values we have developed will be useful, to one degree or another, for museums everywhere—even if the way these values are dealt with will differ from museum to museum, country to country, region to region. The purpose of the essays included in each chapter is to make clear that we can deal with a new indicator in many ways. But deal we must if we are to prove our worth to those who support our existence. Museums and their collections are under threat in many places, whether because of economic crisis, war, lack of interest, or simply decreasing attention spans. We hope to address these threats and their challenges and the opportunities in *Beyond the Turnstile*.

Our set of sustainable values is neither a set of commandments nor is it definitive. Rather, it is a beginning point for a different conversation among museum professionals and their boards, ministries, and funders of all stripes. Reading it will encourage thoughtful arguments for support at a time of new cultural and economic challenges. The provocative and diverse essays that follow each of our ten values are intentionally varied in their perspectives in order to urge an open-ended and multifaceted conversation. This is a handbook that is actually meant to be a spur to thought, and ultimately to action. *Beyond the Turnstile: Making the Case for Museums and Sustainable Values* offers another point from which to begin our articulation and analysis of the success of our own museum's mission and achievements. By taking control of the conversation, we will be better able to contribute to the health of our own museums and, in the end, to the museum field in general.

THE SET OF SUSTAINABLE VALUES

Public Trust

A *public trust* refers to an entity intended for the benefit of the public, not for the benefit of a person or group of individuals. In this chapter we also look to establish the other side of public trust—that is, public trust as the principal sustainable value that the public invests in its museums.

The Primacy of Our Collections

In this chapter we have gathered together a number of perspectives on how we can protect and enliven the value of our collections. We explore ways to enhance the attraction of the permanent collections in the eyes of a public often inured to them due to a steady diet of sometimes-spectacular temporary exhibitions.

Relevance

A museum must be able to locate its relevance to its own constituencies. In this chapter relevance is understood as a dedication to making clear that a museum has meaning and value to its visitors and its various communities.

Inclusion

In this day and age our museums must be demonstrably welcoming. They must also be intellectually open. In this chapter the writers examine how we can articulate that value in the context of a democratic society, and, in one case, even question the limits of inclusion.

Globalization

Whether we choose to embrace globalization or not, we have to be able to show that we are aware of its effect upon our museums—and to claim our niche. The writers in this chapter suggest ways in which they have dealt with the various ideals and consequences of globalization.

Creativity

No museum can claim a future if it does not foster creativity. Creativity can be claimed for a museum in many ways: in its mission, in its relation to creative minds, in its fundraising, and in its education programming. Each museum must be able to make the case for how it encourages a respect for creativity and innovation.

New Alliances

As with creativity, museums have no choice but to forge alliances. Whether for collecting, interpreting, or preserving the legacies for which we are responsible, making and nurturing alliances has become essential for our museums' well being.

Authentic Experience

We need to prove that the experiences we offer cannot be replaced by a theme park, book, or trip to the shopping mall. Whether we are a zoo, a garden, a natural history museum, whether our objects or specimens are alive or inorganic, we must offer a unique approach to understanding the world.

Generating and Disseminating Knowledge

The knowledge we generate, whether it is related to aesthetics, science, history, or music, is a knowledge that comes from tangible experience. We generate that knowledge in our laboratories and our offices, and we disseminate it in a myriad of ways. At the same time, we need to claim our role as participants in the education not only of individuals, but of society as well.

Communication

In this chapter, our writers remind us that no matter what our achievements within our museums may be, the failure to communicate them is something we can ill afford. Communication is necessary in all aspects of museum life—to the external world and, internally, in every aspect of our operations.

This book is meant to be the beginning of a conversation. We believe the opinions and lessons contained in its pages will help all of us consider how we analyze our policies and how we can become more effective professionals. But we cannot approach it in isolation. Directors of museums, boards and ministers and policy makers, individual patrons, nongovernmental organizations, and foundation heads should be reading it as well, so that the complete constellation of stakeholders can together set new, realistic, and defensible indicators by which to measure success and make the case for our museums.

Beyond the Turnstile: Making the Case for Museums and Sustainable Values is driven by our belief that museums, like libraries and great universities, are essential to society, and that society must promote and nourish them if it is to remain civil, open, and creative in the face of the growing forces of incivility, intolerance, and homogenization that threaten our world today. But society will only nurture its museums if it is clear that they, in turn, are nurturing society. We need to be willing to make and prove the case.

Selma Holo is director of the International Museum Institute. Holo is also director of the Fisher Museum of Art and professor of art history at the University of Southern California. She has curated numerous exhibitions, especially on Spanish and Latin American art, and is author of books on museums in society, most notably *Beyond the Prado: Museums and Identity in Democratic Spain* and *Oaxaca at the Crossroads: Managing Memory, Negotiating Change.*

CHAPTER 1

Public Trust

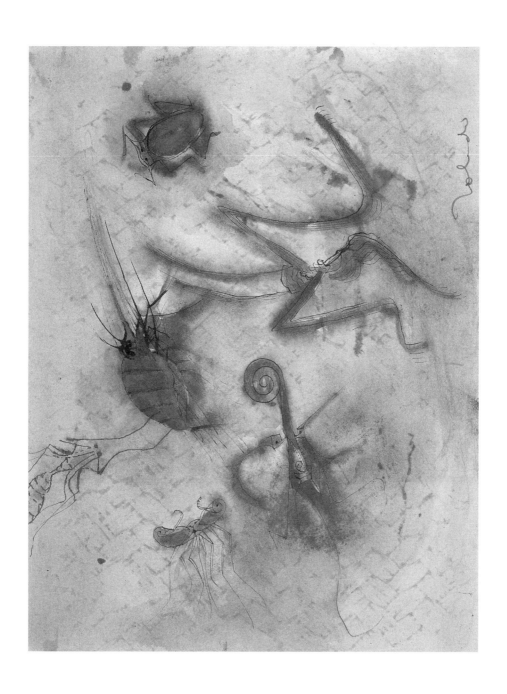

PUBLIC TRUST flows in two directions. Museums exist to serve the public, whether or not they are legally or formally organized as a public trust. At the same time, the public places trust in museums. That trust is profoundly connected, most obviously, to museum collections, but it goes well beyond the expectations of the development, care, and sharing of those collections. Indeed, there has also long been an expectation by the public that museums of all kinds and sizes, whether or not they maintain collections, could be trusted for the integrity of the information and knowledge they disseminate, in matters of authenticity, in the expectations of legal and ethical behaviors, as well as for the propriety of their administrative and financial operations. In this chapter, we ask all museums to assertively make the case that, as institutions founded on the value of the public trust (formal or implied), they deserve the continued trust placed in them.

As recently as a decade ago, this expectation was a given in the United States. Public questioning about either the nature of museum collections or the probity of the information for which they were responsible was rare indeed. An article by Carol Enseld published by the American Association of Museums *NEWStandard* pointed out that when the American Association of Museums released the results of its 2001 survey, it announced that "a vast majority of Americans (87%) view museums as one of the most trustworthy sources of objective information" (summer 2006, pp. 1–2). By 2006, Enseld noted, things had changed. She wrote in that same article that "in the wake of highly publicized corporate, government, and nonprofit scandals, museums today must contend with a broad erosion of public trust. Increasingly, we find ourselves operating in an environment of heightened public scrutiny." This issue was not exclusive to the United States, but also was raised in Germany, Liechtenstein, Norway, Spain, Mexico, France, Korea, Egypt, and China. And, in 2009, one cannot write that the situation has improved markedly. While it is the rare exception when a museum truly dishonors the trust that the public holds in it, it is that very exception that attracts attention, makes the public wary, and undermines its willingness to wholeheartedly support us. It is in the interests of every museum to do its part to rectify this situation. Each museum must, therefore, make the case that it is aware of its responsibilities to the public so that it can proudly, systematically, and transparently claim, or begin to re-earn, the enthusiastic faith of the public in it as a model institution.

We must be willing to be specific. Whether with reference to inflated administrative salaries or expense accounts, illegal or unethical acquisitions of objects or specimens for museums, overly cozy relationships with dealers and the market, conflicts of interest, broken promises, lack of fiduciary responsibility, or inadequate sharing and caring for the objects in our collections, all of us who are in some way involved in the leadership of our museums will need to take stronger and more active roles to demonstrate our awareness of our compact with the public as we steer our institutions through the shoals of the twenty-first century.

Maxwell Anderson's essay places the burden on all of us in such positions to assess the obligations we have to the public as we face pressures to accommodate unforeseen political pressures. We would add that, inevitably, economic stresses are waiting in the wings to test and tempt us to consider loosening our ethical standards to meet financial needs. Writing with an international perspective, Anderson charges all of us to strive to reach our own individual museum's balance between the demands of any given moment in history for an "instrumental" museum practice that might further the demands of a particular political agenda and the core missions of our museum to collect, preserve, and interpret the items in our collections. An early advocate for the use of "other" evaluative metrics, Anderson argues for the imperative of being able to demonstrate our integrity by developing criteria founded on quality of experience rather than only on the raw numbers of people who experience our museums.

Gerardo Estrada Rodríguez, former head of the National Institute of Fine Arts in Mexico, reminds us that the public trusts its museums to avoid identifying with any prevailing ideology so strongly that we would close off the public's ability to openly engage with the objects for which we are responsible. He reminds us, for example, of the extreme intrusion of politics into culture during the Nazi regime in Germany, when museums and museum specialists bent to the will of the state and distorted the meaning and significance of the items in their care. Of course, none of us can be totally free of the constraints of our own time, but we have an obligation, according to Estrada Rodríguez, to try to be aware of the pressures upon us and to resist them when appropriate.

Some of the strongest language about the public trust comes to us from Europe, where Plácido Arango is board president of the Prado Museum, Madrid. He reflects on what his museum owes society as the board stewards the legacy of its superlative paintings collection toward the future: preservation of that collection, transparent and prudent financial management, and the greatest possible public access. Finally, Arango raises the less-oft-noted question of what the public owes to the Prado in return: the highest possible service from representatives of not one but several government ministries or civic groups, including learned societies, artists, collectors, and businessmen—even the press. This essay pushes toward very specific criteria, besides metrics, in evaluating any museum's success. Arango's essay constitutes a reminder that these criteria can and should be enunciated, and by naming them, they can be achieved.

Leonard Krishtalka is optimistic about how we can revive the public's trust in his description of what natural history museums in particular can offer by way of new and renewed possibilities for fulfilling the public trust. In a world threatened by climate change and environmental catastrophe, Krishtalka argues that natural history museums can be the "sentinel observatories of life on Earth." Natural history museums are also the repositories of the DNA of extinct species, and one suspects that the quiet research that has long gone on behind the scenes will come to the forefront as the science of genetics advances—that these museum scientists will be able to locate their own work so as to be ever more central in advancing the public good. Krishtalka thus challenges natural history museums to make the case for their special brand of enduring value to society.

During the last decade, museums have been faced with a growing number of questions involving natural heritage, intangible heritage, living practices, and—more broadly defined—the larger cultural heritage and patrimony that a museum might be representing. Because these questions have come to the fore, mostly around questions of identity, but also around "ownership" or "stewardship," they are now becoming key tests of the public trust. In his essay, Elazar Barkan advances the conversation with respect to museums beyond the now-normative legal and ethical issues about objects to introduce the concept of "cultural justice" as an aspect of the public trust. With that in mind Barkan writes about "cultural offense," a phenomenon that he believes we will no doubt see more of in the future. Cultural justice is an evolving ideal and something that Barkan asks us to consider as we struggle with the ever-more-fluid and possibly inflammatory questions of freedom of expression, of borders, and of boundaries.

The essays in this chapter therefore posit a number of possible approaches to the characterization of our museums with respect to the public trust. As distinct as the essays are in their positions, they are unified in their arguments that museums need to reexamine, reevaluate, and rearticulate their positions with respect to their relationships with the public and the trust we are meant to embody.

MUSEUM VALUES

Maxwell L. Anderson

 Museums as we know them began in the late nineteenth century. Before then, collections of art, artifacts, and scientific and natural phenomena had taken many forms. These included *Wunderkammern* for keepsakes acquired on the Grand Tour through Europe and treasure houses, such as Mexico City's Castillo de Chapultepec, for royalty and nobility to display the fruits of conquest and evidence of erudition and taste. By the 1870s public collections began to be assembled in the United States to ennoble the masses through learning about society's shared natural, historic, and cultural heritage. Beginning in the 1970s, a series of progressive societal pressures combined to awaken museum leaders to the fact that collecting and displaying our collective heritage was a necessary but insufficient mandate. There have followed a succession of approaches to the highly flexible mission of museums, from an educational thrust to service as community centers to, more recently, the emulation of commercial attractions.

At their heart, museums should be separate from other parts of society in one respect: they must be first and foremost a place to provide perspective that may be lost in other contexts. Safeguarding the material evidence of the past and present is no longer an adequate mission, since demands continue to mount for museums to remain vital in a complex, fast-paced, interconnected world. New collections continue to be formed in both public and private contexts. For-profit destinations increasingly imitate the attributes of museums to polish their image. Rapid growth in the number and size of museums over the last decade has challenged the ability of cultural leaders to keep up with the rising fixed costs of operating public institutions—ranging from energy to security to insurance. These expenses continue to rise along with the costs of providing an educational experience through the variable costs of exhibitions and programs.

As museums seek to cope with exponential growth in infrastructure, cost, ambition, and competition for leisure time, it will repay museum leaders to take a periodic measure of what is at the heart of their enterprises.

What museums value is in large measure revealed by what they favor in their budgets rather than by public declarations. As many museums move toward a market paradigm, they have begun to value performance as would-be commercial attractions. These measurements include ticket sales, retail performance, and number of members. But most of all, since earned income represents only a fraction of the revenue of museums, the most closely watched statistic is attendance—a notoriously unreliable indicator of participation, since it is measured according to varying standards, is unaudited, and often is rounded up. Instead of emulating businesses that measure value according to sales per customer or sales per store, museums need to move toward another plateau—one operating within its means but focused on the quality of experience offered.

State-funded museums outside of the United States veer back and forth as governments alternatively privilege socially conscious or business-oriented ideological platforms. In the mid 1990s I served as director of Toronto's Art Gallery of Ontario and began my tenure a few weeks after a social-democrat, provincial government was replaced by a center-right government. The not-so-subtle message emanating from the provincial bureaucrats was to shift our message from education and community service to tourism and economic development. Each of these two ministerial profiles bore a challenge. In the former government, research and conservation were seen as optional emphases that did little to serve the public interest. In the latter government, these necessary features of museum professionalism were seen as distractions from the development of economically significant activities.

In both scenarios, the core mandate as understood by museum professionals—the acquisition, preservation, and research of the collections—was considered subordinate to other aims by government officials. Many public policy leaders outside of museums have fostered a sensibility advocating the "instrumental" value of museums—the extent to which they serve a public interest, whether educational or economic. An instrumental approach has been seen by many to be the best cure for inward-looking leadership, which once relied only on the "intrinsic" value of museums, meaning the extent to which their basic role of safeguarding relics, artifacts, and artworks was of lasting value to society regardless of who might benefit in the short term.

While the instrumental argument has had one desired effect, the fading of a solipsistic museum culture, it runs the risk of completely displacing attention to those functions indispensable to the furtherance of a museum's core mission, which is to collect and preserve what we have collectively inherited.

As the winds of politics and of fashion blow, museum leaders must both be open to new ways of assessing the value of our offer and adhere to principles unrelated to social engineering or economic development. These principles are in service of our primary role: to safeguard the evidence of the past and present and to make that evidence meaningful to a broad audience. The ideal value proposition for museum leadership keeps the intrinsic and the instrumental in proper balance, pursuing research, conservation, and interpretation, while fostering broad public participation in the museum's mission, thereby remaining open-minded about evolving social demands without neglecting the ongoing needs of the collection and its experts.

Maxwell L. Anderson is Melvin and Bren Simon Director and CEO of the Indianapolis Museum of Art, his fourth art museum directorship. Dr. Anderson was a curator of Greek and Roman art at the Metropolitan Museum of Art from 1981 to 1987 and has been a leader in writing about "other criteria" for evaluating art museums.

THE CREDIBILITY OF MUSEUMS

Gerardo Estrada Rodríguez
Translated by Francisca González Arias

The museum is a public institution in which the people place great trust. Large numbers of the population have access to museums' contents, and specialists certify the veracity of the information they present. At the same time, the museum transmits an image of permanence: it is an institution that aspires to endure and make sure that the legacy it watches over is sustainable beyond the winds of political change. However, the trust placed in the museum faces new challenges today, which obligate us to reflect on its origins as an institution, on its role as a means of knowledge, and on its continuing effectiveness.

As opposed to other means of communication, the museum allows for a tangible relationship between people and the testimonies that connect human beings to the world, their history, and its memory. Even if we cannot ignore the importance that reproductions and models have had in disseminating knowledge, those museum objects designated as original or authentic facilitate, beyond their utility for specialized research, a genuine experience of identification with the context that produced the object as well as with the objects themselves. The most immediate aspect of this experience is fidelity: the tangible connection with a trustworthy object is significantly different from the relation with a reproduction.

The original object is something more than a combination of true facts or a vehicle of accurate information. Documentary research may provide us with the approximate number of dead in battle, while the contact with the authentic armor of one of the soldiers allows us to identify with an individual who is at the same time distant from and close to us: we can imagine the historical fact as something that happened to human beings. In accordance with these ideas, we propose that the museum is an institution that facilitates genuine experiences among human beings through the testimonies of history, scientific research, and creativity.

But if the principal activators of this experience are the original objects on display, we should remember that those objects are presented by means of organizational systems that depend on the criteria and viewpoints of those in charge of the museum. This system of organization creates a discourse, the veracity of which is supported by the exhibited items. In the case of an artistic object, its symbolic quality provides the museum with an ontological dimension that has been amply studied in the last three centuries, and that reaffirms the originality of associated narratives.

With respect to the public discourses it presents, the museum as an institution holds first of all an academic responsibility: the offering of information about the items that is as coherent and as accurate as the studies developed around the objects allow. But it also holds an ethical responsibility to remain detached from ideological pressures and political circumstances. We should remember that in 1937 the Ministry of Culture of the German National Socialist Party organized an exhibition that gathered together relevant artistic works of the European avant-garde with the title "Degenerate Art," art that demonstrated so-called harmful Slavic, African, and Semitic influences in Western modernity, as well as the danger of accepting as art the contributions of creators considered to be mentally ill. The eloquence of the museographical discourse of this exhibition contrasted with the lack of methodological rigor applied by its organizers, some of whom were distinguished specialists willing to betray the ethical principles of their disciplines for political purposes.

Despite the fact that a museum's program cannot entirely escape the ideological conditions of its time or the interests of its sponsors, its duty should be to overcome those conditions in favor of a more enduring vision of its social function as custodian of testimonies of patrimony, of a legacy transmitted from one generation to the next. The trust that the public places in museums resides in the museum's ability to overcome short-lived interests and to promote a vision of long-term social commitment. The intimate relation between academic activity and museographical projects guarantees that this trust is nourished and renewed through rigorous research, reflection, and debate, enlarging the spectrum of museographical discourse from the starting point of interdisciplinary collaboration. Likewise, the diversity and plurality of worldviews derived from the dynamics of new democratic societies should be recognized and accepted by the contemporary museum. This confronts the museum with the challenge of abandoning the one-dimensional and univocal museographical discourses of the past, as well as with the danger that the discourse will be dispersed and become meaningless.

The credibility of past museographical discourse was based on its affirmative and comprehensive character: what is exhibited is history, art, positive science, and so on. At the present time, the museum offers partial discourses, and sometimes instead of affirmation it proposes reflection and interrogation. The public has required the museum to extend its cultural offerings beyond museographical exhibitions by incorporating educational services, interactive spaces, workshops, audiovisual sessions, and other activities and exhibits. For its part, the museum asks of the public unprecedented degrees of participation and high critical standards.

The future of the museum as an institution offering genuine experiences and its credibility as a vehicle of knowledge of the world reside in the seriousness and intensity with which we approach new relations between the public and the museums' contents. There are pressures these days to channel the museum toward the entertainment industry or leisure culture. Potential sponsors of museum projects often make their support dependent on the ability of museum projects to draw large audiences, obligating them to develop marketing strategies. Museums and their projects are required to be alluring. In certain cases, this need for attracting audiences produces confusion between museography and scenography, between interpretation and re-creation. The seductive elements are not necessarily contrary to the museum's mission, as long as they do not betray the limits of veracity, and whatever can be affirmed rigorously and truly from a system of museographical objects.

A prehistoric fossil is evidence of past life that is difficult to falsify, but it is necessary to affirm that it is an inert geological configuration. With the goal of attracting audiences toward paleontology, natural science museums present hypothetical reconstructions of a dinosaur's appearance and movements. This initiative can be beneficial to the extent that it directs the viewer's gaze toward—or does not distract it from—the fossil, the object that, both for research and educational purposes, constitutes the genuine testimony of the prehistoric past. Museums' tendency toward re-creation, influenced by media such as film and television as well as amusement parks, can inhibit the public's free and creative capacity of interpreting the authentic museum object as part of a truthful and unadulterated cultural experience.

The attention that museums have been experiencing worldwide, as well as the importance that they are acquiring as activators of cultural dynamics and as indicators of development, is evident. This is an auspicious moment for reflecting on the issues. The modern museum, which emerged at the end of the eighteenth century, derives from both the development of academic research as well as from the need of the secular state to establish public institutions for protecting and fomenting cultural heritage. To the extent that we consider and bring up to date our collections and our original materials, we can be assured of the ongoing relevance of the museum as a true and credible means of knowledge of the world.

Gerardo Estrada Rodríguez wrote this text while holding the post of coordinator of cultural diffusion for the National Autonomous University of Mexico. Of his many other achievements representing Mexico, the following stand out: he was director of radio education, director of Mexico House in Paris, director general of the National Institute of Fine Arts, and director general of cultural affairs in the Mexican Ministry of Foreign Affairs.

TRANSMITTING THE LEGACY

Plácido Arango

As the president of the board of a large public museum, questions of how we administer the institution with which we have been entrusted are often on my mind. The Museo Nacional del Prado is nearly two centuries old, but its collections are much older, and before being a "national museum," the Prado was a "royal museum" made up of collections formed by a succession of Spanish monarchs, beginning with Charles V in the sixteenth century. These include such world-famous works as *Las Meninas* and Goya's *Black Paintings,* as well as many other masterpieces by Raphael, Titian, El Greco, Rubens, and Velazquez, among others. History weighs heavily on the Prado; indeed, the institution is widely perceived as the principal "keeper" of the historical identity of Spain. Conscious of the responsibility of transmitting this legacy to future generations, I am reminded of a phrase much used in the context of environmental conservation but equally applicable to the museum: the Prado is not only an inheritance we have received from our forebears; we should think of it as a loan we have received from our children.

I would like to focus on five areas that I consider fundamental to the profound responsibility we have vis-à-vis the public. First, the Prado is a child of the Age of Enlightenment, and when it opened its doors in 1819 the founding idea was expressed as follows, and its mission was clearly meant:

> to offer the public a copious collection of paintings of national and foreign schools in a museum that is an embellishment to the capital of the kingdom and serves to give luster and splendor to the nation, to provide the occasion for decent enjoyment to those who are interested in the arts and to provide students of drawing with the most efficacious means to improve rapidly in their studies.

In other words, the Prado was established to display works of art for the pleasure and benefit of the public and to provide artists with models to learn from. In seeking to remain faithful to these ideals, the Law of the Prado, passed in the Spanish Parliament in 2003, declared that the museum has the important mission of "preserving, displaying and enriching its collections . . . and letting them be known to all." It is important that the Prado continue doing well what it has always done.

Second, a fundamental responsibility of the museum is the preservation of the collections that are a part of Spain's patrimony. It must be evident to the public that the works of art are being looked after, that they are well-presented in a carefully controlled environment, and that restoration is done according to best practices. An essential part of "conserving" the collections is researching them, both from a technical and an art historical point of view. We will shortly be taking an important step in developing this aspect of the museum's activities through the creation of the Prado Research Center, which will be housed in the seventeenth-century *Casón del Buen Retiro*.

Third, the museum's commitment to access and education is crucial in its broader relationship of trust with the public. At the Prado we have recently extended opening hours, so that the museum is now open sixty-six hours a week—more than any other major European museum—and we have furthermore increased the number of hours in the week that the museum offers free entry to all those age thirteen and younger. Our newly opened extension provides us with the much-needed space to welcome and attend to the needs of our 2.3 million visitors a year. We have worked hard in the last ten years to extend the institution's educational activities in an effort to make the museum and its collections available to the widest possible public, a public that ranges from first-time visitors to those who visit frequently to those who are unable to visit because they are too far away, housebound, or even in prison. Guided tours, lecture programs, family workshops, outreach programs, and the museum website are our principal tools. We are conscious, however, that both in the educational field as well as in adapting the building for universal physical access, there is much more to be done.

The Prado is a publicly funded museum. The Spanish government provides two thirds of our budget, and the highest level of transparency in our stewardship of the institution is required for both legal and moral reasons. Our decisions concerning financial resources must be rational and publicly justified, our strategic objectives clearly outlined, and our procedures for appointing staff, for example, plainly expressed. Philippe de Montebello, former director of New York's Metropolitan Museum of Art, stated in 2006, on page 152 of his article, "Art Museums, Inspiring Public Trust," in James Cuno's *Whose Muse*, published by Princeton University Press, that "It goes without saying that probity should be expected of the museum, as well it should in all human endeavors, certainly where conduct is concerned. But probity should be found deeper still, embedded in our mission, in our thoughts, and in our intellectual approach." This is elegantly put. For the public to be able to trust the museum, it must be confident that the notion of probity is shot through the museum's philosophy, as well as through its finances, labor relations, academic activities, and public programs.

Finally, I believe that in the broadest sense, the Prado exists for the common good, and civil society should be an interested participant in its development and success. Several government ministries, the academies of learning, artists, collectors, and businessmen are already represented on its board. But the museum should seek to have the widest possible network of supporters and friends. By this I mean other museums, both national and international; donors and benefactors; a Friends organization (we are fortunate to have the Fundacion Amigos del Museo del Prado); and sponsors and supporters, including companies, banks, and foundations. The press should be a partner with which the museum must aim to have an open and healthy relationship. Miguel Zugaza, director of the Prado, expressed these aspirations very clearly by frequently saying that the Prado needed to be larger, with new and better services and activities; that it should be more accessible and open to our society; that it should be a museum that illuminates for the world the extraordinary terrain of art and culture, which it represents in the very heart of Madrid.

Plácido Arango is the president of the Royal Board of Trustees of the Museo Nacional del Prado. He was a long-time member of the International Board of the Metropolitan Museum of Art in New York. Arango is a collector of Old Master Spanish art as well as contemporary art.

NATURAL HISTORY MUSEUMS AS SENTINEL OBSERVATORIES OF LIFE ON EARTH: A PUBLIC TRUST

Leonard Krishtalka

 Natural history museums and their collections are sentinel observatories of life on Earth, peering over its past 3.8 billion years and assaying its present condition. But, after three hundred years of the biological exploration of the Earth, natural history museums are at a pivotal point in history for three reasons. First, their collective mission—understanding the life of the planet for the common good—has never been more important to science and society than it is today. Second, their biocollections—their libraries of life—are critical to meeting one of the grand challenges of the twenty-first century: harnessing knowledge of Earth's biodiversity and how it shapes global environmental systems on which all life depends. Third, studies show that among public and private institutions, it is museums—and the information they disseminate—that are most trusted by the populace.

With this confluence of mission, potency, and public trust, natural history museums should be at the center of public consciousness and conscience about the state of Earth's environment. Medical science occupies this ground with respect to the health of one species on Earth: Homo sapiens. Biodiversity science, the business of natural history museums, takes the pulse of the rest of life on Earth, estimated at fifteen million species of animals, plants, and microbes. With current extinction rates and global climate change, that pulse weakens daily.

What confers potency on natural history museums are their biocollections of animals and plants—some three billion specimens worldwide—and the information embodied in them (genetic, morphological, behavioral, etc.). They document the global composition, identity, spatial distribution, ecology, evolution, and history of known life forms, about two million species. One would think, then, that in holding this knowledge, natural history museums would also hold the scientific arena and the public square for informing the stewardship of life on Earth.

Not so. Many natural history museums still seem ill equipped in vision and will to fulfill this mission and establish the fundamental value of their institutions and biocollections in the public arena. As a result, too many private and university-based museums and their collections are being shrunk or shuttered by fiscal shortfalls and perceived irrelevancy.

Whom to blame? Among the culprits are museum cultures that are prisoners of history, remaining specimen-focused and issue-deprived, and protocols, practices, and policies that eschew doing business as a cohesive biocollections community, opting instead to remain local and idiosyncratic, particularly in the global biodiversity informatics arena.

So, unlike the genomics and library communities, museum biocollections have been slow to reap the magnificent advances, resources, and economies wrought by unity of purpose, collective infrastructures, and powerful new technologies. Now we are playing catch-up.

This judgment is deliberately harsh, because previous warnings went unheeded at many museums. Here is Pere Alberch's 1993 deafening alarm:

> Natural history museums are at a turning point in their history. They can now play a central and critical role in . . . the understanding, conservation and sustainable use of biodiversity. To achieve this goal, however, they must radically change their mode of operation and public image, to clearly define goals, objectives, and new research strategies. If museums are unable to meet the challenge, other institutions will be created *de novo* to fill the niche. . . . Museums cannot be dominated by the philosophy of inward-looking curators, working leisurely on their taxa of choice all their lives. ("Museums, collections and biodiversity inventories." *Trends in Ecology and Evolution* 8:372–337, 1993.)

What does this "turning point in . . . history" call for? Museums must invoke their unique potency and trust.

POTENCY

First, potency demands that museums invest as much in modern information management as they do in collection management. In other words, they must use informatics to bring the enormous information content in the world's biocollections into currency for science and society. Essentially, immediate access to collection-based biodiversity information for research, education, and expert decision making is as important as the physical collections of animals and plants. That access must be digital, free, seamless, and interoperable. To paraphrase what Umberto Eco said about books in his book, *The Name of the Rose,* the good of collections and their data "lie in their being read; [otherwise] they contain signs that produce no concepts; therefore they are dumb."

From the information perspective, most of the three billion specimens in the world's museums are, unfortunately, still unread and "dumb." Informatics is a powerful reading instrument. It turns a potent, centuries-old museum descriptive enterprise into a predictive one for the common good. It uses the biocollections data to model environmental phenomena, from forecasting the spread of diseases, invasive species, and biothreats to the biotic and collateral social effects of global climate change.

This is not to disparage the continuing need for descriptive biodiversity. Indeed, potency demands new, industrial strength approaches to species discovery, description, data capture, and knowledge-serving in time to inform smart environmental policy. Solutions here involve deploying the latest computational, technical, digital, and genomic tools. Otherwise, museums should be worried that at the current pace of species discovery— three hundred years to document about two million species—they will be impotent in identifying, conserving, and stewarding remaining biodiversity, some fifteen million species of plants, animals, and microbes. They will fail their mission.

TRUST

Second, public trust deserves the courage of intellectual honesty and visceral advocacy in collection-based public programming. Honesty demands that museum exhibits, such as many dioramas, can no longer pretend that nature is pristine, untouched by humans. Advocacy demands inspiring the citizenry to become the environmental conscience of the nation.

Visitors to natural history museums should learn that our census of life on Earth hasn't gotten very far. Biology, biomedicine, and biofoods are playing with an extremely short deck, perhaps only five percent of Earth's diversity of organisms, given that fifteen million species are left to discover in soils, forests, and oceans. How far would chemistry proceed with five percent of the periodic table of elements? Nothing after boron? Much of unknown biodiversity is essentially a nanoscale world—bacteria, viruses, parasites, insects, worms, mites, algae, fungi, and so on—exploration of which is more difficult but will fuel an explosion in nanoscale science, materials, technology, and ultimately a new economic sector.

Museum visitors should learn that at current extinction rates, Earth would lose a quarter to a half of its biodiversity by 2050. The question of whether there is life on Mars can wait fifty years. Science and society are long overdue for a massive survey of the life of the planet under our feet. And if researchers can do it, why shouldn't the public also have access to web-friendly tools that assemble their backyard biodiversity and predict the effects of an El Niño or an increase in greenhouse gases and a jump in global temperatures?

Visitors should learn the lesson of Easter Island: humans and nature are not breeds apart. When the islanders destroyed the animals and plants of their own island world, they extinguished themselves and their culture.

And visitors should learn that Earth's ecosystems will crash when too many species are removed from its fuselage. Earth's biotas are fundamental for human life, annually providing trillions of dollars of "free" ecosystem services that are irreplaceable with technology.

Finally, all of these lessons are more compelling if nature and culture are integrated, understood, and experienced across the sciences, arts, and humanities. It's time for natural history museums and their collection-based kin in the arts and humanities to unite in an intellectual commons, because they share common ground— understanding and stewarding the planet's human and natural systems and their reciprocal effects.

Leonard Krishtalka is director of the Biodiversity Institute, which includes a natural history museum and biodiversity research center, and is professor of ecology and evolutionary biology at the University of Kansas. He helps lead a global initiative that uses informatics and the data associated with museum biocollections to model and forecast complex environmental phenomena.

INCLUDING CULTURAL JUSTICE IN A MUSEUM'S VALUE SYSTEM

Elazar Barkan

From a lecture given at the Los Angeles County Museum of Art
in collaboration with the International Museum Institute

When we talk about restitution of cultural properties and museum objects, we need to understand that this is a small but significant niche of a much larger movement that has to do with human rights.

We think of human rights as a good thing, something to make us morally better, and something that we really can't have enough of. These statements are partially true. However, by definition, rights are not historical. We think that rights are there. They are timeless. They are global, "universal." But in fact they are none of these. We develop new rights continuously. And those rights are often in contradiction to each other. Furthermore, no one can exercise every right precisely because some are in conflict with others. So, rather, we have an *aspiration* to rights.

In fact, we really only notice rights in their absence. We don't celebrate freedom of speech. Rather, we complain when there is censorship that deprives us of that right. We don't celebrate drinking clean water; we only begin to be worried when we don't have it. We're certainly not happy when we are tortured. You get the point. So it's really with the absence of rights that we are concerned. And what is specifically true about perceptions of universal rights is that we assume those rights operate on a clean slate, that there is a just and fair world out there. But obviously we are aware that the world is unfair. Equality does not exist.

With respect to museums, the topic of redress must be a main focus of the human rights conversation. There is no such thing as a right to redress specifically, but redress informs much of the conversations that we have with regard to rights, especially since the end of the Cold War and to some degree previously.

The question of offense must be very central to museums today. Who has the right to offend? Who has the right to be offended? Do we have the right not to be offended? This is obviously not a new topic. Exhibitions that try to offend the public and make a splash through artistic creativity are not a new thing. What is new is the form of offense that we are dealing with today. This form of offense is precisely what the United Nations addresses in its recently launched "Alliance of Civilization" to advance intercultural understanding. We learn from research that people who are offended are offended differently and in a much wider spectrum than was traditionally the case. For example, the Sensation exhibition, held at the Brooklyn Museum of Art from 2 October 1999 to 9 January 2000, included the display of *The Holy Virgin Mary* by Chris Ofili. The offense of presenting Mary surrounded by elephant dung was a local offense, having caused no offense when it was shown in London. There was global impact, on the other hand, when an image of Muhammad was mocked in a Danish cartoon and caused an international incident. I'm not suggesting that there's a clear way out of this, but I do want to suggest that offense must be taken into account in the way in which museums present controversial representations so as to avoid making those presentations in such a way that they lead to violence. When we think about that aspect of human rights, it is very crucial to consider both sides of the coin.

I think that it is very encouraging that cultural representations intertwined with human rights have become very much a part of the conversation, that the attention of human rights and questions of fairness are both recognized for their complexity, but that at the same time people try to embrace them as part of policy. The fact is that in some respect, vagueness and imprecise answers will always remain with us; it's the nature of humans to be frustrated with that. But that's life. And I am glad to be a part of it.

Elazar Barkan is professor of international and public affairs at Columbia University. He is the co-director of the human rights concentration at the School of International and Public Affairs at Columbia University. He has had a significant influence on museums' thinking with respect to morality and justice, moving the conversation from universal values to include local realities.

CHAPTER 2

The Primacy of Our Collections

"Exhibitions come and go: they are what museums do. Collections are slowly built and stay; they are what museums are."

Holland Cotter, New York Times, *25 October 2008*

MUSEUMS HAVE CHANGED their focus over time. The traditional focus on permanent collections shifted substantially in the last half century to the unsustainable universe of the spectacular temporary exhibition; this shift was deemed necessary to accommodate a host of intellectual, political, economic, and social imperatives. Although collecting continued as an active pursuit in many of our museums, it was the temporary exhibitions that were marketed most aggressively and received most of the public's attention. The goal was clear: to round up the greatest number of people and march them through our galleries. Museums everywhere in the world were being assessed not as much by what was permanent and sustainable in their offerings as by revenues collected (directly or indirectly, through government or private support or by means of the gate and earned income). Whether from government or private support or from earned income, the money that went into the coffers was related to the number of visitors who walked through our doors. Insofar as the public has a taste for the spectacular, extremely popular exhibitions will never disappear; there does, nevertheless, seem to be an appetite for a corrective in the air. And that appetite, based on a renewed interest in sustainable rather than ephemeral values, is beginning to affect how museum leaders see success. We would argue that there is a larger shift toward sustainable values in many of our societal institutions and that this is a good time to make a case for the primacy of our permanent collections—for bringing them back into focus.

Most of our museums—whether encyclopedic art museums or natural history museums, whether botanical gardens or history or science museums, whether representative of the global or of the community—are home to permanent collections. The nature of these collections surely varies greatly from one to the other: one museum's Degas is another's Mercury module; one's singular *Dama de Elche* is another's army of terra cotta Chinese soldiers; one's quilt collection is another's collection of dinosaur bones. It should be no surprise, therefore, that Jon Seydl, in his essay, argues that it is the collections that lie at the heart of our museums. Seydl would surely agree with Leticia Azcue Brea's argument that the permanent collections in our art museums may be compared with DNA banks. Both authors remind us that our permanent collections are the central indicator of our own museum's identity, both internally within our respective fields and externally in the world of our constituents. Certainly there are new trends in museums, such as, for example, museums that protect the intangible heritage of a culture. And norms for their collection, interpretation, and conservation are evolving. But the sustainable value that we are making the case for now is for collections in object-based museums.

Not surprisingly, most visitors recall the museums they care about by summoning up specific, definitive examples of their permanent collections. To some extent, the permanent collection brands the museum. If a great icon of a museum is missing for whatever reason, whether on loan to another institution or undergoing conservation, a visitor is likely disappointed. Yet despite the fact that it is a convention to say that a museum is defined by its collections, over the last forty or so years most museums have minimized the attention they publicly paid to their permanent collections in favor of the excitement created by the mounting of expansive and expensive blockbuster exhibitions. Even small museums felt compelled to have a plethora of changing exhibitions and to participate in large-scale loan programs. In the face of increasing global economic and political uncertainties, that era seems to be coming to an end, or at the very least, a plateau. Shipping and insurance costs are only growing, as operating budgets and security are increasingly imperiled. The interest paid out of endowments and government budgets for museums have dwindled. The permanent collections of our museums appear destined to once again hold the greatest opportunities for our institutions.

The opportunities that the permanent collections offer us can come to fruition only if we put all of the criteria elaborated in this volume to work. We will need to enlist the vast experience we have gained over the last decades in the glamorous presentations of temporary exhibitions to aid us in creatively enlivening our permanent collections. But we must first truly believe that these real things that we are responsible for can be presented to our visitors so as to satisfy a *contemporary* thirst for an authentic connection to our complex past and present. These real things need to be communicated by us (the presenters) to them (our visitors) as part of a body of knowledge that can and should be relevant to their interests and their lives. How to accomplish this? There is an infinity of ways. It is in the area of "permanent collection" that the digital possibilities loom largest and may have the most potential. Whether it is the adoption of Google Earth by the Prado or the more prosaic digitizing of collections for universal access, the possibilities are endless and increasingly accessible to our museums as we strive to make our works available, search for new connections among our collections worldwide, and awaken potentially new visitors to our museums and to what we have in store for them.

Surely the fuller stories behind our permanent collections will need to be more generously shared, and a new transparency about collecting histories, ownership, provenance, condition, and authorship of information made available to the public. The exciting, traditionally behind-the-scenes stories, so long taboo, should be communicated more than ever with the public. By curating into these exhibitions carefully orchestrated smaller loans of related materials, we can begin to craft fascinating stories for our public—narratives that until now only we, on the inside, were privy to. These are the mini-blockbuster exhibitions that can and are now being invented by some museums. More of us in leadership positions in the directorial, curatorial, education, and conservation worlds will likely become charged with generating excitement around our own collections. The selling of this newer, sustainable model revolving around and based on the permanent collections in our possession will make our museums viable for the duration. But being successful in convincing the public of the validity of refocusing on our permanent collections depends on many things: internal communication, scholarly research, external marketing, and, often, a political will.

This renewed thinking is, indeed, in the air. Edward Goldman, a Los Angeles–based art critic, claimed in his 28 July 2008 "Art Talk" radio review on radio station KCRW, after the opening of the museum's new pre-Columbian galleries, that the Los Angeles County Museum of Art "decided to raise the bar and reintroduce its permanent collection of pre-Columbian ceramics with a highly theatrical, eye-popping presentation, due to the unique vision of another well-known Los Angeles artist, Jorge Pardo." Although Goldman wasn't absolutely sure what to make of this radical approach, it certainly caught his attention! Across an ocean, in the guardian.co.uk, on 27 March 2009, Jonathan Jones quoted Nicholas Penny, director of London's National Gallery, as saying that his museum would no longer "put on exhibitions just because they will be popular, and we'll do them with consideration of the needs of the permanent collection." Penny is understood to be moving in the direction of captivating his visitors by focusing on his own great museum's treasures and their potential. At the same time, the Louvre has been inviting artists to put occasional contemporary artworks in the heart of some of their permanent collections. Thus, visitors may have surprise encounters with an enormous, unsettling Anish Kapoor mirrored sculpture in the middle of the usually tranquil Assyrian galleries or perhaps with less well-known contemporary artists displayed cheek by jowl with Renaissance or eighteenth-century masters. The unexpected juxtapositions of ancient or older masterpieces with works of art that reflect our own time invite powerful reactions to works in the permanent collections that are too often just taken for granted.

The last two essays in this chapter are dedicated to expressing other concerns, equally pressing, about collections and cultural patrimony. Former director of the Baghdad Museum, Donny George Youkhanna, poses hard moral questions around the issues of the illegal acquisition of stolen art for permanent collections. He proposes that we expand our definition of what constitutes the "permanent collection" to encompass long-term loans or permanent exchange programs, or even shared ownership, once we have dealt with restitution of objects and collections to their proper owners. This would be a way of reinterpreting the word *permanent* to suit new times. It is no accident that museums in the United States are working with museums in Greece and Italy not just to restitute objects, but to invent alternate ways to share works of art and archaeology. The British Museum remains on the forefront of finding legal, moral, and ethical approaches to building their collection. In 2008 the museum was busily working with archaeologists from Sudan to save important endangered early rock art. As a result of that cooperation, twenty of the Sudanese blocks were granted to the British museum. All things considered, the conversation in the museum world about collecting antiquities remains extremely lively—ranging as it does from the position of James Cuno, president of the Art Institute of Chicago and ardent defender of museums and their ability to construct antiquities collections "responsibly and for the public's benefit," to the position of Donny George Youkhanna that stewardship of these collections, rather than ownership, is the proper way of the future.

On the other hand, İlber Ortayli expresses yet another attitude toward permanence, forcefully defending his museum's conviction about the inalienability of the materials it acquired during the heyday of the Ottoman Empire. Ortayli's passionate interest is not in restitution but rather in preventing smuggling and looting. If we are to engage in international conversations about the "permanence" of collections, it is critical that we do not assume that all countries look upon the issues surrounding cultural patrimony similarly.

So we present here some of the many options for considering and reconsidering how we want to express the sustainable values that come along with a renewed focus on our permanent collections. Most importantly (and most traditionally of all) we need to ensure that we are properly caring for and celebrating the collections we have in our keeping. Then we need to convince our supporters and our visitors that the objects in our care are actually a part of our cultural DNA and that we, and our world, would be diminished without them, not just as the foundation but in the forefront of our institutions. We need also to make the case that the permanent collections tell a specific story, that this story is interesting and relevant to the place where they happen to be, and that they therefore contribute indispensably to our own sense of identity.

The purpose of this argument in defense of the primacy of the permanent collections is to help us command the human, intellectual, and economic resources that will allow us to regularly revisit and update their display and interpretation. We need to argue that our policies with respect to our permanent collections must be regularly reviewed. In sum, we need to be able to demonstrate that we are commandeering our smartest, most ethical, and most creative minds to guarantee the ongoing vitality and passionate interest in our permanent collections.

IT'S ALL ABOUT THE PERMANENT COLLECTION

Jon L. Seydl

It's all about the permanent collection. Now, I love exhibitions—in fact, before I came to Cleveland to reinstall the European galleries, I considered myself an exhibitions curator. I love the creativity, novelty, and pace; I love experimenting with ideas, design, and interpretive strategies. Yet when visiting other museums I found myself going to the permanent collections instead of exhibitions. The turning point was my last exhibition at the Getty, in which—instead of a conventional "masterpieces of" show—I took twelve paintings from

Dresden's Galerie Neue Meister and interspersed them throughout the Getty's permanent collection, with some pictures blending in seamlessly, and others leaping off the walls in startling contrasts, but always transforming the experience of the Getty's own pictures. The gap between the temporary exhibition and the permanent collection closed.

While the permanent collection is the touchstone of all museum activity, it should never be considered static. Most think about collections evolving with acquisitions (or objects returning to their legal owners), but I find it better to think of the long-term (and therefore constantly changing) installation along with the permanent (if occasionally changing) collection.

Of course the best temporary exhibitions are highly resonant experiences, but they also customarily convey a single idea (however profound it is). Museum collections can do something else: sustain multiple interpretations over a long period. It's the only arena for a sustained experience of objects by the museum staff and the returning visitor, permitting a depth of knowledge and experience that temporary exhibitions can never provide. Only through the collections can these deeper connections occur—it's the real site for lifelong learning for the curator, the educator, and the returning visitor, and still a place where the first-time visitor can have a meaningful experience.

Think about the permanent collection as objects on view. By the time this book publishes, my museum will have unfolded new installations of the collections after years of closure (aside from temporary exhibitions, presented as a stopgap measure). For the first time I'm in an institution cut off from its collection. When I arrived, I couldn't believe how the community starved for the collections: my mechanic, professors of art history in the area, the bagger at Trader Joe's, and colleagues at cultural institutions around the museum all vigorously expressed their sadness, anger, mourning, and depression, as well as their anticipation and concerns about the new installation, feelings mirrored and intensified by museum staff and volunteers. This story repeats over and over in other institutions, such as the Brooklyn Museum, with the joy that greeted the reinstalled American galleries and the hollowness that accompanied the recent quiet disappearance of the European collections into storage.

Curators often justify changes to the permanent galleries by arguing that they enliven the visitors' experience. But depending on this transformative experience is optimistic (remember, a large percentage of museum visitors are coming for their first and only time, and we know people consider themselves repeat visitors if they come once every few years). Expecting that kind of sensitivity to every change from your broad visitorship is asking a *lot*. On the other hand, installations should be—must be—constantly retooled, certainly for the staff and the small, core group of frequent visitors—but also because a long life of constant reinterpreting is a key value in itself. Every take on the permanent collection must provide a powerful and coherent single experience, but that experience has to evolve to stay fresh and alive. The interpretation grows along with the visitor, while for visitors from far away, the great works become a touchstone experience, providing a definition of place.

This rethinking and evolving happen in the following ways:

1. Reorganizing and reinterpreting the collections. Spinning new narratives from familiar objects heaves new life into static collections, seen dramatically (and not always successfully) in the recent reinstallation of the Detroit Institute of Art's European galleries. More creatively, one of the Autry Museum's recent experiments in retooling the permanent collection, Encounters, spun an entire exhibition out of a resonant confrontation of five objects never before placed near one another: a precontact pitcher; a postcontact Chumash basket; a Spanish mastiff collar; and two spurs, one a colonial reinterpretation of Amazoc forms and the other an Amazoc imitation of colonial forms.

2. Exhibitions from unplumbed parts of the collections, such as the important show of portrait miniatures at the Cincinnati Art Museum. These shows can be temporary or incorporated into long-term installations.

3. Small in-house exhibitions or installations, possibly with selective loans. Think about the decades of thoughtful exhibitions of prints, drawings, and photographs at the Philadelphia Museum of Art. They can also make up for lacunae in the collections—consider the remarkable installation of native Southeast pottery lent by the University of Alabama to the Birmingham Museum of Art, creating the local (and thus the most important) component in their encyclopedic story of Native American art.

4. Interjections, or placing single objects from another collection in the galleries. These can be loans completely consonant with the gallery's theme. Or they can jolt us out of the gallery's expected narrative. These interjections have often been spoiled by the bad or boring—particularly because of the persistent idea that adding contemporary art to galleries of later art inherently adds hipness and energy. We can do better.

5. Collaborations with local institutions. This is the most underutilized but ultimately the most productive of these strategies. At their best, they should reach further than occasional loans and reorient the local community of museums; for example, Scott Schaefer, curator of paintings at the Getty, coined the phrase, "the greater museum of Los Angeles."

Think about the permanent collection as every object in the museum. While all of the proposals outlined here work with collections on view, we also have to consider the whole collection, the stored *and* the exhibited. We all know the reasons collections can't all be out at once: insufficient space, too many objects, and issues of quality, state of conservation, and resting sensitive materials. But while storage is a given, museums have long struggled with how to engage works in storage meaningfully.

1. Visible storage projects have been among the least successful. Often fueled by a comfortable ideology of democratization, these projects often fail museologically, since they generally give a false sense of museum practice because very few installations actually bring any meaning to the displays. Moreover, they often undermine their democratic purpose with displays that create more physical distance with the visitors, cramming art into cases that forbid close viewing, and highly damaged or otherwise problematic works often remain off view.

2. More successful are imaginative projects spun from collections in storage. Many have become nearly impossible with current standards for security, staff time, and conservation: for example, the Cleveland Museum of Art for decades placed hundreds of immensely popular small exhibitions in community centers across the region. Indeed, large repositories of objects should distribute exhibitions or long-term installations of their collections in other places: the Kress collections are probably the best example. Works that would have lived in storage at a large institution now appear perpetually on view across America, yet retain their coherence as Kress objects. Other institutions—such as the Blaffer Foundation in Texas—have pulled back from this approach, but it would be well worth reviving. The largest, encyclopedic museums with vast troves of storage have a particular responsibility to share collections. Finally, museums closely connected to universities are especially well suited to these kinds of projects, reinterpreting objects in storage for exhibition elsewhere.

3. Since all our communities are global, electronic representation of collections is axiomatic. It starts with the dreaded data and photography projects: uploading and verifying information, which is rarely given full institutional support or funding priority. Nonetheless, it *must* be a key agenda item. We must surpass our fear of sharing provenance and conservation data and our fear of admitting flaws of the past. The Met's pioneering Dutch seventeenth-century painting show, which placed all works in accession order, represents a breakthrough, but it's something that could be represented online at all times. These kinds of projects open a window on collecting practices and ultimately allow others to participate in our research: shared information means errors get caught, attribution questions get answers, and under-explored gems surface.

Jon L. Seydl is the Paul J. and Edith Ingalls Vignos Jr. Curator of European Painting and Sculpture, 1500-1800, the Cleveland Museum of Art. A specialist in seventeeth- and eighteenth-century art, he was awraded a Ph.D. in art history from the University of Pennsylvania (2003). Prior to taking his position at the Cleveland Museum of Art, Seydl was curator in the Department of European Paintings at the Getty Museum.

BRINGING OUR PERMANENT COLLECTIONS TO LIFE

Leticia Azcue Brea
Translated by Francisca González Arias

Our permanent collections are our history. They are our past and our present. We must build and maintain them (if I may say this, knowing that it is not very fashionable) as a library does. That is, a library would not only want to own the great first edition of *Don Quixote*, but it would also want to possess the complete production of the *siglo de oro*, the golden age of Spain. So with that in mind, like a great library, our museums should strive to contain the artistic production of its designated periods. Only in such a way will museums ever have the masterworks as well as the context within which they were created. It is a shame to only care for, value, and keep the greatest of the great objects. (We must not forget that even the best masters produced lesser works.) It is very productive to know and to preserve the largest possible trajectory of a great artist's oeuvre. In that way we learn about not only the artist's social and cultural context, but also about the personal artistic context.

Our museums are, it must be remembered, the DNA of our cultural and natural history. And that is the reason that we have and must maintain museums of all types: history, archaeology, sacred history, science and mineral museums, ethnocultural museums, military museums, and art museums. We must also maintain museums that mix art and culture: archives and libraries. We should be able to bring together all of our continuing and living traditions, all of the oral traditions with traditions that no longer exist. Not only is this essential to knowing our cultural DNA as a species, but museums are another wonderful way of teaching and learning. Sometimes what is static in a book of history can be very powerfully communicated by the authentic objects, whether through the more traditional museums of science, history, and art, or even through museums of, let's say, fashion. And, wonderfully, with new technologies we can today sometimes understand mere fragments of the past, their uses, and their evolution up until our own time.

With that being said, we must stress that this is why we must be very vigilant against selling objects from a museum's permanent collection. De-accessioning is an idea that springs from the private museum tradition, a tradition such as we see in many museums in the United States; in Europe there is another tradition springing from the fact that the great bulk of our museums are publicly owned. Because of the idea of public ownership, the notion of selling from the museum is not considered here. But, in any case, it is always, *everywhere*, a risky thing to sell in this way—because a work that is considered to be minor or by an unimportant artist can radically change its stature over time. Let's be reminded that El Greco was not valued throughout much of the nineteenth century but since then has become one of the most prized of Spanish and, indeed, world painters.

At the same time, one cannot talk about permanent collections without taking into consideration the craze for temporary exhibitions. It seems that it is possible to learn lessons from the popularity of temporary exhibitions so as to add an excitement to the permanent collection. How might that be done? It could be accomplished by dedicating to the permanent collection significant attention and resources, by presenting smaller numbers of pieces within meaningful contexts, by producing brochures, text panels, audio guides, better and more exciting layouts and design, or guided visits. In other words, we need to do for our permanent collections what is done for our temporary shows. Our permanent collections need to be the objects of as much creativity and resources to support that creativity, of education and marketing efforts as passing shows are. There is no doubt that greater interest could be generated around our permanent collections if they were considered to be dynamic. Our public must come to believe that they can come back to our museums and see different interpretations of the permanent collection over the years. In a certain sense, I am talking about the creation of temporary exhibitions using the museum's own great *and* contextual material.

And keep in mind that people need to enjoy their visits. I am in favor of, for example, period rooms (again another unfashionable idea) because our audiences learn a great deal from them. And I am not only speaking of art museums employing highly contextualized pieces from the past. I observed a similar delight in children at military museums when they were able to see historical objects from historical paintings. In that way they both observed and experientially learned, piece by piece, about, for example, arms and armor. And they retained that knowledge.

At the same time, we must be clear that a great or important museum always does have a key collection, *un nucleo duro*. These are the pieces that are key or most famous and that the public expects to see. But we can display temporarily other pieces from our permanent collection: enriching that *nucleo duro* with other perspectives and activities by exhibiting those other parts of the collection that can be periodically rotated.

And, finally, I would like to say a word about a trend toward using the permanent collections of museums for temporary exhibitions in, for example, banks, inside and, above all, outside of Madrid. This is a trend proving to be quite attractive for institutions that do not have their own collections and that by default find it advantageous to organize these kinds of temporary exhibitions. It is especially good when they are activating a relationship with a museum that has a big permanent collection, part of which is not normally shown at the temporary location. In such a case, if the bank (or other venue) can provide for restoration, publicity, and education for and about that collection and can provide financing for the museum itself, it could be a very good idea. Works in storage then have the possibility of being seen, studied, and known outside of their own museums, being available in such an instance for a structured and coherent project that is both interesting and rigorously scientific. Indeed, it can be a good idea if it benefits both sides of the equation: the museum and the host institution—and of course, the public.

In these ways, the permanent collection can be both respected and enlivened at the same time.

Formerly administrative director of the Prado Museum and presently its chief curator of sculpture and decorative arts, Leticia Azcue Brea was also president of the Spanish Committee of the International Committee on Museums. She was deputy director of the Royal Academy of Fine Arts, San Fernando, and deputy director of culture and historical patrimony for Spain's Ministry of Defense. Azcue received her doctorate in art history from the Complutense University in Madrid.

WHAT ARE WE SHOWING IN OUR MUSEUMS?

Donny George Youkhanna

When I was nine years old, we moved from one of the towns outside of Baghdad into the city. The first day after we moved, my father took me to visit the Iraq National Museum (otherwise known as the Baghdad Museum). I was struck by the colossal guardians, the Assyrian, human-headed winged bulls, as well as the remains of a Sumerian early dynastic grave. For a long time after that visit I thought to myself, why would people show such huge statues? And why would they show dead people with the material that was buried with them to the visitors?

Some time later, as a teenager, I came to the conclusion that these pieces were on display because museums are the places that you can see, watch, and wonder about those who came before us, about their behaviors and experiences. Our lives are full of achievements that are based on the achievements and experiments of the people who came before us. But do we recognize this? Do we recognize the achievements of the past? While we are working or traveling, we are so busy that we can only see in the parameters of our work or our family—this is our immediate awareness of life in our busy environments. But museums have the ability take us away from our myopic vision, to transport us to a different place, to show us the experience of human beings other than ourselves. Museums enable us to enrich our own experience in this life with the physical evidence of the achievements of others—in other words, to go beyond what we enjoy and know about our lives, to the enjoyment and knowledge of what other people have done in their lives.

But we have to ask: where do these museums get the objects or artifacts that they are showing? Of course, museums get their material from different sources: from excavations if they are archaeological museums, from donations, and through acquisitions. Now, as we are more and more aware, moral problems may occur in the case of acquisition. Sometimes the object or artifact is brought to the museum without the owner's knowledge and approval. What I mean to say here is that material that has been taken from a country without the official approval of that country poses large moral as well as legal dilemmas. In that case an object or artifact has become a looted object. That is, it has been taken out of its original country without the approval of the owners or the authorities of that country.

Big questions arise: How can a piece of antiquity that had been looted from a country—a criminal act—become legitimate material in this country? Morally, how can we reconcile displaying stolen material in our museums? To have such works in our collections would seem as if we were teaching our children that it is quite right to steal something from someone since you like it! Can we do this? Can we teach our children that? Of course not. To do this is a crime we are committing against our future generations.

If we are really looking for an honorable trade in antiquities, I believe we cannot treat these objects and artifacts as legal. We need to consider not only the national laws of the countries of origin and the laws of the United States, but also international laws and the agreements of the United Nations Educational, Scientific, and Cultural Organization, and the arm of these international laws, Interpol. I believe if Interpol had enough means to act in the United States, ninety-nine percent of the dealers in non-American antiquities would have been put in jail, and some museum curators, too. The real problem in this country is that the international antiquities that enter the United States are dealt with according to the laws of the United States, not according to the national laws of their countries of origin or according to the international laws. Currently the burden is on the country of origin to prove how items illegally left the country. The dealer or museum that has the item does not have to prove whether the object is in this country legally or illegally. I believe that this should be reversed; the end owner should prove that the item was imported legally with legal and official documents.

Now, are we ready to do this kind of work? If we are not ready to take this on, we should stop meeting and discussing this subject. If we are ready, we should pressure legislators in the United States government to start creating new legislation to stop this kind of cultural heritage crime, the kind that is committed every single day. Only then will other countries stop accusing the people of the United States of stealing the cultural properties of the world to put on display in U.S. museums.

There are other ways for museums to obtain antiquities for the permanent collection, through loan or exchange of important materials between nations and institutions. To do this we need to train museum staff or give scholarships to members of the institutions of the countries of origin so that they can be retrained. This will allow those in the countries of origin to improve their professional skills. Most countries' national laws already permit the loan of antiquities to museums all over the world for a specified period that can be arranged between the two institutions. We could arrange long-term loans or exchanges for an extended period. These steps would allow visitors to see the antiquities, without having to ask the hard question: where did you get these antiquities?

Cultural properties are valuable and should not be owned and traded by one person for commercial purposes. These things are the property of all mankind, and it is a human right that they be seen, studied, and appreciated by everyone. But these items must be displayed in highly moral ways, ways that might extend beyond current laws into another framework yet to be devised.

Dr. Donny George Youkhanna was director general of the National Museum in Baghdad and chairman of the State Board of Antiquities and Heritage. He was also president of the Iraq State Board of Antiquities and Heritage. Author of books on the architecture and stone industries of Tell Es-Sawaan, Dr. Youkhanna is visiting professor of anthropology at SUNY Stony Brook.

FROM THE PERSPECTIVE OF TURKEY. . . .

Ílber Ortayli

From a lecture given at the Los Angeles County Museum of Art in collaboration with the International Museum Institute

There is a long history of collecting and collections in my part of the world. Peoples such as the Hittites collected Sumerian texts; the ancient Babylonian kings were fond of archaeology and led a kind of archaeological excavation at a number of monuments. Indeed, every sovereign in the Eastern Mediterranean led a kind of archaeological excavation; they also collected texts. This tradition went on, as evidenced in the Renaissance period by Spanish, Portuguese, and German gentlemen, and of course by Mehmet the Conqueror and his great-grandson Suleyman the Magnificent. Turkish cultural patrimony and collecting was characterized by a long-lived cosmopolitan attitude. But it was not until the nineteenth century that the marshall of the Imperial Artillery, Akhmet Fethi Pasha, established the first real public museum in Turkey. The St. Irene Church became a military museum. This military museum accepted and received, among much else, many antiquities from different parts of the empire. It was a storehouse of the palace and later became Turkey's first national museum.

The Istanbul Archeological Museums—the imperial archaeological museums—were intended to tell visitors the history of the Trojan excavation, how Schliemann destroyed and plundered it. But certainly the most wonderful achievement of all of our archaeological museums is the Museum of the Ancient Orient, founded in 1910 as the cultural achievement of the young Turkish government. It has around twenty thousand cuneiform texts in its collection. A few thousand of these texts were loaned to the German empire so that they could read them, clean them, and return them. Years and years passed, and, in the end, they did not return these texts.

When Germany became partly communist, the German Democratic Republic signed the international treaty convention to give the antiquities back to their owners. I do not agree with this at all. I don't understand why some circles of our government supported this convention. If Germany does return this material to us, then we also will have to give a lot of material back to Syria, Lebanon, and even to Greece. During the war of 1894, the chief of the Ottoman army invaded southern Greece and got many wonderful pieces that are still in the Istanbul Archeological Museums today. So, as I understand it, the convention requiring the return of the texts from Germany is not for us.

Relating to the specific issue of smuggling out of Turkey, in the nineteenth century Turkey created new regulations for antiquities and excavations. Egypt, Turkey, Greece, and Italy are unfortunately subject to smuggling. In Iran smuggling has slowed to some extent, but I'm sure it will change. If money can be made from smuggling, it seems people cannot be expected to resist the temptation. There are stories about how easy it is to pass this or that illegally. In our world, only Israel is not a victim of smuggling. The great majority of the people of Israel are amateur archaeologists, and they love their country and try to preserve their history. They are very aware of that history and the possibility of smuggling, and they are very rigid in this sense, so no smuggler would dare take something away from this country. Israel is not a country for smugglers. Therefore, I advise everyone in other countries to follow the example of Israel. Archaeology should be a national sport and everyone should belong to the nongovernmental parallel unofficial security forces; that is, they should be involved in caring for their own patrimony. I have watched it. It works.

Let me conclude by talking about the international, or encyclopedic, universal museum. Let me be frank here: American art lovers are quite naïve. Maybe they don't always really know that something is smuggled. Sometimes, I find them shameful, but on the other hand they are very different in their attitudes from the Europeans. Some American museums, one must admit, are not so honest. Some of them, on the other hand, are *quite* honest. The Smithsonian Museum is an excellent example. They do not buy any object without proper provenance. Honest museums exhibit a custodianship of their collected artifacts. For example, take the case of Tibetan objects: because they have been destroyed by China, I would say that museums who possess Tibetan artifacts should keep them.

The history of Turkey is the history of hundreds of centuries of being plundered and robbed by everyone, not just native Turks. So what can we do? We need security organizations, as they have in Israel, with good, humanistic motivations. Every country has to take care of its own archaeological sources. People talk about the destruction of Armenian and Greek and Hellenic heritage in Turkey, but the destruction of Turkish heritage continues to go unrecognized. The smugglers continue to work. And that's the trouble. Turkey as a country does have the consciousness and desire to end smuggling, but we do not have the money. And it should be remembered that Turkey also does have museums—just as in the United States and Europe. Of course we have lots of problems, but we do have the museums, and we do have archaeologists!

İlber Ortayli is a leading professor of history at the Galatasaray University in Istanbul and at Bilkent University in Ankara. He is a popular defender of Turkish culture in Turkey and appears in the media frequently. He graduated from Oxford University and received his doctorate at Ankara University in 1978. He was the head of the Topkapi Museum in Istanbul Cultural Patrimony, during which time his 2006 book, *Rediscovering the Ottomans,* became a best-seller in Turkey.

CHAPTER 3

Relevance

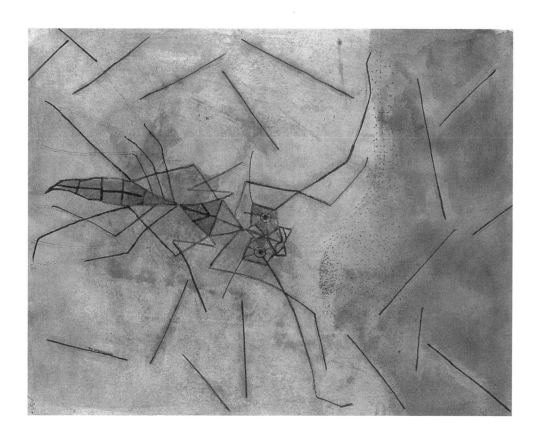

"Time for Talking Is Past, Time for Action Is Now. "
Artists' chant at 1970 Association of American Museums meeting protest

I N 1970 the annual meeting of the Association of American Museums held in New York was marked by protests demanding both the end of the war in Vietnam as well as an end to discrimination and racism as manifested in our museums. The presumption was that our museums were irrelevant to our communities because they represented or spoke to an elite class. Whether in New York or Paris or Mexico, the1960s and 1970s constituted an era that questioned institutions and "the establishment."

Exhibitions such as Harlem on My Mind: Cultural Capital of Black America, 1900–1968, at the Metropolitan Museum of Art began addressing African American artistic contributions in a manner that the museum thought to be honoring those contributions. However, the whole enterprise was seen as a condescending gesture to what the museum seemed to cast as "other" audiences. The museum both ran into and created problems. It was a time that emotions in the African American community ran high; Martin Luther King had been recently assassinated and New York City had released a report documenting high numbers of incidents of prejudice. By hiring a curator from outside of the African American community to in effect interpret the culture of that community, the Manhattan museum generated outrage and charges of irrelevance, ignorance, and paternalism. "Relevance" became the most value-laden measure of the period as social consciousness spread in the museums of the United States, and it began to be used ubiquitously when critiquing museums. Although this criterion for the success of American museums is no longer as singular as it was in the 1960s and 1970s, the issues that were raised at that time have entered our consciousness and are still to be reckoned with as one of many valid evaluative tools. While it is no longer the overriding question, we still must ask, "Are we sustainably relevant?"

As we have seen, a museum must be a model of public trust and it needs to have great collections that are dynamically and creatively curated and presented. But if a museum, wherever it is in the world, does not seem to matter in some essential way to its community, it will not be supported and will ultimately fail. However, framing and claiming relevance is not as easy as it might seem on the surface. The very concept of relevance, of mattering, leads only to another question: "Relevant (or mattering) to whom or to what?" Since museums address a number of audiences, that which is relevant to one audience for one reason might be irrelevant to another for still other reasons. For example, a small museum of an indigenous municipality in Oaxaca, Mexico, might be relevant to its citizens solely for the transmission of its own local memory and identity. But that same museum would possess another relevance nationally, perhaps demonstrating to the rest of the country or to tourists from abroad the acceptance and promotion of diversity within Mexico. On the other hand, it might demonstrate a vital key link in the development of a craft or a religious sect and be relevant to the history of art or anthropology. There could be many more criteria for relevance, even in a tiny local museum. All in all, relevance can and should be argued for in a number of ways. But the bottom line is that our museums must matter in some way or ways that we can and are willing to articulate and verify. The verification could be by sophisticated surveys, by informal conversations with visitors, by reasonable estimations of visitorship and activity in the galleries. Each museum needs to devise its own means of detecting the relevance of the museum to the community it serves.

Museums have long been taken for granted as one of the foundational institutions of a democratic society, as an indisputably relevant amenity that contributes to a richer quality of civic life, as a kind of "open university" based on the perceived value of original, real material. During the nineteenth and early twentieth centuries, American museums described themselves as building "better citizens" and "better cities." Brazilian museums work to make better citizens by virtue of their educational missions and their vital contact with the public. By the end of the twentieth century the interrelationship between museums and civic life, political identity and even urban renewal, along with a concomitant sustainable economic city life had come to be one of the tests of relevance. The relevance of museums to their communities became a global raison d'etre, heard in manifold ways from village to megalopolis.

Guillermo Barrios, in his essay in this chapter, explores how changing the location of a national museum, in his example, the National Gallery of Art for Venezuela, might revitalize a part of Caracas. He reflects on the resonance and the relevance of the "Bilbao effect" throughout the museum world and the potential that it might still have for Latin America. Inspired by the fabulous Guggenheim Museum designed by Frank Gehry, the now famous "effect" refers to how a single museum spurred enormous economic investment and became the keystone in the revitalization of a dying Basque industrial city. As the effect of this museum became legendary, more and more famous architects were commissioned for ambitious projects all over the world. However, with the passage of time, this kind of investment in the "starchitecture" of a museum has begun to be questioned. It remains to be seen whether that approach is a sustainable one: how it might play out in Venezuela or the rest of Latin America is a story that remains to be told. Barrios wants us to consider all of the possibilities carefully as he reflects on the relevance of building projects that could (anachronistically, perhaps?) conceivably have similar aspirations as those ignited in Spain in 1907.

It is not a big leap from Barrios's essay to thoughts of China and her museums. China's was, throughout the early twenty-first century, the world's fastest growing museumscape. It was frequently reported that the Chinese government planned to build over one thousand brand new museums over the next ten years. Many of these have huge construction and exhibition budgets; all of them are expected to be relevant to the economies of the cities in which they will be built. It is noteworthy that there is already a publication called *New Museums in China*, which promises to be an invaluable guide for companies interested in exploring this huge market. The global financial crisis has not spared China and the effect on museums is yet to be evaluated over the longer term.

But China's example is not meant to argue that relevance can only be assessed by economic plans and intentions. In 2001 it was proposed that the Iziko Museums in Cape Town, South Africa, collaborate with the International Museums Studies Program at the University of Bergen, Norway. The purpose was to develop innovative ways, including mobile vans, web sites, and computers, of linking oral storytelling with the new technologies. They would also connect satellites of the Iziko Museums with schools in the south and north of the country. Known as the "Iziko Stories Project," it is characterized by Soul Beat Africa as a museum endeavor "aimed to redress what organizers described as unbalanced representations that have developed within South African museums during the colonial and apartheid periods." The Iziko Museums would have no trouble making the case for this project as relevant to its populations, reconnecting them with their essential cultural narratives. What, after all, could be more relevant?

Beyond a museum's relevance in nation/city building and restoring cultural and connectivity, museums have held special places in communities and in the evolution of group identities. Selma Holo looks, in her essay, at the role of museums in the United States with respect to its many culturally specific groups. These museums hold a unique place as mediator and cultural advocate between a strongly identified ethnic culture and the devouring maw of American culture. Even as they preserve the unique stories of immigrants to the United States that might otherwise be lost, they are also authentic evidence of the shared humanity of refugees and immigrants, not to mention the process of assimilation and identity preservation that is part of the United States' meta-narrative.

On the other hand there are personal stories that can communicate to us the relevance of museums that one would never find in a museum brochure or an economic prospectus. Brother and sister, art historian Cherise Smith and Major League Baseball player Gary Matthews Jr. reveal their own reasons why museums have been relevant to their lives. We can gain another kind of understanding about the value and relevance of our own institutions, beyond mass surveys, by taking into account that individual stories can be multiplied infinitely. Perhaps we should collect and relay more of these individual stories such as theirs when making the case for our own museum's relevance.

In 2005, after hurricanes Katrina and Rita, Jay Wiegel, director of the Contemporary Arts Center, asked himself, "Will our museum survive?" Four years after the hurricanes, many New Orleans museums remain closed, and some may never reopen. Wiegel's reflection is relevant to our own meditations because, although our cities may not be facing natural disasters, some of our museums are facing potential financial disasters. Not all museums are, in fact, sustainable as autonomous institutions, and one of the challenges of the future will be to seek out the areas of indisputable relevance and figure out how we can best defend our ongoing existence. Should that not be possible, we need to consider other sustainable configurations or reconfigurations that maintain our museum's relevance.

Each museum needs to be able to demonstrate and articulate its own criteria of relevance in its own disciplines, whether science, natural history, gardens, or art museums, whether hybrid in mission or interdisciplinary in reach. Each needs to be able to provide evidence that the institution remains relevant to the public and that society would be worse off without it. Even our mission statements need to be reexamined with some regularity to spot-check for ongoing relevance. No museum can be all things to all people, but every museum needs to know to whom and to what constituencies it intends to be relevant and then be able to assess both its successes and weaknesses to identify areas that call for improvement. Only then can we expect to garner the economic support we need to carry on.

THE REVITALIZATION OF THE URBAN ENVIRONMENT: A MEASURE OF THE MUSEUM'S SOCIAL VALUE

Guillermo Barrios

Translated by Francisca González Arias

 The new location of the National Gallery of Art (GAN), the first large-scale museum built in Venezuela in the last decade, offers an opportunity to reflect on the tendencies that are now redefining or broadening the range of the museum's relevance as an institution. Founded in the mid-1970s by an independent collective from the cultural community and supported by public funds, the GAN's inauguration of its new galleries merits special attention, given its location in an area of central Caracas that is both important and problematic. To begin with, we are finally aware of its visual impact. With the completion of the project's first phase, the shapeless mass of concrete and steel bars incorporated into the city landscape for more than twenty years by intermittent construction has disappeared. Beyond this initial effect, this institution must grapple with city and worldwide challenges to the ability of museums to contribute to the regeneration of the fiber of the urban fabric.

As has been profusely studied in specialized literature, one witnesses today the unfolding of a true chain reaction that has impelled large and small cities to search for what could be termed the "Bilbao effect," with reference to that Basque city whose successful strategy of rehabilitation and repositioning on the national and international map undoubtedly took off with the opening of the Guggenheim Museum there in 1997. From that moment on, the race to incorporate museum building into large-scale urban redevelopment planning has undeniably come into vogue. Without going into other implications that invite meditation, like the growing "syndrome of the empty cash register" that worries experienced thinkers in the museum field, it is clear that the tendency to integrate notable buildings into urban renewal programs continues to be reinforced, not only in Europe and the United States, but in other parts of the world as well. This demonstrates that the museum's physical presence, rather than its grand mission, seems to be the focus. Architecture's star system has capitalized mightily on the rhythms of newly minted urban fortunes. A Frank Gehry for the small city of Herford, Germany; a Zaha Hadid for Cincinnati; or a Santiago Calatrava for Milwaukee constitute just a portion of the many initiatives in progress that attest to the recognition of the museum as a catalyst for change and of its architecture as the most effective way to express this change. Rather than debate these issues a priori, careful observation is necessary so as to highlight important aspects of the phenomenon in the contemporary dynamic.

In Latin America, where investment in culture has long been at odds with the urgent needs of pressing social realities, the formula of the pivotal insertion of the "catalyzing museum" has been tried successfully. Apart from some new, already-constructed projects like Oscar Niemeyer's for Curitiba, Brazil, or others in the proposal stage like that of Enrique Norten for Jalisco, Mexico, there are other examples of this trend. Among these is the Museum of Antioquía, occupying the former City Hall of Medellín, a praiseworthy initiative in a series of promising renovation plans undertaken by the Colombian city. Apart from the plans for the museum itself, this institution's achievements can be measured in its physical surroundings. In this sense, the austere, unspectacular architecture of its new building stands out. The museum's activity has extended to exterior spaces in what today is known as the Plaza Botero, in honor of the artist whose large-scale sculptures create a pleasant gathering place in an area that, like the rest of the city, was beset in the recent past by violence and urban decay.

In the early years of the twenty-first century, as these projects from far and wide were being carried out, museums in Venezuela went through a period of clear regression and redefinition that prevented them from partaking in global tendencies. With the troubled course of the so-called Bolivarian Revolution unfolding in the background, the construction of cultural buildings was limited to the fabrication of a series of perishable, multiuse structures (many of them swept away by time); few had any architectural value, and many were located far away from the big cities. That public cultural management devoted no attention to the capital was in keeping with the lack of interest in public spaces on the part of city government, a fact that took on truly alarming proportions in the context of the new building. As part of the Venezuelan architect Carlos Gómez de Llarena's project presented in the early 1980s for the recuperation of the failed main thoroughfare of modern Caracas, the GAN could act as a mediator in this situation, especially if the original plan for the construction of open spaces goes ahead, and the museum begins to face its surroundings to establish with them a supportive relationship. It must shed as soon as possible the "bunker" image that it has begun to take on and open its heart to the eroded dynamics of the site, undertaking programs that will breathe life and lend warmth to its surroundings.

This is a plan of extraordinary promise, not only for this museum, but also for a group of new museums that have been projected for different cities throughout the country. It heralds a new policy enabling the museum to rise above its special function of extolling human creativity, in all its richness and complexity, proposing now to stimulate, enliven and increase creative activity within the landscape where it is placed.

Guillermo Barrios is an architect who holds a PhD in architecture from the Central University of Venezuela, where he is currently dean of the School of Architecture. He has worked since 1983 as a leader in the museum field, working both in public institutions and in academia as the former chair of the graduate program in museum studies. Barrios is also an independent curator and exhibition designer and a philosopher of museums.

ETHNIC-SPECIFIC MUSEUMS: WHY THEY MATTER AND HOW THEY MAKE A DIFFERENCE

Selma Holo

As a country made up of many cultures and ethnicities, America's encyclopedic museums might be perceived, superficially, as eminently relevant to all of its peoples. Encyclopedic museums, with their collections ranging from prehistory to the contemporary, have as their purpose the representation, through art and artifacts, of the history of the best creative contributions of all peoples throughout the world. In the sense of "cosmopolitanism," as promoted by Anthony Appiah, they are, by definition, relevant: they display a great swath of the world's cultural production under the umbrella of a single museum. Encyclopedic museums have traditionally represented a history through art that is true to Western mainstream narratives. Normally collections in encyclopedic museums are displayed, interpreted, and framed in a cultural context that emerges from the academy, especially from art history.

In the last forty years of the twentieth century in the United States, these encyclopedic museums began to be seen as actually *irrelevant* to many peoples living and thriving in that country's dynamic cultural and ethnic mix of communities. The unrest of the 1960s led to demands that new museums be created that would have special relevance to discrete cultures. That demand eventually undid the general acceptance of the universal validity of the kind of contextualization of art that had until then been normal in the encyclopedic museum.

So, at the end of the 1960s, after a long season of social disturbance, a new model for a museum sprang up in New York: first the Studio Museum in Harlem, dedicated to advancing the art of black artists, and then the Museo del Barrio, initially intended to represent Puerto Rican artists and later all Latin American and Caribbean artists. These museums and others with the same desires to celebrate ethnic cultures in the United States began to open throughout the 1970s. They fulfilled an emerging need in the United States, a need not expressed anywhere else in the world, and they did so with intensity and urgency. It was a need determined by cultural insiders, representatives of living and evolving communities, for there to be museums that were demonstrably relevant—on terms set by the communities themselves.

This model of ethnic- and culture-specific museums swept the United States. It was replicated in various forms and combinations of missions from coast to coast. It took special root in New York, Chicago, and Los Angeles in alternative institutions—often combining art centers with gallery spaces and communal gathering places—and helped to redefine the institution of a museum. A museum became a more flexible institution than it had ever been before: sometimes collecting and preserving objects, sometimes not; always exhibiting, advocating for, and interpreting the specific heritage from its own perspective; supporting artists; educating about the past and nourishing the future, but always a bastion of memory—preserving and disseminating narratives and collections that might otherwise, over time, become lost or, at the very least, assimilated and diluted in the overwhelming mainstream culture in the United States.

Rather than presenting the museum as a world in microcosm, as the great encyclopedic museum does, the new model claims that the particular ethnicity or culture that the museum is celebrating is the center of its own universe. The museum assumes the responsibility for telling you, the visitor, what it will pass on for you to take away as truth. There are many submodels of the culture and ethnic-specific museums, but I will point out here only one, highly developed in the United States, but springing from this country's globalized nature. It is the "Hyphenated American Museum."

In all cases, the success and sustainability of the Hyphenated American Museum has depended on it having the following characteristics: a clear identification as American, but through an "other" prism and a genesis with a unified, coherent, and agreed-upon narrative that has been framed from the inside and is transmissible to both insider and outsider audiences. In all cases, the hyphenated American population that creates this kind of museum has had unique struggles and challenges in white, Anglo-Saxon America, but it also wants to be known for its achievements. The people who build such a museum are dedicated to spreading greater understanding of themselves to the outside world. They want to keep their histories alive for posterity. They have a narrative they don't want to be forgotten. They have a strong desire to be both particularistic and universalistic. They have objects or the ability to display objects as any art museum would, but ethnic- and culture-specific museums most often combine history, art, and cultural artifacts. They are also expected to be safe gathering places. They collaborate with other hyphenated American museums—on their own terms. They are supported from within and without, by private and public funds. They are ongoing, dynamic, and living communities that have re-rooted in the United States. Inevitably a museum that has all of these characteristics thrives in the United States.

Let me briefly mention four extremely successful more recent museums of this model, all of which epitomize these characteristics, but in their own ways.

THE SKIRBALL CULTURAL CENTER AND MUSEUM
OF THE AMERICAN JEWISH EXPERIENCE

The Skirball Cultural Center and Museum of the American Jewish Experience originated with and has stayed with a unified, optimistic narrative of America as "refuge"—as a place of aspiration for all who came to it. The Skirball is inspired by the parallels between Jewish values and American democratic principles but is profoundly ecumenical and inclusive in all of its programming. Notably, although Jews have had special struggles in white, Anglo-Saxon America, very little space is given to anti-Semitism or even to the Holocaust. In the balance, it is less about the struggle than about the success and the achievements that have been possible for Jews in the United States. The Skirball's programs have ranged from exhibitions on Einstein and Bob Dylan, to one-man shows for artists George Segal and Larry Rivers, to the wildly popular ZAP! POW! BAM! The Superhero: The Golden Age of Comic Books, 1938–1950, where, as the Skirball writes in its promotional materials, "the creative processes and influences that drove young Jewish artists" to draw for comic books are explored. The Skirball reflects Jewish desire to keep the memory of becoming American alive for their children who are inevitably being absorbed into and reflective of the larger American experience. It is a collecting institution that frames its story through the objects it collects, displays, preserves, and interprets.

THE JAPANESE AMERICAN NATIONAL MUSEUM

The Japanese American National Museum (JANAM), an adamantly American museum, also has a coherent and unified, clearly articulated story line. Unlike the Skirball, the core story of JANAM is the most painful part of its history. The JANAM wants to memorialize the time during World War II when Japanese Americans's property and money were confiscated in their own country, America, and when they were transported to concentration camps. They want that struggle to be known in a tale told by their own people. JANAM, however, is not just a "victim" museum. Its recently created National Center for the Preservation of Democracy is intended to inspire and educate all people to live by democratic principles so as to prevent what happened to Japanese Americans from happening ever again, to any Americans in the United States.

Like the Skirball, JANAM is a combination history, material culture, and art museum. Art exhibitions range from celebrations of the important contemporary artist Isamu Noguchi to shows featuring younger Japanese American artists. It is therefore a place of collected memories by means of objects and performance, through dialogue and research, and in the safety of a profoundly communal space.

JANAM has a broad funding base. It has raised money, for example, privately from Japanese Americans and from Japanese corporations and private citizens, from California state and from municipal governments—both for its museum and its democracy center. After years of lobbying, the Japanese community received an apology from the United States that came with restitution money, much of which was given to the museum by

Japanese American individuals. Notably, JANAM and Skirball, which are essentially private institutions, also receive private and public moneys from inside and outside their respective communities.

CALIFORNIA AFRO AMERICAN MUSEUM

The California Afro American Museum (CAAM), a state-funded museum, began with a coherent, unified, and clear story line from the African American perspective focused on the history of slavery in the United States and on the Civil Rights Movement. There is one difference, though, between CAAM and the other hyphenated American museums mentioned in this text that permeates the museum: all of the other ethnicities and cultures celebrated in those American museums came voluntarily, looking for refuge or opportunity. African Americans came as slaves, and for years that was the principle guidepost of the museum.

But that story line is now growing to include other examples of the larger black experience. It has evolved to include, for example, Africans who have migrated to the United States recently from the Caribbean or Africa who do not share the slavery or Civil Rights narrative that forms the cornerstones of CAAM. Nevertheless, they do share a racial reality and a perspective that is special to that reality. According to its director, Charmaine Jefferson, of the big challenges of the CAAM today is to build on this newer and larger racial perspective that includes a changing and evolving contemporary experience. In doing that, CAAM functions in much the same way as the Skirball and JANAM in its balance of inclusivity and particularity, of presenting struggle and achievement, of the past and a dynamic now. It is also a collecting institution featuring art and history.

THE ARAB AMERICAN MUSEUM

The Arab American Museum was opened in Dearborn, Michigan, in May 2005. Ambassador Bader Omar Al-Dafa from Qatar was quoted (by Sean Barlow, on 12 May 2005, in his "Afropop worldwide" guide) as having said at the inauguration of this museum,

> After September 11th, which was a horrible occasion, the media here played a negative role in portraying Arabs and Muslims and relating them to terrorism. Yes there are some, those who committed this horrible act. But those are few. They do not represent the whole of the Arab and Islamic community all over the world. I think part of the message of this Museum is really to give the American people, especially the younger generation, a different picture about the achievements of Arab Americans—in politics, sports, entertainment, business and art.

This museum was modeled very closely on the other museums we have already discussed—with a permanent exhibition based on the tropes of "Coming to America," "Living in America," and "Making an Impact." The temporary exhibitions celebrate artists and great achievers in the Arab American environment. And, as always, the museum struggles to maintain a healthy balance between victimhood and success—between a bad past and a good future. Like the others, it is also art center, cultural center, and gathering place. Above all, it is a safe place. As are all of the others, this museum is basically a public place created by insiders and made for insiders and outsiders alike to demonstrate the particular and universal humanity of the Arab American in the light of the shared immigrant experience.

As the other museums have, the Arab American Museum has been able to develop an economic and a political base from the inside and the outside that allowed it to gain economic support from, in this case, major corporations. It receives support from Arab Americans and the Arab world at large. And, as always in the United States, the federal government helps support this museum by its system of tax relief for donors.

COMMONALITIES IN HYPHENATED AMERICAN MUSEUMS

The proliferation of culture- or ethnic-specific museums, especially the Hyphenated American Museum, has served two significant societal purposes. The first is that they have come to be agents of stability—conceived as such by groups who feel themselves misunderstood or mischaracterized in American life as a way to retain and tell their stories, and to present themselves and their histories in their own way. And, second, they can be agents of positive change in that they promote tolerance and understanding to outsiders by insisting on the notion of a shared humanity. The best of these museums promote a more universal understanding of their culture to the outside world and a sense of pride in themselves and their achievements.

What could possibly be more relevant to any museum's sustainability?

Please see Selma Holo's biography in the introduction.

WHAT IS THE RELEVANCE OF MUSEUMS? CAN YOU IMAGINE A WORLD WITHOUT THEM?

Cherise Smith and Gary Matthews Jr.

 Answering those questions is at once deeply personal and profoundly public, striking nerves both on individual and on communitarian levels. Some might argue, for instance, that museums are places of leisure for the wealthy or the intellectually oriented. Those same people might say that there is no power in the objects in museums in that they are dead or, at the very least, controlled by the elite. Others might argue that museums are profoundly public places—here we mean *public* in the sense of the public sphere, a place where ideologies and identities are negotiated. There are still other ways of answering that question. And, even with people in the same family, the answers are idiosyncratic and shifting.

Though we grew up in the same house, we have different conceptions about art and museums. Gary is a Major League Baseball player, and Cherise is a professor of art history. Stereotypes dictate that the division of our labor is pretty clear: he lives a life of the body, and she lives a life of the mind. But we do not partake in such stories, for they inevitably prioritize one set of cultural values over another. We realize instead that each of our chosen careers requires dedication to the mind and to the body, and we respect the interdependence of those two entities, which have been cast as rivals. Gary's career mandates that he maintain a tremendous level of physical fitness, continually improve his already exceptional skills, and track the history, statistics, and strategy of a sport that many liken to art. Cherise's career requires that she constantly increase the breadth and depth of her knowledge and improve her ability to communicate to diverse audiences textually and audibly while preserving the physical fitness to stand in front of the classroom, sit at a computer for hours at a time, and walk through museums. Each profession involves significant acuity and discipline, mental and physical, and each necessitates periods of recreation. For rejuvenation, the professional athlete engages his curiosity about art, and the academic trains for triathlons and plays tennis. Clearly, we have fairly distinct reasons for visiting museums and diverse understandings of their relevance.

Growing up, we lived with our parents, who were first-generation Californians, and our grandparents, who fled the poverty and racial discrimination of rural Texas after World War II. Ours is a rambling family, with certain members shuffling in and out and temporarily sharing our living space, while others were stalwarts whose presences were consistent and deeply felt by us. It goes without saying that we grew up in a household with a plurality of generations and worldviews.

Black Los Angelenos, we were raised middle class, living in largely white areas and attending mostly Anglo private and, occasionally, public schools. While our grandparents did not attend museums or other arts events until they were middle-aged and could afford to take their children on occasional visits, our parents deemed museums important because we could learn about history and culture and be exposed to new things. They were perhaps persuaded by advertisements, such as the Norton Simon Museum's campaign featuring the glamorous Candice Bergen, which extolled the virtues and serenity of art and museums. Fortunately, we were surrounded by great art collections. As children, we visited museums during school field trips. The California Museum of Science and Industry (now known as the California Science Center) and the La Brea Tar Pits were frequent destinations. Likewise, there were regular family outings to museums. When we were young, the Children's Museum was a favorite, and when we were older, we made trips to the then-newly-opened Museum of Contemporary Art, to the Geffen Contemporary (which, at that time, went by the name Temporary Contemporary), and to the Los Angeles County Museum of Art. Some of these trips were made possible by passes—the result of corporate sponsorship of certain museums and exhibitions—that waived admissions fees, thereby encouraging employees to take their families for visits.

Later, Cherise attended, on partial scholarship, an expensive, private high school that had mandatory art and music appreciation classes. In retrospect, she realizes that these classes were a holdover of a bygone era when wealthy young people were supposed to possess at least a cursory knowledge of the arts. Sensing that they were old-fashioned, students approached these classes as a nuisance: they must be taken, but students were doubtful that the knowledge, which they perceived to be arcane, would be useful. Students quickly learned that the arts appreciation classes had advantages. In fulfilling the assignments, which included attending performances of five different musical styles and visiting five different museums, students were given carte blanche to explore Los Angeles's diverse arts scene: they heard Gregorian chants sung in south-central Los Angeles, listened to jazz on the affluent west side, and strolled the gardens of the Huntington Library in San Marino. Looking back, these assignments were designed to show students how to locate cultural events, get them to sometimes far-flung places, and open their minds to diverse artistic styles and practices.

It was on one such trip, to what was then called the J. Paul Getty Museum and is now called the Getty Villa, that the idea of having a life in the world of art took root in Cherise. Walking the gardens of the reconstructed Italian villa, seeing the perfection that ancient Greek sculptors pursued, and admiring the grandeur of the Pacific Ocean transported her to another time and place. It was an overwhelming experience for a seventeen-year-old: she wondered how she could live a life surrounded by such beauty.

A few years later, as a junior in college, Cherise switched her course of study from pre-medicine to art history, unsure about what art historians actually do. Her ambition to dedicate her career to studying beautiful objects was met with resistance; our family thought it was folly and urged her to pursue a financially rewarding field such as law or medicine. Despite their protests, she persevered, and over the next decade, she received master's and doctoral degrees in art history and worked in the curatorial departments of six major museums. This was during the 1990s, when questions surrounding audience, viewership, multiculturalism, and diversity were affecting museums' collecting, exhibiting, and educational practices in significant ways. An intellectual fire was ignited inside her: she wanted to encourage disenfranchised individuals and people of color, like members of our own family, to attend museums. She wanted them to feel a level of comfort and ownership in museums that, she thought, rightfully belonged to everyone. Here, *ownership* has a plurality of meanings: everyone who wants access to the aesthetics and ideas that art offers should have it, and anyone should have the opportunity to enjoy the respite, refuge, and critical insights that museums offer. Equally important, *ownership,* by our reckoning, means that museums should collect, display, and maintain art that addresses the experiences of diverse constituencies and that members of diverse communities can encounter art that speaks of their experiences.

As a professor of art history and specialist in American art after 1945, especially that made by African Americans, Cherise charges herself with teaching students to appreciate and understand the materiality and forms art takes; she also instructs them to think critically about the intellectual, political, and social histories surrounding artworks. Toward that end, her students see art that hangs on walls of museums and galleries, and they visit rooms where they can view prints, photographs, and other objects that have been retrieved from storage. Experience tells her that the goal of increasing students' feelings of comfort around and ownership toward art and museums by increasing the amount of time they spend in art institutions and pulling the curtains back on museum practices works: students feel more knowledgeable, which makes them more at ease in museums and around art.

While seeing art and visiting museums is a pleasurable but nonetheless intellectually demanding experience for Cherise, it is, for Gary, a relaxing activity. He is content when experiencing the architecture and space that museum environments create, and he appreciates the silence. He attributes his comfort in museums to two things: regular visits during childhood and the attitude of openness he assumes. "I leave the specialization of art to you," he says, preferring to approach art and museums from an inquisitive and humble position: he is open to learning new things and feels empowered to ask questions of museum staff or "his sister, the art historian."

That Gary can assume a posture of modesty while in museums and around art is significant. He is a specialist of baseball after all, having played in the major leagues for nine years, been named to the 2006 All-Star team, and made it to the playoffs. The level of seriousness and professionalism he applies to his own craft allows him to put aside momentarily the expectation of mastery he assumes in his own professional sphere. Still some of his concerns in the area of baseball translate directly to his interests relating to art. For example, his concern for the diminishing number of African Americans playing baseball in the major leagues leads him to question why certain objects enter museums and others do not. Similarly, his ability to sequence several disparate activities, including running, jumping, twisting, and catching, into "stealing" a home run from a batter guides his curiosity about how an artist constructs a two-dimensional painting so that it represents the three-dimensional world accurately. Likewise, his attention to the precise mechanics of swinging a bat and to the particular physics of sending a baseball on a home-run trajectory directs his inquisitiveness about the materials artists use and their methods of application.

While Gary's frequent travel lends itself to visiting some of the country's best museums, the unrelenting schedule leaves little room for exploration in museums. Nevertheless, Chicago's Field Museum, with its wonderful cabinet-like collections of artifacts and art, is one museum he visits regularly, for, as a child, it captured his imagination. As an adult, he enjoys its assortment: on one visit he might encounter an exhibit on African art, while on another he will find a display of ancient Egyptian artifacts. When visiting the Museum of Fine Arts, Houston, to see an exhibition of Jean Michel Basquiat's work or the Getty Center to see a temporary display of Manet's *Bar at the Folies Bergere,* he walks in a leisurely and meandering way, wandering around and lingering at objects that catch his interest.

For Gary, museums are pleasant environments to spark thought and clear his mind, where he looks forward to encountering school groups, scholars, and tourists from diverse ethnic, cultural, and class backgrounds and witnessing how they interact with the art and with one another. Perhaps in mutual realization that, in a different time, our race and class might have precluded us from being museum visitors, we share the belief that art belongs to everyone and that museums have wide social and political relevance. We picture, in our minds' eyes, a child's life being transformed by passion for a single work of art or a meaningful interaction with museum staff, and we see opportunity and possibility.

Cherise Smith received her PhD from Stanford University in 2005. She is assistant professor of art history at the University of Texas at Austin, where she is at work on the manuscript *En-Acting Others: Identity Performance in Works by Eleanor Antin, Nikki S. Lee, Adrian Piper, and Anna Deavere Smith.*

Gary Matthews Jr. was an All-Star center fielder, now playing for the Los Angeles Angels. A graduate of Granada Hills High School, he attended Mission College before pursuing professional baseball. After spending several years outside the state, he is pleased to have returned to California and the closeness of family.

WILL MUSEUMS SURVIVE?

Jay Wiegel

First, let me identify myself. I am a composer who has run the Contemporary Arts Center (CAC) in New Orleans since 1996. For twelve years before my appointment as executive director, I was the CAC's music director. I state this to let you know that my personal expertise is in performing arts. However, the CAC is, and has been for all of its thirty-plus years, a multidisciplinary institution, with the visual arts at the core of our programming. We employ a staff that includes a visual arts director, currently Dan Cameron, who is responsible for the curatorial decisions of this program area. I oversee the overall artistic direction of the CAC, including approving any exhibition before it is slated into our calendar and making the curatorial decisions regarding our performing arts season.

Several issues pertinent to this meditation have become evident to me since my days as music director. Over the past twenty-four years, I have observed vast changes in the arts landscape. Although many of the challenges confronting visual arts institutions and programs have been around for decades, it seems to me, at times, that many of us who manage the field of nonprofit presenters have our heads in the sand. We oversimplify and underestimate our community and audience, putting the blame on the larger community who does not attend our institution. Instead of taking a critical look at our work and how we do it, we blame education and believe that if only our community and audience were more educated, they would surely understand how important our work is. The issues do not stop there. Our institutions depend too heavily on a few foundations and wealthy individuals for our finances. Our definition of art tends to be biased. I could go on.

About ten years ago, I sat on a panel that was distributing travel money to performing artists. The applicants were requesting travel support to participate in eastern-

European festivals. When the panel had finished its work, the results showed an interesting cross-section of selected recipients. We had selected symphony orchestras, string quartets, opera singers, blues musicians, and brass bands, as well as traditional folk musicians. We were then asked for feedback as to how the process could be more effective, which prompted me to inquire about their parallel program that funded travel support for visual artists and exhibitions. I was distressed to learn that the support had gone to only the most traditional visual arts organizations and exhibitions. By traditional, I mean exhibitions and work that reflect the standard view taught in art school, which tends to hold a biased and narrow view of art. Had we on the performing arts panel approached our musical decisions with the same limited view, we would not have funded the blues artists, brass bands, or folk musicians. When I asked why this double standard was allowed to happen, I was told that the visual arts world was much slower in embracing a broader description of relevant art. I suggested that this probably had more to do with who was selected for the panel than the larger communities' ideas regarding visual art.

This last statement is at the core of the problem. As long as schools continue to teach an extremely singular view of art and as long as major institutions offer the best opportunities to young professionals who support this narrow view, the problem will only persist. At the CAC in New Orleans, a city rich and diverse in artistic activity, we face the same problem now as we have over the years. Our ethnographic art is excellent. The visual influences that are prevalent in our community are profoundly informed by non-European sources. Yet many of our curators have always vacillated to the most "traditional" contemporary artistic work. The work that does not neatly fit into the "box" propagated in art school has been given its own label, such as folk art, outsider art, and so on. These labels insinuate that this art is not really part of the main thrust of the art of our time, but some kind of aberration. Believe me when I say that our community feels this insult. As a result, they too often choose not to participate.

This lack of broad participation has led many organizations to program "blockbuster" exhibitions. These exhibitions are designed to attract large audiences by showcasing the work of the most famous artists or that revolve around an exotic theme. Too often for my taste, these exhibitions are focused on the narrowest definition of art and its origins. Thankfully, these exhibitions can give the institution unique educational and outreach opportunities, and some can even create opportunities to engage new segments of our community.

As an example, our institution presented an exhibition by Dawn Dedeaux entitled Urban Warriors. This exhibition, presented in the 1990s, examined the urban culture of New Orleans and the way in which black youth are characterized as "warriors." Dawn, though she lived in a neighborhood where this reality existed, also came from a place of experience and sympathy and as a result could be viewed as an outsider to this reality. You see, Dawn is a white woman. Her reflections on black urban youth could be viewed as an outsider looking in, commenting on a culture that she can only observe. While the exhibition was excellent and the subject matter was treated with respect, we were concerned about how our city's black community would respond. Would they feel exploited?

Fortunately, we had a strong relationship with Carol Bebelle, an African American woman, who, rather than attack our curatorial idea, instead presented us with an accompanying exhibition. Artists from New Orleans's black community, taking an insider's view of urban life in our city, created this exhibition entitled Efforts of Grace.

Urban Warriors pleased our general audience and supporters, who came in sizable numbers. The accompanying exhibition, Efforts of Grace, allowed us to balance the point of view and attract a new, broader audience. The relationships forged by this decision remain intact today. Afterward, Carol joined the CAC's staff, and while there conceived and later created the most prominent African American cultural arts institution in our city, Ashe Community Art Center, which she now runs.

Moving on, what about our dependence on foundations and wealthy patrons? Are we too dependent on too few sources of revenue? While I would never suggest that we not raise investment from these sources, I believe we often fail to think about alternative ways of creating revenue. Our sector employs some of the most creative thinkers in our country. Certainly the "product" we present comes from these creative minds, so can't we think of new ways to raise revenue?

At the CAC, we have been able to build several viable "businesses" inside of our institution. Our hospitality program employs a sales force that accounts for twelve percent of our earned revenue (before Katrina, it accounted for thirty percent). This "division" of our institute works with the New Orleans tourist and convention community to secure clients. Through this program, thousands of visitors to our city experience our exhibitions, many of whom might not have otherwise. Currently, we are now strategizing and beginning to work with other nonprofits with the goal of our sales force representing their facilities. This allows us to increase earned revenue, while helping others to keep their overhead down. They will not need to hire a sales force because they will instead rely on ours.

We also initiated a financial services program. Simply put, our financial department solicits clients who need financial services and charges a fee for performing those functions. After twelve months of operation, we have five clients. The fees from these clients have allowed us to hire staff accountants, freeing up our chief financial officer to focus on strategic thinking by relieving him of administrative work.

These two examples can be used to summarize our approach. We examined the staff skills of the CAC, areas of growth capacity, and underutilized intellectual capital, and devised ways to create positive cash flow by helping others. I would add that these strategies have also had a positive effect on contributed income. Many funders see our work to increase earned revenue as a positive indication of increased stability. This understanding has increased their confidence in the institution and allows us to have a proactive relationship with them.

I would like to point out one major shift I see that has been led by artists and not institutions: community engagement. Again, let me start with performing arts. It is my observation that performing artists have had to be somewhat accountable for attracting an audience to their presentations. To build that audience, they hold workshops and master classes, visit community organizations, conduct interviews, and have their press agents assist the presenters' marketing departments. Much of this is accomplished through short- or long-term residencies. It is exciting to see that visual artists are often instigating similar activities around their work. More visual artists want to create work that is informed by the community in which their work is presented. They not only visit art schools, universities, and so on, but also really dig deep into the community, often making visits to organizations and people they find on their own. This increased tendency among visual artists is one that our institutions need to support, nourish, and make a crucial part of our institutional culture. I believe this can have a positive effect larger than most anything else we can do. The implementation of this may be easier for those of us who focus on contemporary work, but expanding presentations to include artists engaged in community-based work can result in a broadening of the audience involved in your institution.

Finally, our sector has many incredible opportunities ahead. Our relevance to the general health of our community is talked about more today than ever before by many of our state and local political leaders. While talk is not the same as financial support, we need to focus on the opportunity to turn talk into reality. We can work together as a united sector to raise awareness collectively and to provide real services, artistic and otherwise, that prove our relevancy. If we lead the way, our artists will follow, and our country will benefit.

A New Orleans composer and musician, Jay Wiegel is executive/artistic director for the Contemporary Arts Center in New Orleans, Louisiana. In the wake of the 2005 Hurricane Katrina disaster, Wiegel has overseen the New Orleans Museums Rebuilding Consortium and has launched the New Orleans Concert Series to preserve and celebrate the city's rich musical heritage.

CHAPTER 4

Inclusion

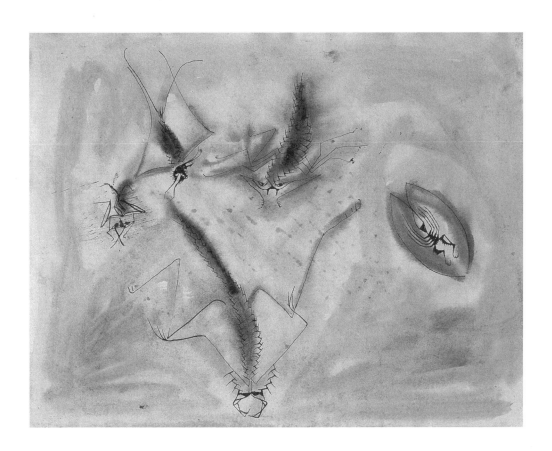

WHAT IS INCLUSION with respect to museums? How can we define inclusion in a meaningful manner for those of us who are committed to the world of museums as democratic institutions? Is inclusion an ideal related only to physical accessibility for our visitors and the success we achieve in making everyone feel welcome and therefore included? Or is it a larger, more complex and multifaceted ideal that also touches on the intellectual, philosophical, and moral aspects that we encounter every day in any museum? We argue that inclusion must encompass both ideals. Still, each museum needs to determine how much and how well it has fulfilled its own mission with respect to the value of inclusion, as this is the value that particularly marks its success in a democratic society. Each museum needs to determine how far it has come and how far it is willing and able to go to provide a sustainable, inclusive institution.

Museums have been working long and hard to shed the reputation of elitism. We have spent enormous time and expended untold financial resources creating environments that are intended to be more welcoming to greater and greater percentages of the population. Nevertheless, even as museum architecture, interior design, exhibition strategies, restaurants, non-stop programming, and more seductive shops make our museums appear more inclusive and accessible, the simultaneous, almost ubiquitous embrace of ever-higher admissions charges has effectively excluded many more people than the populist approach can possibly have attracted through our portals. It could be argued that museums have become embroiled in a problematic contradiction by creating a situation in which we must keep increasing our admissions fees to help balance budgets that have to get larger and larger to pay for our increasingly expensive exhibitions and special projects that are apparently necessary to make our museums more inclusive! So what was once free or inexpensive became costly—too costly for some of the lower-income people we most wanted to reach—and the cycle, ironically, can be traced back to the ideal of inclusion. Perhaps the time has come for us to analyze how we can be more truly inclusive, more accessible and welcoming to all, and in so doing we might succeed in finding sustainable solutions to the unintended negative consequences that have accompanied our most expansive and populist plans.

These are some of the questions we must ask about our respective institutions as we analyze the issues around social and intellectual inclusion: Is the museum perceived to be intimidating and, if so, what are we doing to enhance a sense of welcome? Are we encouraging diverse audiences to enter our doors by providing contextualizing experiences that might be of special interest to those audiences? Does the museum, even if it is dedicated to the defense of a specific narrative in a show or in its mission, acknowledge the rights of others to disagree, to bring their own narratives with them? Does it allow that there might be a variety of valid points of view about the history of art, history, science, or archaeology, or any other aspect of the material culture with which our museums are engaged? If so, how? Conversely, how much inclusion of other perspectives is positive, and when does that value begin to break down and start being counterproductive? These are only some of the questions. The answers themselves are diverse, and that is as it should be. There is no overarching answer about how to achieve the ideal of inclusion. The point of this chapter, though, is to argue that a sustainable museum philosophy with respect to inclusion must be considered and that the philosophy must be able to be assessed in practice.

Each of the essays in this chapter presents an example about the value of inclusion and develops how it has been approached in museums with which the authors have been associated. As a whole, we hope the essays will provide fuel for conversations with your boards, staffs, funders, governors, and even forums with the public. We need to remember that almost all museums, whether public or private, whether in Latin America or Europe, Asia or the United States, whether as direct recipients of government funding or more indirect beneficiaries by means of tax relief (e.g., uncollected revenues by the government, as in the United States) do benefit from the public purse. And with those means of support come the responsibility to include a broad and generously conceived range of people and programming in a museum's accounting of its aspirations and achievements to inclusion.

Our first essay, by James Walvin, directly attacks the questions around inclusion as related to the extended national effort in England to stimulate a heightened historical awareness of the abolition of the slave trade. The broadest possible inclusion was successfully achieved through coordination by history museums with schools and even, surprisingly, by a special issue of abolitionist stamps by the Post Office! Inclusion was undertaken as a mass national ideal that supported the efforts not only of museums, but also of other public institutions to underline the importance of remembering Great Britain's positive historical marker with respect to the correction of a grave historical wrong.

Bernard Müller stakes out a different realm by including a counter-perspective to the official French philosophy that prevailed in the creation of the Quai Branly museum, which opened in Paris in 2006. Müller demonstrates how he was able to subvert the old-fashioned, colonial ideas that characterized the museum through the installation of contemporary exhibitions that questioned the overriding thesis of the museum. He was thus able to help realign the Quai Branly more harmoniously with the increasingly inclusive approaches to public life widely held both by intellectuals and the general populace in France—approaches that exist in opposition to the governing ideas of the political class that shaped the museum as the container of the art and material culture of "the other."

The Huntington Gardens and Art Gallery in San Marino, California, labored under the perception of being generally aloof and, particularly, of being not especially family-friendly. Its garden director completely changed that perception by creating a special place in it for children. James Folsom, by giving more than lip service to the reality of children being the cornerstones of our museums in the future, built an inclusive, interactive, and, above all, fun garden haven for children, one where they could gently develop curiosity and an understanding of physical phenomena through joyful experience of the world in bloom. Carlos Monsiváis, on the other hand, struggles with the broad notion of cultural inclusion in Latin America, but principally in Mexico, where, he writes, the elites do not consider museums or cultural institutions a natural right for all but rather as a gift from "us" to "them." He distinguishes cultural inclusion from political and economic inclusion and laments that cultural inclusion only happens when pushed from below. His philosophical essay is a meditation on the nature of that push and the museological possibilities that it can generate.

And finally Vanda Vitali, writing from New Zealand, challenges us to face the limitation of what can be achieved with respect to inclusion. Museums, she writes, can help society be more open, both in the social realm and in the realm of ideas, but there are limits to what they can achieve as well. She explores those limits here, leading us to end this chapter not with any answers, but with an assertion of the ongoing ambiguities around the nature of inclusion in museums. By extension we will make our cases more credibly if we do not aspire to more than is realistically achievable.

As with the values we have already explored—the public trust, the primacy of collections, and the requirement of relevance—each museum must stake out its own goals and objectives with respect to inclusion. As our writer, James Folsom, says, ask around, inquire into the community how it feels about the inclusiveness of your museum. Observe who comes and who stays away. Costly surveys may not be necessary. You will be more credible when making your case to supporters that your museum is really emblematic of inclusion, that you really represent this sustaining and sustainable values if you can summon up the history to prove it.

REMEMBERING ABOLITION: BRITAIN AND THE SLAVE TRADE, 1807–2007

James Walvin

 The year 2007 marked the two hundredth anniversary of the abolition of the British slave trade. It was remembered in a remarkable series of commemorations in galleries, museums, and libraries—indeed, in most institutions—from Parliament down to small local schools. Throughout, there was a strong and influential political interest (and a plethora of government publications) along with substantial funding made available on a competitive basis by the National Heritage Lottery Fund. The outcome was the most pervasive and eye-catching public commemoration in recent years.

This cultural interest in a single historical moment—the British abolition of the slave trade in 1807—seems easily explained at first sight: here was a "feel-good" event that showed the British at their benevolent best. Abolition saw the ending of a violent and miserable episode in British history (before 1807, British ships had carried 3.5 million Africans across the Atlantic). Yet closer scrutiny of 1807 reveals a much more problematic issue than a simple triumph of good over evil. Why did the world's leading slave trader transform itself in a generation into a global abolitionist power? For curators, the initial and pressing problem was how to present abolition—an act of Parliament—to a viewing public not merely on its own terms, but set in the context of a longer history of slavery itself. To take a simple example, the Parliament, which passed abolition in 1807, had, for more than a century before, passed dozens of acts to assist and make possible the British slave trade.

In the three years before 2007, the urge to commemorate 1807 grew into a broadly based—almost irresistible—cultural force, encouraged by a government that saw the commemoration as a means of speaking to a range of important contemporary social issues (of social inclusion, human trafficking, and democratic access). The year 1807 had a resonance for 2007. Here, after all, was the first successful campaign against human trafficking—all issues that were troubling Europe in the new century. And here, too, in 1807 was an effort by the British to turn away from its slaving past and to usher in a world of social inclusion: black and white as equals—"Am I not a man and a brother?" For politicians, a glance at the story of 1807 seemed to reveal an uncanny reflection of many of today's critical social problems.

As this cultural surge toward 2007 increased, British institutions scrambled to find an appropriate way of presenting their own distinctive interpretation of 1807. All agreed that it was pointless simply to replicate the broad story of abolition in 1807. What quickly emerged was an extraordinary variety of interpretations; a host of local, specialized, and specific commemorations, all of which added up to a national picture. Not surprisingly, the story of 1807 looked very different in Manchester, Liverpool, and Bristol. Even highly specialized museums (e.g., natural history) found a way to link their holdings to slavery and abolition. Libraries and archives in small towns were equally inventive in teasing out local connections to 1807. And schools everywhere found ways of engaging local children in the debate about abolition. The end result was a mosaic of interpretations, clustered around the same theme, but each speaking to a unique vision.

If there was a "national" vision of 1807, it was offered by the remarkable output of the BBC. Scarcely a department within the BBC failed to respond to the challenge of the commemoration, and the end result was, in March 2007, a rich complexity of programs on TV and on radio, all analyzing, portraying, and debating the significance of 1807. Add to this veritable blizzard of news coverage in the press a shoal of scholarly books, essays, and meetings. The end result was that it was almost impossible to avoid the two hundredth commemorations, culminating in a memorial service before the Queen and Prime Minister in Westminster Abbey. By then there were also available a new set of abolitionist stamps (two of the six portraying African faces) and even a new abolition coin.

From this profusion of commemorations perhaps the most striking—because of its origin and location—was the parliamentary exhibition in Westminster Hall. It emerged from an earlier desire to make public display of Parliament's own ample art collection and to provide greater public access to Parliament. The parliamentary abolition exhibition (for which I acted as historical advisor) sought to explain the Abolition Act of 1807 as a consequence of popular politics: to see the Act of 1807 flowing from grassroots discontent from men and women, black and white, high and low. This was a very different view from a traditional interpretation of abolition as being largely the work of Wilberforce and the Evangelicals. Equally, the parliamentary exhibition set out to attract large numbers of London schoolchildren (many of whom also walked the "slave routes," which conducted them along some of the main sites of British black history in and around Westminster en route to the exhibition). Here was an elite institution—Parliament—opening its doors to young Britons and others and addressing a history that had previously been the preserve of small numbers of academic historians. It was, at once, an inclusive commemoration and an expansion of popular historical awareness.

A different and distinctive exhibition spawned by the anniversary of 1807 was that devoted to the life of Olaudah Equiano, a major figure of African descent who was a part of the British advocacy for the abolition of the slave trade, in the Birmingham Art Gallery (again, I was advisor). This sought to link both the local black community and schools to the development of the exhibition and to its appeal as a public commemoration. A smaller "traveling exhibit" toured regional schools and libraries and (like the parliamentary case) a catalogue and set of essays was published in parallel. So too was a "teachers's pack" for use in schools. Forty years ago Equiano was virtually unknown, but now, in 2007, he had found a home in a major provincial gallery and his face was draped along the sides of major civic buildings in Birmingham. Equiano now appeared on the city skyline and even appeared on national postage stamps. All this represented a major transformation for a man known, until recently, only to specialist scholars. At the very least, 2007 represented a huge spread of historical information and awareness.

In both exhibitions I worked on, the curatorial teams worked hard to foster links to local communities and to schools. Through all this activity, museum leaders and their teams worked in harness with academic specialists in the appropriate fields. As the process emerged, it became clear that public history had outpaced academic history in confronting major historical issues and in styles that embraced a wide and varied public audience. Stated crudely, tens of thousands of people became aware of the importance and complexities of the abolition of the slave trade in 1807 via exhibitions and public commemorations rather than via the published work of scholars. Armies of people shuffled through galleries and made their own judgments about the significance of 1807. But what *did* they really think about what they saw and experienced?

With that question in mind, colleagues at the University of York launched a major research project that probed both the origins and creation of exhibitions (what were the aims and ambitions of the curatorial teams?) and the reaction of the visitors to the finished product. The intention is to blend interviews with exhibition visitors with data gleaned from exhibition planners, with the aim of producing a rounded analysis of the commemorations of 1807.

We await the outcome of that work, but other outcomes of 2007 are already clear. The study of slavery and abolition became part of the nation's compulsory school curriculum in 2008: this is a major social change—a direct consequence of 2007 that few could have predicted. There has also been a remarkable flowering of local research projects on the back of 2007 exploring the links between the locality and slavery and abolition. This has often flourished in the most unlikely of places (Newcastle and Norwich, for example). What we have witnessed in 2007 is the British rethinking their history, scratching away at the surface of the physical fabric around them. And there, as the galleries and museums revealed in the course of 2007, they find an abundance of links to Britain's slaving past: stately homes founded on slave profits, business and finance shaped by the Atlantic slave trade, local radical traditions forged initially in the drive against the slave trade.

What the public commemorations of 2007 have illustrated is that the British slaving past is to be found not merely in the Americas and Africa or on the high seas, but it can be found closer to home, in Britain itself. As creators of public history in 2007 scratched the surface in their institutions they have revealed slavery and abolition in all of its local— and often surprising—diversity.

The inspiration behind this array of exhibitions was, of course, varied. There was, however, a shared determination to embrace as wide a visiting audience as possible. There was a vague, shared sense that each institution had a unique opportunity to speak to a national issue (abolition) with a distinctive, local voice. The events of 2007 have been both imaginative (and varied) and sometimes even commercial. The surge of people through the major exhibitions has surpassed expectations and has fulfilled the ubiquitous aim of popular public access.

A minor but no less interesting story reveals why some institutions chose *not* to do anything commemorating 1807. The National Archives, for example, canceled an initial plan to create an archival exhibition—and did so allegedly on commercial grounds: there seemed no money to be made from 1807. It was a strange decision, which did not reflect well on the nation's archival service. That aside, however, promoters of public history in 2007 have shown themselves to be in the vanguard of advancing public awareness about a major episode in British history. The events of 2007 prompted expanding public historical awareness. Inevitably it also opened a Pandora's box of historical argument and debate. But it was a debate that quickly enriched Britain's cultural life. It is no exaggeration to say that the events of 2007 have enabled us to rethink our historical past in ways no one could have predicted. Public history and commemoration in 2007 proved instrumental in encouraging a cultural debate that was both historical and contemporary—hence its great appeal to both politicians and the public alike.

Dr. James Walvin, OBE, recently retired professor of history at York University, has written more than thirty-five books, mostly on the subject of the slave trade. He functioned as curatorial advisor in the national effort to celebrate the abolition of that trade in England and to heighten national awareness of it. Walvin continues to write and lecture the world over.

INCLUDING CONTEMPORARY ART AT THE MUSÉE DU QUAI BRANLY: A WAY OF COMING TO TERMS WITH THE COLONIAL PAST *À LA FRANÇAISE*?

Bernard Müller

Time is the genuine treasure of a museum of mankind, not its collections. Time is what conservators actually conserve, preciously, and what they distribute cautiously. This is especially true in the case of the musée du quai Branly (inaugurated 23 June 2006, and seen by 2,520,470 visitors as of the writing of this essay), in the French postcolonial context in which the issue of France's colonial past remains a museographic taboo, not to speak of restitution or any kind of concept of reparation. This French postcolonial syndrome, which can be seen as paradoxical "French insularity," is probably more due to the culture of its elites, and notably of its civil servants, than to a real national outlook, since the public opinion seems to be much more in favor of a kind of *Vergangenheitsbewältigung* ("coming to terms with the past") *à la française*, as suggests the Taubira law declaring slavery from the fifteenth century onward to be a crime against humanity. In France there is a fantastic gap between the values of its elites, including academicians and researchers, and its very dynamic nongovernmental organization network supported by independent artists and intellectuals who realized the importance of opening the debate about French responsibility concerning its colonial past, beyond the fixation on the Algerian war of independence. This gap clearly appeared when the parliament passed a law to put an upbeat spin on a painful era, making it mandatory to enshrine in textbooks the country's positive role in its colonies before their independence. The law had finally to be abrogated after the pressure of a number of nongovernmental groups, supported in that case by inspired schoolteachers who refused energetically to apply this law.

As such, the musée du quai Branly remains a basically conservative institution in the quite conservative province of the world called France, founded on nineteenth-century rigid republican and ethnocentric principles, meant to be universal, and definitely reluctant to encompass the co-temporality of the societies whose objects are displayed in the museum. The museum works as a jewel case that freezes the object. The aim is to congeal its historical dimension, and thus the relation between France and the others in a *beautified and beatified* form that cannot be grasped, sealed in an ultimate figure out of political reach. It may sound unbelievable, but it is possible to spend an afternoon in this museum without knowing exactly where the objects come from, who produced them, and how they arrived where they are today.

Nevertheless, a museum is an institution that reflects numerous tensions, at the meeting point of local sociocultural conditions and global geostrategic considerations. The object is probably the hostage of this situation. These tensions are mainly defined by the present state of the relationship between France and its former colonies, these formerly colonized who are now called the "other" in order to erase once again the historical dimension and its still-problematic dimension (motto: *"musée du quai Branly, le musée des autres*"). The fissures in the walls of the "fortress of time" are numerous; the "other" is indeed finding the way to the treasure of the fortress or at least for now, tracing the itinerary for others to come, using contemporary art practices—from visual arts to performance—as a kind of Trojan horse, by bringing in surreptitiously time and history (i.e., relationship and interaction).

The hope is certainly that they will all do it as peacefully and ironically as Yinka Shonibare did it during his exhibition *Jardin d'Amour*/Garden of Love (April–July 2007). Yinka Shonibare's installation precisely attempts to counterbalance the *allochronic* trend of the musée du quai Branly when it expels the people who did the objects out of time. His position, as expressed in an interview, is quite clear:

> Interviewer: What does it mean for you to perform this installation in a "museum of mankind" where it will be surrounded by so called "traditional/primitive" objects?
>
> YS: For me the context of the quai Branly, because of the ethnographic collections, is the perfect context for this work. As an artist of African origin, I know that somehow there is an expectation that I am still connected to traditional African art . . . even though I am a twenty-first-century person and it would be rather odd to imagine that a French or English artist is remotely interested in Medieval art. But in the case of an African, for some reason, he is somehow meant not to have experienced Modernism. Of course this is a fallacy! Saying that, I do not mean that I do not equally value traditional art from Africa, Oceania, etc. Of course I value them in their historical context. I have to understand them historically. It's a very complicated issue. I certainly will not say that as an artist, that all ethnographic museums in Europe should be abolished. And in a way, I also feel a contradiction, as I don't like the way the objects were acquired, politically. Quite a number of these objects were indeed looted and as such they are symbols of conquest. But culturally, I am happy that some of the objects are there and where I can see them. The question arises of course whether they are preserved in the right context or in the right way? Most of these objects were used in religious contexts such as rituals, and they were not art in the way we put art in a gallery now. They were very much part of initiation and ritualistic ceremonies. So Modern art is different from that point of view. Yes, of course they were art, they were aesthetic but very much linked to different types of ritual. It's a dilemma and I can't give you the answer: do I think the objects, all of them, should be given back? If the objects were given back, will the objects be looked after? I don't know! Is it important that the objects are looked after? Because also in some cultures the point might be to throw the objects away after the ceremony, so it is also possible that the idea of preserving these objects is just a Western notion. (*Yinka Shonibare, MBE: Jardin d'amour. Garden of Love, Exposition.* Paris: Flammarion; musée du quai Branly, 2007.)

Paris's new museum on the Quai Branly has chosen as its motto "the place where cultures dialogue." Its president, Stéphane Martin, is generally understood to possess the ambition for the museum he directs to play a political role: "We want to play a role in the city, as the centre George Pompidou does." But to really create the conditions of such a political dialogue, a statement is not enough. Equality between the interlocutors is the result of a long process based on numerous interactions and a complex of relations based on mutual respect. This should be the role of a relevant contemporary art and research program in a museum of humankind in a postcolonial context. A museum should be a place where conversation and not only conservation is made possible, here and today.

> An independent curator and dramaturge, Bernard Müller teaches social anthropology at the Ecole des Hautes Etudes en Sciences Socials, Paris. Bernard works on special projects such as the Yinka Shonibare installation *Jardin d'Amour* and acts as an independent curator for the museé du quai Branly. He is presently working on a multimedia program on the "memory of slavery."

THE HUNTINGTON'S DECISIONS ABOUT AUDIENCE AND SERVICE: HOW AND WHERE COULD A CHILDREN'S GARDEN BE BROUGHT INTO PLAY?

James Folsom

In the wide array of nonprofits in the Los Angeles, California, area, my own institution, the Huntington, has had a broad challenge in regard to "inclusion." As a collections-based institution, with significant library, art, and plant resources, the Huntington is guided by an indenture that directs the institution to benefit the general public, with the measure of success being what it produces. There is no further definition of "general public" and little direction as to how the product might be gauged—it is for people, for the public. But who is the public and how does it benefit? And how is that benefit measured?

For the Huntington, the ultimate audience is society at large—and the question of benefit depends on which audience is directly served. The immediate audience for library collections is the researcher. The benefit afforded to the public comes with pure archiving and organizing of important material and educational exhibits, but most importantly in the knowledge produced by research that flows from use of materials. The museums and gardens are dedicated more completely to exhibitions and benefit the public in multiple ways, through nested layers of audience engagement—from interpretive research of curators and involvement of donors and supporters to the nourishing of teachers and the legacy of meaning-making that object-based exhibits can bring to those who visit. The fact that the museums and gardens could serve the general public indirectly through servicing a narrower professional audience introduces a conundrum. Why open more than absolutely necessary to the public, given complex issues of directly serving the public writ large, when the public could benefit ultimately from the work of researchers serviced by the institution?

These are the issues we considered a decade ago, specifically in regard to the botanical gardens. With an established collections function and 500,000 visitors annually, the Huntington already had a good-sized audience and could claim success. But our community has changed greatly over the past few decades and the makeup of our visiting population represents only a narrow segment of the regional constituency. What would be achieved by engaging a broader audience, and how might that be accomplished? And how would the Huntington determine, in the end, that the change proved worthwhile, both for the institution as well as for the public?

For the Gardens specifically, the answer to the question of serving the public through direct engagement was easy. We were already doing that. Moreover, since the greatest cost of maintaining the Gardens derived from keeping them open to the public, it became clear that given insufficient endowment, the only way the Gardens could survive into the long-term future would be through increased public support. Because the Gardens are able to appeal to a broad audience, the logic of appealing to the broadest possible audience was undeniable.

At this point, other institutional issues fell into place—issues and discussions that could fill volumes. A significant outcome was the decision to move ahead with a project that had been in the ether for two decades—construction of a children's garden. This was actually a serious matter; both insiders and outsiders perceived the Huntington as a place of gravity, a very adult place. How and where could a children's garden be brought into play? Why? And with resources stretched already, how would it be funded? Thus began a journey into our own enlightenment, a story more lengthy and complex than we have space to present, but a tale with lessons.

The first lesson is that supporters should not be sold short—they see opportunities and worry when an institution will move ahead. The idea of a children's garden so challenged staid perceptions of the Huntington and held such promise for bringing gardens and art to new audiences that support materialized quickly. At the very first presentation of the concept, Helen and Peter Bing adopted the project and have remained engaged through development, design, construction, and implementation. Supporters are often waiting for institutions to make bold moves.

The second lesson is that one way to develop a new audience is to grow it—starting with children and families who then have the opportunity to discover and appreciate other aspects of the institution. The connection with institutional programs meant the children's garden could not be an adjunct playground; it had to bring delight and discovery to the landscape as a prelude to adult appreciation of plants, gardens, and the natural world. The simple goal was to ensure that children think of the Huntington as a special place for them, a place of memory and wonder. The result was more profound. The garden is designed for young children, but that brings parents and other caregivers, and nothing delights parents more than discovering an engaging, supportive, learning experience for their children.

A third lesson reminds us that children learn the same way we all began—through hands-on activities that shape a mind for future intellectual endeavor. This mode of learning remains the easiest path to understanding. As we grow up, past experience allows us to delight in the mere thought of encounters and activities. However, exhibits that engage children through opportunities to touch and interact can be just as welcome for adults—we do not forget how we first learned. Moreover, like Montessori education, we can often use the same materials for adults as we do for children. We underestimate children when we assume they always require saccharine or nauseatingly whimsical paraphernalia. Indeed, children developed very nicely for centuries in adult settings, devoid of the infantile trappings with which we dutifully surround them today. In the end, the extra thought dedicated to distilling themes and concepts to a level intelligible for children could play out for people of all ages. Sometimes, in an effort to reinforce how seriously we take a topic, we insist on exhibits and signage that are too arcane, even for educated adults.

A fourth lesson is that learning must be, as today's science educators say, a lifelong endeavor. Moreover, studies suggest that multigenerational learning is powerful, in that family experiences retold and reinforced after encounters outside the home have a greater chance of becoming permanent memories than concepts that do not surface again. A museum or garden that engages families in the joyful pursuit of learning may be seeing the greatest heart-to-heart educational effect that is possible in society at large.

And then there is humility. Some of life's greatest lessons are the simplest ones, learned early and reinforced continually. As we age and become more introspective, we grow away from learning through physical engagement. We come to think of working with our hands as drudgery, associating manual activity with things demeaning. We become effete and distant. Expanding programs to include children and families keeps us young and connected, reminding us to use all of our faculties, to make exhibits immersive, experiential. Indeed, reaching out to any nontraditional audience will likely bring new genius to a program by forcing curators to expand their own thoughts.

These are bold claims. How could you test the idea that inclusiveness makes an institution more productive, more beneficial? If a clear strategy were established, real baseline and formative studies could inform expansionist agendas, with summative evaluation planned for drawing conclusions. Alternatively, there are surveys and comparisons that can be designed to yield data and conclusions as subjective or objective as is desired.

Or you could talk to my daughter, who, at the age of five, spent an entire day in the San Jose Children's Museum, where she came to the opinion that the word *museum* meant joy unconfined. Indeed, the next year we went out of our way to drive through San Jose, just to spend a couple of hours at the museum to see if the excitement could be replicated. And the magic was still there. The next year, on learning that her second-grade class would be visiting an area museum, Molly could hardly contain her excitement. The day came for the class visit, and I was anxious to learn how her day went. That afternoon I asked, "How was your trip to the museum?" She was clearly let down, so I asked what happened. Her response: "They just talked at us." You can't just "talk at" a group of second graders, and you could do better than just "talking at" a group of adults.

Though such audience feedback is anecdotal and unscientific, I believe it is crucial. The greatest way for the curator or director to stay connected is to spend time on the floor, asking visitors for their thoughts, giving lectures, teaching a class from time to time, and conducting occasional tours. Leaders need to take an unconventional leap into the roles occupied by people in the admissions booth and interpreters in the galleries. They must eavesdrop on family conversations, gently of course, and observe the behavior of visitors. You can pay as many consultants and staff as you wish to make these observations, but the same lessons that apply to visitors apply to curators—there is no substitute for firsthand experience.

Leaders should inquire in the community to come to understand how the institution is viewed. One time I was at the muffler shop, sitting next to a retired fellow. I asked him if he had ever visited the Huntington, and he told me no, he hadn't: "That's just a place for a bunch of rich people." A few years later we hired a costly evaluation firm to conduct focus studies in the community and come to the same conclusion.

In the final analysis, a museum or public garden is about people—those who know you as well as those who do not. Yes, it originates with a subject, which is usually a collection of objects, but any collections-based institution attempts to create public benefit through preservation, study, and promotion. We are tempted to measure institutional worth by the strength of our collections, but I would argue that the greatest museum or garden is the one that affects as broad a component of the public as possible in the most fundamental and profound ways—by becoming a place of cultural memory and pride, by enriching the educational level of society in ways that help people to develop social units and improve their own lives and the lives of others, by bringing joy, beauty, and pleasure to the world, and, most importantly, through helping us all learn to live together happily, productively, and sustainably. An institution that ceaselessly adapts with its community and yet grounds the community in significant and timeless ways is one that serves well, and should survive well.

James Folsom, director of the Huntington Botanical Gardens, received his PhD in botany from the University of Texas at Austin. With the goal of establishing the Huntington as a national leader in botanical research and education, he created the Botanical Center, the Children's Garden, and the Rose Hills Foundation Conservatory for Botanical Science, aiming to educate new generations of children in basic plant science.

MUSEUMS (A RAPID VIEW OF GUIDED TOURS): THE RUINS OF THE FUTURE SHOULD BE IN SHOP WINDOWS

Carlos Monsiváis

Translated by Francisca González Arias

In memoriam, Olivier Debroise

The demographic explosion (an overpopulated planet, ravaged resources of all kinds) commands our attention even beyond neoliberalism's aptitude for plundering. It simultaneously renders moral sentiment stricter and less absolute, provides daily redefinitions of scarcity, and, by its very devastating effect, foresees and foments all kinds of disasters. But let us not pile everything on top of the similarly jam-packed apocalyptic vision. The surplus of people renews and enlarges ideas and cultural practices, among them, for example, visiting museums. At first, about three decades ago, and only within the group of great American and European museums, voluntary attendance was generally, if only partially verifiably, attributed to a variation on the tour: cultural tourism. Cultural tourism is a limited explanation because it does not take into account growing information about creators and artistic tendencies, and also because the devout attitude toward art, characteristic of elites during the early decades of the twentieth century, is making a furious comeback and transcends mere tourism when it insists in several ways on *the spiritual benefits* for those who view the plastic arts. This is an expression that reeks of affected religiosity but that was already ensconced in secular territory where it seemed, and continues to seem, unassailable.

"The religion of art" is an old expression, which became popular with a specific purpose as secularization prevailed; the purpose was to disseminate certain states of mind called forth by artistic power and to attest to "the apprehension of the sublime." People glimpse or delve deeply into the artistic experience through devotion. To be moved in front of images of Christ, saints, or virgins in cathedrals or country churches is equivalent, even though the contexts are different, to what is felt in contemplative attitudes in museums or in churches that the visitor's eyes turn into museums. Some harmonize their experiences and others do not, but outside the space of prayer, the work of art is the subject/object of reverent attention that facilitates entry into the unknown or the extraordinary: the sense of genuine wonder. Oh, the great paintings, the great sculptures, the marvelous carvings, drawings, engravings! Many beholders of the extraordinary could cite the verses of Saint John of the Cross: "Now you can look at me / after you looked at me, / what grace and beauty you left in me!"

From the nineteenth century on, the religion of art has been the privilege of the happy few whose number is increasing; then came cultural internationalization, the mass reproduction of works of art, and the diversity of social and artistic phenomena just after World War II, when going to Europe implied giving other opportunities to travelers who were already desirous of experiencing new things. Enthusiasm spread from the cultural elites to all social classes: "You've got to see *The Last Supper*." "I don't want to die without experiencing one of Goya's great works." "Don't tell me you've never seen *The Mona Lisa* up close?" And the stream of visitors who refuse to take their last breath unless they have stood in amazement in front of a Rembrandt or a Tiépolo increases in the face of interventions of the culture industry: "Charles Laughton was brilliant as Rembrandt, but Kirk Douglas was matchless as Van Gogh, and Anthony Quinn was the best Gauguin ever." Droves of people come to museums impelled not only by curiosity but also by something new, in the following proportions: the sense of duty and the desire for sudden spiritual well-being.

In Mexico there is an emphasis on the right to culture (something which, by the way, should not be made part of bureaucracy and allowed to die like a clause in a constitutional article), which is and should be an essential human right. Yet what has not been duly taken into account is an international movement from the bottom up governed by the feeling of doing one's duty and the vow to do it again. These are the dynamics of the many who, despite distraught guards, linger as long as possible before Michelangelo's murals in the Sistine Chapel, in front of *La Giaconda* in the Louvre, before Turner's paintings in the National Gallery, or while viewing *Las Meninas* and El Greco's saints and virgins in the Prado, before the Elvises and Jackie Kennedys of Warhol wherever possible, in front of *The Two Fridas* in major exhibitions, and before a work by Richard Serra in the Guggenheim of Bilbao. With the intensification of secular "sacralization" of architecture, and with more time than that allotted in museums, aesthetic enjoyment flourishes in front of works by Frank Lloyd Wright, Le Corbusier, Mies van der Rohe, Luis Barragán, Frank Gehry, and many more.

The marveling multitudes are gripped by a thesis that can perhaps be expressed in this way: "It is my right to be here, in this museum, because it is also my duty." This rallying cry of museumophiles of the past explains today's massification: "Why should I miss out on the chance to make the most of my time and to mentally record this visit?" (Mental videos replace memories.) And the so-called classic questions reappear: "Who came first: the public or the museum?" "What came first: the wish to admire or the object of admiration?" "What was seen first: the art or the aesthetic?" These questions are misleading: museum attendance is enormous.

Although the notion of acceding to one's rights, centering on the term *inclusion*, has become generalized, it is very recent. Beginning ten or fifteen years ago, in programs and projects, it has been a basic characteristic of democracy that is still utopian and almost unachievable and requires huge political battles, but which can no longer be dispensed with. Political, social, and economic inclusion, however difficult it may seem to the majority, is now a ubiquitous demand, but *cultural inclusion* is not even taken into account: "That's an individual matter." However, the mere enunciation of the topic favors its reason for being, its definitions, and its mobilizations, and if it is not yet perceived clearly, this is due, among other things, to the old prejudice. Culture is the gift bestowed on those who, albeit sporadically, accept it in the way it is given. In this sense, and to the contrary, cultural inclusion is, and can only be, a demand from below, while from above it is still considered a gift.

Is there a demand for cultural inclusion? It should be emphasized that this demand is not expressed as such, but the desire for it does strive to be seen and heard. The commotion following worthy offerings (opportunities) in art, music, and sometimes in literature is irrefutable proof of this. Furthermore, it is not only a question of offerings but also of pressure by groups and sectors: young people who are demanding cultural centers in the city or the suburb, who buy books and CDs on sale, who are involved in any kind of creative effort—from the graffiti artist, to video filmmakers, to poetry workshops, to amateur installation artists, and so on. I'm not referring to the quality of their products, but to their attitude, whether verbalized or not, that characterizes cultural inclusion as a civil right, or, if you will, a most noble demand, even when it is not, or could not, be presented in this way because it is a recently coined term, and because culture does not carry enough weight in the educational system of Latin America and Mexico.

An examination of textbooks shows that culture occupies a very minor place, while what is considered important is devoted to fundamental social studies: national and international history, grammar, geography, the sciences, and so on. Two or three pages and a series of illustrations are devoted to culture: a fragment of a mural by Diego Rivera, a painting by Tamayo, a picture of Octavio Paz, a text by Juan Rulfo, a poem by Sabines or José Emilio Pacheco. This occurs in Mexico, and similar situations exist in other Latin American countries where culture is the sum of unique qualities that highlight a country's wealth from another point of view. In the predominant educational perspective, culture and the arts do not have a role in daily life, however much they may have it on occasions of bureaucratic and social pride.

For the same reason, which is true in too many countries, museums are not seen as providers of fundamental experiences. In Mexico, the first occurrence of cultural inclusion as a right of the masses (without that qualifier) was the inauguration of the National Museum of Anthropology (Museo Nacional de Antropología). In 1964 the Museum's presence caused noteworthy changes: first, the great indigenous art became a national and personal heritage, which it had not been before due to internal and external racism. After visiting the Museum of Anthropology one could no longer dispense with the admiration of indigenous art, and the pre-Hispanic past became *our* cultural past; it was not the only one, but it could not be ignored. Second, the Museum of Anthropology was vastly aided by the recognition of foreigners and the cultural tourism that turns into museum ritual transferred, for example, to ceremonial centers previously devoted to the bewilderment of those interested in nature and in the "primitives" (note the quotation marks); these are now the subject of persons who extract from identity the heritage of subjective affirmations and who go to museums to reaffirm commitments, belongings, and ways of admiring. In the 1960s and 1970s the lessons of the Museum of Anthropology were not fully taken advantage of because of a lack of institutional (that is, business) confidence in the other great creative elements of the past: the art of the Viceroyalty, nineteenth century, and modern and contemporary art. It is also true that the value of archaeological heritage is not subject to controversy, since no more will be produced, and none of these majestic works will ever make it to auctions at Sotheby's or Christie's because they are barred from the legal market.

I offer the example of Mexico, with which I am more or less familiar. In the area of painting, for example, at the start of the 1960s, the state lacked the museum impulse (the impulse to collect) that it placed in international exhibitions of Mexican art organized by Fernando Gamboa. In those traveling exhibitions in Europe and the United States the fundamental canon of national art that is still in effect was created. However, the state bought just a few pieces of the art it circulated and, relying on the existence of mural art, did not seek to acquire important paintings it had access to. The federal or state governments could have easily purchased major first-rate collections; this did not happen. The state did obtain some extraordinary pieces, but the majority went abroad because the bourgeoisie of that time neither bought nor gave away ("Isn't my presence decoration enough?"). Pressure was not brought upon museum administrators to acquire international twentieth-century painting and paintings by Diego Rivera, David Alfaro Siqueiros, José Clemente Orozco, Frida Kahlo, María Izquierdo, Agustín Lazo, Juan O'Gorman, and so on. It is extraordinary that the major state collection of Frida Kahlo was the gift of Dolores Olmedo, because, despite the fact that Fernando Gamboa admired Frida, the persons in charge of acquisitions were still guided by the idea that there is no point in purchasing a painting if many viewers have already seen it.

The acquisitions process did not occur because, without ever being expressed, the belief existed that viewers of paintings do not require the continued presence of the works; having already contemplated them, they will possess them mentally forever or will forget them because they are not needed. (In accordance with this idea, memory is an illusive and hierarchically arranged catalogue of eternal or volatile possessions). Those who drive state indifference toward museums are not followers of Heraclitus, and for that reason do not know that no one sees the same work of art twice. Each person's artistic memory is a combination of adjustments, revisions, constantly refined enthusiasms, disavowals, and forgetting. But the people in charge of cultural policy do not believe that this is so, and this error will last until the paintings become inaccessible due to extraordinarily high market prices.

The state, which, for whatever almost always nationalistic reason, promotes the canon of national art, does not value it beyond catalogues and homages and does not anticipate speculation. Beginning in the 1960s, the state's narrow-mindedness—the belief that buildings are the only permanent symbol—favored the showcasing of residences. Also, there were no public cultural officials who proposed the meaning of museums as open systems of ever-growing audiences. There was a belief in one sole, more or less unchanging, group of spectators that increases just a little each year but no more. The museographer Gamboa was putting something specific into practice—the idea that the art community would receive a boost if *the state* highlighted the quality of the artists. But the Ministry of Finance and the Ministry of Public Education disregarded this notion.

The museographer Graciela de la Torre asked me if, in my view, every museum's goal—individual visits that produce meaningful messages or experiences—is something of the past because today museums summon the masses, as is seen throughout the world and as was proven in Mexico in 2007 with the Frida Kahlo exhibit. I certainly do not think this is so, not only because of Kahlo's personality and talent (there are only so many one-eyebrowed artists!) but because I have another hypothesis: the transformation of museums into receptacles of multitudes is linked to the right of the spectator/reader to avail himself or herself of spiritual stimulus, to "expropriate" (once again, note the quotation marks) what each person judges to be the substantial part of an exhibition. To see the paintings, is, for as long as the fireworks or the deep recesses of memory last, to establish a dialogue with their creators, with their images and symbols, with their colors, and with the sensitivity—a key word—of the individual's mind. This is valid for the grand retrospectives of Van Gogh and Gauguin, for the raging fashion of exhibitions of Egyptian or African art, and for the appeal of Mayan art. A phenomenon that must always be taken into account is neoliberal speculation and the ostentatious expenditure that is proof of power in the patronage market. The Reina Sofía Museum paid three and a half million Euros for the loan of a Picasso collection.

It is clear that museums not famous for attracting crowds should keep on trying. But what is really contemporary and what determines the direction that museum projects take is the rise of what is at the same time a great artistic experience and a noteworthy mass phenomenon; that is, the ritual act or virtual expropriation of what has been seen there in the purchase of catalogues and memorabilia and the incorporation of several images into daily life. Without glorifying or minimizing them, I appreciate the calm or dizzy involvement of these multitudes who wait hours or weeks to enter a museum. This, together with the yearning to hear first-rate concerts is the most noteworthy demand of cultural inclusion that we know. I do not deny, since it concerns me personally, the very central importance of individual viewers who demand quality, but who do not promote, nor should they, the cultural inclusion that occurs in a large number of museums, including the Louvre and, of course, the Museum of Modern Art (MoMA). Also, the contributions of creators and of artistic genres and themes should be taken into account in the development of regional or neighborhood museums.

Two simultaneous matters must be considered: there is no cultural inclusion without themes and artistic experiences that are added to the known map; it is the expansion of themes and artistic genres that social demand assimilates most rapidly. The basis of cultural inclusion is technology; its second foundation is the demographic explosion; the third is the incorporation of art and culture into daily recreation—not something outside experience, but something that participates in different ways in experience, thereby opening up perspectives of understanding and enjoyment. The development of a civilizing influence requires a collective sensibility, and this is a way of clarifying cultural mobility.

It is a good idea to debate the truth of whether the inclusion of the masses in the observation of museums modifies the social role of works of art, not because their viewing is cheapened, but, on the contrary, because a certain phenomenon that occurred a long time ago with *La Gioconda, The Last Supper*, Michelangelo's *David*, Velázquez's *Christ*, or Duchamp's *Nude Descending a Staircase* is still rooted in national and international society. To a similar extent in Mexico this occurs with specific works like *La Vendedora de Frutas (The Fruit Vendor)*, some of Siqueiros's oil paintings, the *Portrait of Lupe Martín* or *El Matemático* by Diego Rivera, engravings by Orozco, Leopoldo Méndez, or Posada, works of art that upon incorporating fundamental personal iconography, change their meaning, for example, *La Indígena que se Quita la Espina (The Thorn)* by Raúl Anguiano or some images by Carlos Mérida. Because they are widely seen, as well as because of their quality, they represent the most extensive artistic context of collective admiration.

Cultural inclusion is most vigorous in nations with large library systems and consolidated today by the Internet. The English and French, the Americans and the Nordic peoples have outstanding libraries at their disposal, and that infrastructure helps museums. In these countries, the very existence of exhibitions sparks debate. The "Primitivism" (in quotes) exhibition at MoMA brought to the fore racial prejudice, as did the High and Low in Art exhibition, also at MoMA, posing an already indispensable debate in Latin America. The canon has been a force behind *Christina's World* by Andrew Wyeth, *American Gothic* by Grant Wood, and Edward Hopper's works, including *Gas,* the painting of the young woman alone in a hotel room, and *Nighthawks,* all of which form part of the collective imagination and are iconic not only for Americans in this time of globalization.

In Mexico there will not be cultural inclusion and participation that is truly meaningful for museums until there is a coming together of the state and the potential or already existing enthusiasm of wide sectors of the population. The dialogue with individuals should be preserved and enriched because that is the basis of museums, but it is necessary to systematize the dialogue with the masses through exhibitions that have a collective appeal that does not signify "making concessions to the common people" but rather a search for other incentives, fostered by the methods of today. To insist on works with the ability of drawing crowds is not a populist concession but a kind of cultural politics, which is already the norm anyway. Is there still any difference between the exhibitions that invite the individual and those that have as their intention attracting the masses? *Yes,* because of the complexity of contemporary art and the limitations of artistic education in different countries; *no,* because the learning process proceeds very rapidly and because what is not understood intellectually is captured through emotion, an accepted step in the process of cultural inclusion if it originates in the effort to enrich sensitivity, that place where channel surfing has yet to prevail.

Carlos Monsiváis is one of Latin America's most well-respected public intellectuals. He has written extensively as journalist, novelist, and critic. Monsiváis has recently created his own museum in Mexico City. This has naturally brought him to think more personally and professionally about the nature of museums and the role they play in Mexico and the world.

GRAPPLING WITH LIMITS: MUSEUMS AND SOCIAL INCLUSION

Vanda Vitali

As the world has become more globalized, museums—simultaneously local and universal in scope—have become more vital than ever in advancing their cultures' conversations. The potential for and number of challenges this presents is formidable. Today, the Louvre hosts some eight and a half million visitors per year, more than double its optimistic predictions a decade or so ago at the time of its major master planning renovations.

A few years ago, the United Kingdom decided to offer free access to the permanent collections of public museums, which has, almost overnight, doubled the attendance for most of the museums there. Over the past decade, the number of museums, regardless of which statistics one might use, has been growing. Today, exhibitions are developed on almost every aspect of history or collecting in the world. The physical expansion or renovation of facilities has been on the "planning list" of almost every museum. As well, almost all leading museums have come to rely strongly on continuous growth in museum visitorship as a measure of their performance.

Given the rapid proliferation of Internet-based communication vehicles, most museums would like to increase their presence on the web, including podcasting and vidcasting projects, in an effort to reach out as far as possible and engage "visitors" with their particular mix of offerings. Museum annual reports, on their websites or elsewhere, provide evidence of a broad concern for programs, particularly exhibitions that are accessible and comprehensible (at least at some level) to all visitors. The opportunities this presents to museums that were at one time reliant on a purely local demographic are immense. But they bring up significant questions regarding exhibit conceptualization, questions that cut to the core of how museums define themselves in this age of visitor statistics as a primary measure of success.

The Natural History Museum of Los Angeles County prides itself on the demographics of its visitors, which reflect the overall makeup of the city. Its Friday Nights programs, which I conceived and established as evenings of diverse live programming, attracted upward of fifteen hundred visitors per evening in a city that represents one of the toughest and most competitive leisure-time markets in the world. In addition, it was principally young adults who frequented these programs, a demographic segment considered by most museums to be very difficult to attract at any time of the day.

From this kind of data and other research, it is evident that museums today have much larger and more diverse audiences than a few decades ago. But what does this mean when one begins to survey a museum's level of "inclusiveness"? In spite of the importance of parameters such as the quantity and kind of visitors that museums draw, is "inclusiveness" really just about the number and diversity of the public attracted? Or is inclusiveness about the variety of topics addressed across time or geography? Should numbers alone be used to measure museums' performance as it relates to social equity or inclusion? Should a museum be satisfied with providing a single experience, elite or not, to all those who are interested? Should a museum be concerned about other aspects of its relation to its visitors? And is there a dissonance between the culture of museums and the culture and identity of some groups, such as young adults, and should museums acknowledge that?

For me, the issue of "inclusiveness," to be a relevant metric, must recognize the inherent limits of insight that a museum can provide and should be measured against the museum's willingness, in general, to acknowledge limitations and be open to other points of view. This would be true regardless of a museum's particular approach to its audiences, or the degree of inclusiveness the museum seeks.

Museological literature is rich in its analysis of past museum displays and the shift in their emphasis and philosophy. For instance, in the concluding chapter of *Exhibiting Maori*, Conal McCarthy writes about how the display of Maori culture changed so dramatically from the nineteenth century to the beginning of the twenty-first century. He points out in this book how the meeting house, "Te hau ki Turanga, for example, has been seen at various times as a symbol of chiefly mana (authority), a trophy, a curio, a specimen, an artifact, a model of arts and crafts, a national treasure, a masterpiece of primitive art and then as a taonga (cultural treasure)" (Berg).

Examples such as this can be found in the literature pertaining to other kinds of displays, not only to those concerning indigenous artifacts. Worldwide, historians, researchers, collectors, and museologists recognize and accept the notion of changing perspectives with time. What about the multiple perspectives that also exist at any particular time? Rarely does the opportunity present itself to have a multiplicity of institutions exhibit on a single theme; when it happens it is an occasion of note.

When a museum is more commonly making any kind of presentation it is faced with a vast number of choices. The resulting choices are made on the basis of who the presenters are—in terms of their time, their mental and physical space, and their social awareness.

As institutions making presentation in the public realm, museums make choices that can become very transparent. This is particularly true with exhibits, a museum's principal communication tool, which are, in essence, visual communicators and rather limited in the amount of information they can transmit (although rich in their capacity to inspire).

Why not then acknowledge the inherent limits of insights and wisdom that may be provided by any museum, together with the limits inherent to any presentation? How can or should a museum address a more complex matter, particularly one that is attempting to find a fit between different cultures—culture that presents (internal to the museum) and the culture that views (the museum's visitors). A respectful scientific research program requires, indeed, demands the inclusion of assumptions and limitations and invites comments and debate. Why not the same for museum presentations?

Practically speaking, in addition to its principal presentations, should not a museum set aside a "However" (or "On the Other Hand") exhibition space and offer it on an ongoing basis, together with professional curatorial help, to groups with a standpoint different from the presenter's? This can and should be done only as long as the added perspective is constructive and non-hateful. It is a concept suggested at one time by Ursula Franklin, a University of Toronto professor and former head of its museum studies program.

Moreover, the possibilities for museums to represent alternative viewpoints increase exponentially when new and emerging media strategies are taken into consideration. Museums have a special opportunity with respect to creating and nurturing online dialogue, as they can act as a convener of debate as well as a repository of content from which more informed and refined debate can emerge. The ability of museums, with their depth of content, to create both virtual and real alternative viewpoint spaces will not be lost on complementary channels as well. One foresees a future in which online news providers, television broadcasters, podcasters, social network forums—all the myriad communication channels in our 2.0 and eventually 3.0 web world—look to museums as the agoras of knowledge, debate, dialogue, and change. What museums must do to live up to that promise is understand that they do not represent a solitary notion of "truth."

At the heart of this notion is the overriding belief that in today's world there is no single "truth" and that museums may not continue to blithely present their perspective as the ultimate version. Films, books, and other scholarly or entertainment vehicles acknowledge authorship of their presentations openly and thus indirectly acknowledge a perspective that is singularly theirs. Museums' presentations, although equally the result of a "single" perspective of the team that produced them, rarely in public acknowledge this fact. They continue to present exhibitions and galleries as the institutional "truth" while within the profession their perspective and presentation may well be debated.

This becomes a more serious issue when the subject matter being presented carries a high degree of sensitivity for one or more aspects of the viewing demographic. At the moment, when abstract concepts such as "justice" and "fairness" become part of the conversation between institution and public, a museum must face the subjectivity of its choices or run the risk of marginalization in the cultural debate.

Acknowledgment by a museum of the intrinsic and existential limitations that can and do exist in its insights and wisdom is a way for museums to strengthen rather than weaken their authority. It is also a way of strengthening the quality of a museum's presentations and of responding to museums' overall imperative for social responsibility.

We are now in an age that requires each of us living on this planet to consider and acknowledge the various aspects and degrees of limitation that prevail everywhere, at all times. Museums are institutions that need to feel and express the pulse of society. By providing access and insights into their own limits, museums would lead the way, rather than follow.

Prior to being director of the Auckland War Memorial Museum, Dr. Vanda Vitali was vice president of Public Programs and director of Content Development at the Natural History Museum in Los Angeles. Vitali was director of the Royal Ontario Museum's Institute for Contemporary Culture and before that, director of international heritage and museum projects in France, Tunisia, and Canada. Vitali obtained her doctorate in solid state physics.

CHAPTER 5

Globalization
Finding and Claiming Your Niche

CLAIMS FOR and about globalization are not new. From earliest history, as human beings came to understand that their world stretched beyond their places of birth, adventurers set forth to explore, to conquer, to trade, to colonize, and inevitably to change the world. This is the repeated history of human conquest: the conqueror takes from the conquered that which is most useful to them, while abandoning to history those aspects of the defeated culture they deem inferior to their own. At the same time the conquerors, as they become colonizers, make public examples of those qualities that they will brand as barbaric, eccentric, or beautiful, from nature or culture. The material display has usually been wrested from the conquered by violence or guile. Sometimes globalization plays out in sheer buying power, such as when the kings of Spain in Renaissance and Baroque periods purchased and commissioned the greatest European contemporary art of the day to be housed in its royal palace (eventually the Prado Museum), or when Japanese businessmen in the 1980s bought European art for Japanese museums and collections. From *wunderkammer* to the Musée de l'Homme, the Louvre to the Metropolitan Museum of Art, museums have been the repositories of the fruits of the historic global adventure.

Our museums need to be able to articulate their own role in the phenomenon of globalization now. By being able to defend its own positioning within the framework of a truly "global" world, each museum moves closer to being able to demonstrate its role in today's global enterprise, a time when this force touches us all. The essays in this chapter suggest a dialogue around some of the many aspects of globalization as they affect our museums. We hope they will be helpful to ponder as a beginning point to clarify and prepare to articulate your own stand on globalization.

From these articles we can see that as museum professionals there are many ways to address the issue of globalization. The particular address we choose will be a reflection of our own museum and its mission. Your own decision might relate to any of many aspects of globalization: exhibitions, collecting practices, conservation, scholarship, and exchange of knowledge with colleagues. But, still, these essays only present a few of the responses your museum might be making to globalization. They are meant to inspire individually crafted ways of dealing with this reality. Because, respond we must. Whether we see the positives or the negatives of globalization for us, the awareness of it and a clarity with respect to it for us will help us be sustainable as institutions as we continue into the twenty-first century. We are all, like it or not, a part of the phenomenon.

Anthony Appiah reflects on the ethics of collecting antiquities throughout the world as a positive way of making humans more cosmopolitan people. Encyclopedic museum collections (which he calls "universal" museums), this worldly and engaged philosopher argues, enable us to appreciate the unique creative contributions of people other than ourselves. That Appiah's is an outspoken and controversial position should not prevent us from considering it as a means to enter into the conversations that are needed to test our own museums and their relationship to collecting the patrimony of other nations. Charles Merewether reflects on perhaps the most daring and ambitious effort in our own time to globalize a society from scratch, by using museums, universities, and other cultural institutions as the means. The creation of the Cultural District of Saadiyat Island will bring to Abu Dhabi art from both the Louvre in Paris and from the Guggenheim in New York. Merewether explains the dream of the leadership of the project, roundly criticized though it was by some of the Western world's most well-respected museum leaders, including Philippe de Montebello. Montebello expressed this widely quoted view at a meeting of museum directors during the conference, "Opening Museums to the World," in Venice on 8 May 2008. Quoted in the *ArtNewspaper* in its June 2008 issue, he was responding to a plan for sending art to countries when he remarked, "to lend into the emptiness becomes an abuse of art." Later, Montebello himself became a part of the Abu Dhabi plan when he joined the faculty of New York University's Institute of Fine Arts, which will have a campus there. Montebello has adapted to the inevitability of an art-filled Abu Dhabi: he will help fill the "emptiness" of Saadiyat Island by participating in creating a much-needed intellectual foundation for the collection, preservation, and interpretation of that art. Abu Dhabi is betting that by embracing globalization it can put the Arab world in the forefront of museum and world culture. Faya Causey takes another approach to globalization, one based on Washington, D.C.'s, National Gallery of Art program for training museum staff worldwide. In her view, one could say that another means of embracing globalization is to share expertise with museum professionals internationally while at the same time learning from them to better and enrich one's own museum practice. Finally, Shelly Errington warns about the dangers to humble folk artists due to the "museification" of popular art by virtue of the global market place and the increasing taste for "high" folk art.

Because of the nature of communications today, it is not just the mega-museums that are a part of the story of globalization. Our major national museums represent their countries' histories with respect to colonialism and economic power by means of their collections and exhibitions, but it is evident that even the tiniest museums in the most isolated places in the world can and do participate in the globalized arena. Indigenous communitarian museum leaders in the remote mountains of Oaxaca with no staff at all and with only brief consensual terms in office find their ways to meetings at, for example, the Smithsonian Institution in Washington, DC. At those meetings, they have been joined by leaders from First People's museums in Australia, Latin America, and American Indian reservation museums. Such museums' leaders from the world over now learn from each other about everything from best practices in fund-raising to useful philosophical positions on any number of important issues. E. M. Forester's directive to "only connect" can empower the relatively powerless in our field. This, too, can be another response to globalization.

Oddly enough, making the case for our museum's relationship to globalization might be situated in co-opting globalization as a way of strengthening local cultures—but in a way that can afford local cultures the benefit of communicating with other local cultures in relatively inexpensive ways. An example of that approach was inaugurated by the New Museum in the Bowery in New York City in its new program called Museum as Hub. Called Hub, the small New Museum invited four other museums or arts organizations from four other cities on four different continents to take a single specific neighborhood as their subject for contemporary artistic investigation. Insa Art Space in Korea chose the long-militarized neighborhood of Dongducheon; the Tamayo Museum in Mexico City took the Tlatelolco neighborhood where the infamous massacre took place in 1968; the New Museum selected the indigent Bowery; the Townhouse Gallery of Contemporary Art in Cairo worked with downtown Cairo and the neglected Said Halim's Palace; and finally, the Van Abbemuseum in Eindhoven chose its own urban neighborhood in the Netherlands as its subject. This profoundly specific examination of neighborhood became a globalized endeavor as artists investigated their particular histories and perspectives and then participated with their Hub partners by means of Internet-based conversations and collaborative projects.

It should be added that globalization also carries negative baggage, and a considered response *against* it could also be the position that a museum might take, frame, and claim. When globalization translates as a kind of conventionalized homogenization, this can lead to fresh new thinking. Manuel Borja-Villel, the new director of the Reina Sofia, Spain's national museum of contemporary art, is an example. In 2008 he decided that the Reina Sofia should not be just another museum spreading the mainstream Western perspective of modern art. From now on, the Reina's brand of globalization is to embrace alternate art histories from Latin America and Africa and other often-discounted places so as to better fill out the story of contemporary art. He will demarginalize the margins and mix center and periphery together in a bold statement.

Certainly there are countries that find the universal museum an unpardonable exploitation of their cultural heritage in favor of richer countries. In such cases the notion is that artists can thus lead the conversation about provocative subjects such as expressions of power, property rights, and social justice. Presented within a knowledgeable global framework, under the auspices of our museums, this could only be an enriching project. The possibilities are limitless.

Globalization, positive or negative, remains an indicator, a force to be reckoned with, a means of articulating and evaluating a museum's success. We would all serve our institutions well if we were able to make the case for our museum's positioning in this arena, taking into account our own mission and various constituencies with their sometimes conflicting cultural needs. Chris Bratton, in the *Art Newspaper* (no. 191, 2008, p. 38) proposes that globalization and our work in museums might be better communicated as "thinking" the world, our work, our lives, the objects that surround us, as inextricably bound up in a complex web of local and global relations. "The point is," he writes, "to make these interconnections visible and understood."

DEFENDING THE UNIVERSAL (ENCYCLOPEDIC) MUSEUM

Anthony Appiah

From a lecture delivered at the Getty Museum in collaboration with the International Museum Institute.

 There are new models of globalized collecting and collection sharing that need to be considered and developed today. Thinking about a more cosmopolitanized cultural world, let me suggest examples stemming from the world of traveling exhibitions that might extend to a model of building exhibitions based on long-term or permanent loans.

I think people should try to develop, through organizations like the United Nations Educational, Scientific, and Cultural Organization (UNESCO), traveling exhibitions that would go places that do not have the finances to import such programs normally. To achieve that goal, I am thinking of what the British Museum did recently in helping to develop the national museum of Kenya. The British Museum invited Kenyan curators to London and trained them. When the training was complete, the British Museum said to the Kenyan curators, "Now, what do you want to take back with you from our collection of Kenyan art, to Kenya, on permanent loan or indefinite loan? We have enough Kenyan material here, so if you want to take some, feel free to take it back with you." And one of the greatest things about the response of the Kenyans was that they said: "Why should we just take Kenyan art?"

The British Museum helped them with the development of the preservation and conservation side of their museum, so as to create an environment in which some of the more sensitive objects could actually survive. The British Museum thus added another layer of training to the project, acknowledging that one of the tasks of museums is to preserve things, not just to display them. This is a great model.

There was another traveling exhibition being sent to China. And again the Chinese, when asked what Chinese material they would like to have, replied: "We've got lots of Chinese art and artifacts." And so they received a show that begins with a carved stone made by early man from Africa and includes artifacts from around the world: they borrowed material from outside China, rightly recognizing that that was what they needed most.

And so, if we build on these models of cultural exchange and sharing (which I think is quite consistent with UNESCO's fundamental aims) we can see the way ahead. We need to work to create more sharing of actual objects, as much as possible, to expand the cosmopolitan idea.

Also, I would like to note that if we were to solve the wider problems with respect to the rest of what the UN is working on, there would be less of the kind of inequality in the world that makes it hard right now for most museums to organize these types of exchanges by themselves. Museums throughout most of the world don't have the resources to go out—even if the government officially permitted them to do so—and compete for works. So the help of UNESCO and the bigger museums in richer countries is invaluable in allowing either kind of sharing.

There is, by the way, another model that is also current that I think is great, and that is based on the continuing encouragement of using and developing technology for the sharing of collections and the creation of exhibitions. The musée du quai Branly in Paris opened a virtual museum at the same time as it opened its physical museum space. The web is now accessible in every country in Africa, but, still, of course, we recognize that this is not enough. There is a reason why people come to the Getty and don't just look at the website. There's something about the thing itself, and of course it's what Walter Benjamin talked about: it's the magic of the actual object that's not easy to explain or give a rational account of. I believe that anyone who doesn't have that response to the actual object inhabits a different aesthetic universe from you and me.

So I think the cosmopolitan thought would be to suggest that what, for example, Italy should be doing is not importing and demanding back more Italian materials. They should be working with their embassies and agencies and so on to try to create venues all around the world, places where local people can come and see the great treasures of Italy outside of Italy! There's an awful lot of Italian art in Italy. If some percentage of it were traveling around the world people from all over the world would be able to see Italian art. The reality is that Italy is not presently a great place to look for non-Italian art, and that's bad for the Italians. So, the Italians themselves would be better off if they spent the same amount of energy trying to get interesting non-Italian art into Italy as they are currently spending trying to get Italian art back to a place that's crammed full of it.

So I think that these answers give an indication of the cosmopolitan response to the question of what might be done in the future with respect to collecting antiquities: my answer would be that we all have something to gain from exposure to the widest range of culture. At the moment one of the greatest pities in the world is that such exposure is not possible for so many people in so many places.

Anthony Appiah is Lawrence S. Rockefeller Professor of Philosophy at Princeton. He was educated at Cambridge University, where he took both a BA and PhD in philosophy. Appiah has been influential, especially in his recent book, *Cosmopolitanism,* in broadening the conversation about restitution of cultural patrimony to include a universalist approach.

PROFESSIONAL MUSEUM TRAINING PROGRAMS AT THE NATIONAL GALLERY OF ART: FROM THE SHORES OF THE POTOMAC TO A WORLD VIEW

Faya Causey

The National Gallery of Art (NGA), conceived as a "Gallery *for* the Nation," opened to the public in 1941. From the beginning, it took its educative role to heart. The new education and publication programs were as important as the display of great works of art. Guiding visitors, providing publications for a wide public, and training future museum professionals—these were considered to be essential and *modern* responsibilities.

Why was the institution so committed to a role beyond the aesthetic, historical, and cultural experiences that might be provided by the art and a museum of art? In 1941, the NGA, now sixty-seven years old, was a relative newcomer to the international art museum scene. It took as its mandate the incorporation of the best of the past as well as innovative approaches. There was a sincere belief that the Gallery's combination of great works of art, a photographic archive, and a first-class library supported by the august presence of specialists (the director, curators, and visiting scholars, and beginning in 1957, the Samuel H. Kress Professor) made it a fertile ground for the production of philosophically educated connoisseurs. The Gallery joined a growing number of museums in the training of future museum professionals, especially curators and future directors.

During the 1930s and for the next decades, the internship and fellowship programs at the Gallery and elsewhere in the United States were much influenced by two great luminaries—Bernard Berenson, living in Italy, and Paul Sachs at Harvard's Fogg Museum. Berenson, who had done so much since the late nineteenth century in "perfecting" and popularizing the connoisseurship of art, was the model for many museum curators. By the early 1960s, with an eye to furthering its national and international responsibilities, the exhibition, education, and publication initiatives expanded. Among them was a new internship and museum fellowship program. Added to the small but active program of predoctoral fellowships for advanced American students in art history, in place since the 1950s, was a new federally funded program of summer internships. Now American college students competed for places in the traditional museum departments: curatorial, education, and conservation. The approach and methodology was based on connoisseurship, and the "curriculum" reflected Harvard's Fogg Museum program.

During the last fifteen years, the internship and museum fellowship programs of the Gallery have been augmented and modified again, having been much affected by corresponding changes in the relevant academic disciplines and in the museum field. New funding sources became available, including individual gifts, grants, and endowments. In the early 1990s, academic-term internships were added; in 1995, the programs became international, no longer restricted to U.S. citizens; and in 2000, interns and fellows were working in the library, administration, horticulture, design, architecture, exhibition installation, and publishing departments. In 2003, an additional three-year fellowship program was added to the mix: the Andrew W. Mellon Curatorial Fellowship offers an experience equivalent to that of an assistant curator. Since 1993, there have been interns and museum fellows from all of the states in the Union and America's territories and from forty-four foreign countries.

In addition to these internationally advertised programs, the Gallery began offering in 1996 an in-service professional training to non-American museum staff. This, too, is privately supported, with funding from various internationally minded foundations. Curators, educators, registrars, conservators and other specialists from Spain, France, India, China, Korea, Japan, Cambodia, Argentina, Brazil, and Chile have been in residence for periods ranging from three months to a year.

These international fellows have joined the other interns and museum fellows in an ongoing weekly seminar, which introduces the Gallery's programs, departments, and staff, and includes discussion based on current topics and readings. Critical to the success of the program, interns and fellows (art historians, educators, conservators, administrators, and scientists) all attend a weekly seminar. Current topics and issues are discussed, and the projects, departments, functions and staff of the institution are introduced to the group. Sessions are led by senior staff and sometimes involve tours or in other cases lectures or conversations. The Gallery's executive officers are committed to this program, and consider it an essential role of the museum to help in providing a well-educated body of museum professionals.

The administration of the museum training programs is through the education division. The head of the relevant department provides mentorship and daily supervision. This double administration has many advantages. One is the opportunity to see various roles in museums, and how much interchange there is among staff throughout the institution. Interns and fellows are treated as temporary staff members. In addition to a placement in a department with a mentor, a project, desk, and computer, the interns and fellows work on an ongoing departmental project, either an independently supervised project or a discrete portion of a major project. Inclusion is critical. The goal is sharing and learning through engagement. It is essential that participants are encouraged to learn from one another and to collaborate on projects wherever possible. The top-to-bottom model of management is eschewed in favor of a collaborative one. Discourse is key to the success of a program dedicated to the future of museums and their management of cultural properties. Innovation has joined tradition, for the legacy of Paul Sach's ideal are still tangible, the emphasis on individual works of art and connoisseurship is inescapable.

The goal of each one of these museum training/experience programs is to provide the field with professionals who are experienced in theory and practice with the most current thinking and experience. The "multiplier effect" is a goal for staff, interns, and fellows. That is, the hope is that the knowledge and experience at the Gallery will be passed on directly and indirectly to a larger group, through teaching and institutional practice. "Each one, teach one," in the words of Mrs. Harry Lenart, an early funder of the Gallery's internship program.

There is another active saying at the Gallery: "Once an intern or fellow, always an intern or fellow." The experience does not end with the internship or fellowship; the door is always open to further questions, information, resources, and training. Exchange is key. Program participants are encouraged to consider the Gallery a lifelong resource, and vice-versa; former interns and fellows continue to contribute to the institution, with advice, aid, or publications.

One example of this is the 1997–2007 special initiative program of museum exchange with Argentina, Chile, and Brazil. Modeled on an American Association of Museums (AAM) program, it was funded by the Lampadia Foundation and its daughter foundations, Andes (Chile); Antorchas (Argentina), and Vitae (Brazil). Gallery staff made site visits to the South American museums, agencies, and universities wishing to send its staff or students to Washington, DC. This helped in the selection process because the goal was that each staff member or student from the Southern Cone should be an active participant in passing on information and skills upon return. However, the experience has not been one-way or paternalistic. Much of the best part of the program is the active role the participants have taken in introducing new ways of thinking, techniques, or programs to their Gallery departments and to the institution more generally. Many of the museum exchange fellows bring with them an excellent background in museology or museum studies and have actively contributed to the weekly seminars, especially with contemporary issues, including the role of connoisseurship or museum metrics.

Of the thirty-one Southern Cone participants who trained at the Gallery, twenty-six are now working professionally in their countries and encouraging their students and colleagues to apply to programs around the world—and many have developed on-site professional programs of their own. Claudio Gómez (at the NGA in 1997–1998), now director of the Natural History Museum of Chile, maintains that his Washington experience was crucial to his vision for his institution. He was certainly crucial to the Gallery, for Claudio helped perfect a method of measuring works on paper by using an ordinary scanner.

The goals of the internship and museum fellowship program are being realized: more than 150 graduates are currently working around the world in museums and comparable cultural institutions, often sending back suggestions for continued development of the program. Although the number of participants may be small in comparison with the number of museum workers worldwide, the desired "multiplier effect" is hopefully the more important metric. The Washington, DC, professional training experience, with its underlay of concern with "object" modified by global perspectives brought by the program participants and international exhibitions, will continue to evolve, and it fits in with the original mission of the Gallery. These programs are among the ways the NGA participates in a world no longer valorized by or limited solely by nationalism: professionals learn together, and then act in an increasingly globalized world.

Faya Causey is an art historian who heads academic programs in the Division of Education at the National Gallery of Art in Washington, DC. Causey develops the museum's extensive internship, fellowship, and public programs as well. She earned her doctorate in ancient art at the University of California, Santa Barbara. Her *Catalogue of the Ancient Carved Amber in the J. Paul Getty Museum* is forthcoming.

A WORK IN PROGRESS: CULTURAL DISTRICT, ABU DHABI

Charles Merewether

A VISION

My most optimistic dream for the Cultural District of Saadiyat Island was to contribute in developing an environment in which the creative arts could be fostered and given a home. This home would be a place where the creative arts could be critically appreciated and serve as a platform for valuing the cultural heritage of a country and people alongside an intercultural dialogue with others. Such a dialogue would provide a means of sharing knowledge and appreciation for one another's cultures and the often-shared histories as well as differences they embody. I saw this as a model for what globalization could positively offer insofar as encouraging countries, institutions, and individuals to exchange, collaborate, and share their cultural and intellectual wealth as much as their knowledge and expertise. With that said, I believe this could be viewed as a worthy aspiration, especially in the light of decreasing resources for the arts and humanities as well as the sharing of richness of some cultures whose institutions have built extraordinary collections and bodies of expertise.

The plans for the Cultural District encompassed a series of stages that would unfold over the course of several years, beginning with the opening of the Sheik Zayed National Museum in 2012 and the Louvre Abu Dhabi and Guggenheim Abu Dhabi in 2013. Moreover, these museums were a part of a larger master plan for a small city to be developed that included other noncommercial and commercial cultural institutions, residency community, schools, and a commercial sector to service. Opening gradually, the Cultural District would then be followed by the building of other museums such as a science and technology museum, a maritime museum, and a performing arts center. Both the Louvre and Guggenheim projects have come under considerable scrutiny and sweeping criticism in part because they were seen as motivated by the need to support their own public institutions or as a form of governmental "soft power" in regard to geopolitical relations. However, I believe the potential of each constituted a significant step from any previous historical model, whether during the period of imperial and colonial expansion or under the aegis of Western modernity. What differed about each was that, on the one hand, the Louvre project involved a consortium of different French museums and collections as well as a dedicated organization to help develop the project and, on the other hand, a Guggenheim that was only part of a complex of cultural institutions (unlike Guggenheim Bilbao) dedicated to the visual arts. Not only should they be seen as a step in recognition of mutual needs, but also as a fundamental belief in the value of public culture and public cultural institutions that serve in the movement toward cultural emancipation. Ironically, contrary to the criticism of the endeavors taking place in the Emirates, these projects reaffirm the continuing value of the museum as a public and relatively autonomous sphere. It is this sphere that, when faced by the diminishing support of government funding and increasing intrusion of the market, can provide a site for the viewing of historical memory and the ongoing significance of the arts and humanities in terms of innovation, experimentation, and level of insight and reflection they can bring to understanding the contemporary world.

The vision of the leadership that brought me on board was to provide Abu Dhabi with a world-class range of cultural and educational facilities that could benefit the Emirati and people of Abu Dhabi and the United Arab Emirates (UAE). To achieve this ambition, the leadership understood the need for developing the means by which to train and professionalize an Emirati workforce in culture, the arts, and education. This is seen as part of a long-term plan and an essential component in the growth of a knowledge-based economy and the in value of developing advanced research opportunities for future generations of the Emirati. The ability of the country to provide cultural and educational institutions of an international standard of excellence becomes a symbol of the country's progress and security in delivering services and investment opportunities and hence an ability to participate at a global level.

POINTS OF VIEW

While it has been a tremendous accomplishment to secure and make possible the iconic architectural buildings of Nouvel, Foster, and Gehry, it is quite another matter to develop the conceptual framework and substance of what will go on inside and around them. In reality, the challenges are manifold when faced with planning a cultural district that has not organically developed over a long period. While one can argue against an organicist cultural district and the implicit notion of progress that underwrites it, one has to ask, what is an alternative model? How would it work? How can one put the process of perception and learning on a fast track, what steps need to be taken, and what goes first? What is the point of view that sufficiently allows for recognition of different cultures that embodies different and often opposing beliefs as much as shared values and aspirations and hence forms of exchange? Does the "shock of the new" work best? Perhaps not, but then does one present other histories in their own right or rethink them interculturally or from a perspective that claims universalism? Yet, even universalism has a point of view, disguised as it might be. So it means returning to the local as the perspective from which to begin. But what precisely is the local in this instance of the UAE and, moreover, is it not now multilayered with differing levels of education and degrees of access, knowledge, and open engagement with other cultures?

Perhaps Islamic culture could be taken as a starting point on which to build a program or museum that, like a *souk* (marketplace), has a central spine along which the story can be told, but that also has passages and alleyways branching off that provide the connections, exchanges, and, in turn, lead to other points of axis with their own branches, and so on. A maze or labyrinth, indeed; who has such a collection? And what does one do with fields of interpretative dispute, such as the period of the Crusades or when the origin of a work lies precisely within the field of exchange such as with the "fetish" objects that emerged in the trade between Portuguese traders and West Africans or the uneven development of modernism? Moreover, is not the field of creativity far more serendipitous and less about the story of influences than an aesthetic achievement that embodies a complex set of values? How does one approach the building of a historically nuanced program that both enables people to appreciate the critical importance of aesthetic experimentation and innovation, while at the same time providing a historical framework for its reception? How does one develop such a perspective within a short span of time when there is an absence of preparation on the ground?

From within this context, it seems to me that, however delicate it may be, there is an extraordinary opportunity for Abu Dhabi and the Emirates to establish a framework that enables and shapes a critical relation to, but is still intertwined with, the cultural history of the Middle East and the region. By region, I especially refer to the subcontinent and its long history of engagement with the Gulf States. There is a wealth to the cultural histories and contemporary practices of the Middle East that, while radically distinct from that of the Gulf, are imperative to address not only because of their long history of entwinement but precisely because of the current climate in which there is an increasing crisis over Western military presence, armed conflict, foreign occupation, energy resources, nuclear armament, the rise of radical Islam, the destruction of cultures and their histories, the ongoing displacement of peoples from their homeland, and an enduring refugee crisis.

And yet, having said this, one must acknowledge, too, the kind of radically different historical trajectories these countries have taken, especially over the course of the past one hundred years or so with the end of colonialism and different forms and stages of modernization undertaken and accomplished. There is no simple unifying thread here and the cultural practices that characterize each of the countries within this larger region have taken on their own particular character and significance as well as differing relations between themselves and with the Western world. And yet none of this should be sufficient to deny that the opportunity is there to be taken, most especially given that the Emirates' population is composed also of large communities from the Arab world and from India, Pakistan, Bangladesh, and Sri Lanka. This raises the issue of creating audiences across a hugely diverse public and providing educational opportunities in such a way as to benefit both them and the country in which they live. Equally, the Emirates could provide an extraordinary platform for the Middle East and region as much as for themselves. This sense of cooperation and mutual recognition would also assist in overcoming the prejudices and racism that exists between these countries. The opportunity, then, is not simply one of identifying or serving diverse audiences, but of collaboratively exploring together with them their distinct and shared cultural histories and overcoming the social distinctions that currently prevail across and between the Emirates.

To try to bring the current situation into alignment with the vision, or, in other words, to realize the vision, exposes the need to undertake the development of a strong humanities-based curricula (not just vocationally oriented)—including the teaching of critical studies, art history, and those of the other arts—as much professional and vocational training in and for the Emirati people. As has been undertaken successfully in other parts of the developing world, this is being done in the Emirates by establishing institutional relations with foreign universities and organizations. Some of this has been quietly done in smaller and larger ways and proved successful in providing opportunities for exchange. However, while one can admire the desire to embrace and learn from the West, the project also reveals an overly dependent relation on the West for building the necessary infrastructure on which to create a vibrant contemporary culture locally. What needs to be done is to create connectivity between the locally existing habitats of knowledge. This allows for a network of perspectives to be brought to bear on one's ability to make choices and to ensure that such projects are calibrated to engage with those cultures in which they are developed. Further, it is precisely these networks, which are informal and socially based, that are at the heart of creativity and the making of culture as distinct from its consumption. This is what is meant by the idea of the "fabric" of a city, a city where creativity thrives by way of urban mixing and opportunity to participate in the everyday life.

At an institutional level, this cultural fabric already exists in Abu Dhabi, led by the Cultural Foundation and its tremendous program of events as well as those hosted by governmental agencies such as the British Council, the Goethe Society, and the Alliance Francaise, as well as Zayed University and the Sorbonne. There are other organizations, too, and also such events as the Abu Dhabi Music and Arts Festival, Art Paris Abu Dhabi, the Abu Dhabi Book Fair, and most recently the arrival of an independent newspaper, the *National,* which seeks to offer a serious cultural section in its daily. All of these to a lesser or greater degree of quality provide the basis and platform for the creative arts. But then the question of what counts and what is quality also matter and the question of who decides and on what basis benchmarks are established is not a simple question to be answered. It is not enough to leave it to the Westerners or whoever they may be, but then neither is it enough to leave it to the locals to decide. The problem is knowledge of one another, of what is being offered and why. A good Picasso exhibition may be done and received well, but this does not mean it is sufficient when perhaps there is a better show that could have been done. The people of Abu Dhabi and the Emirates, like anywhere else, deserve only the best. And, one might add, is Picasso the right choice in this context? Is it personality that counts because marketing has become a more powerful tool than understanding the history of art? Perhaps Manet, Cezanne, Duchamp, or even Malevich would have taught us more not only about the great art in the Western modern era, but, equally, how each of these artists were great exponents of modern art at different moments during the course of its development.

In the context of a building program, schedule, and deadline, these kinds of questions can be swiftly consigned as being overly academic or peripheral to the immediate tasks to be done and therefore given neither time nor place in which they may be conducted. This is precisely the challenge of such a timetable that is determined by an end date of delivery only five years away in 2012. Institutions such as the British Museum or the Metropolitan do not have such pressure, and they have great collections and staff of immense learning and competence with which to begin.

This involves a complex of perspectives representing very different cultural values and interests, and hence collaboration should lie at the very heart of the project. Few Western cultural institutions with which Abu Dhabi or the Arab world could work have been faced with these kinds of questions insofar as their programming has been for their own audiences. To address these issues for a local audience is then a different and radically new enterprise. Moreover, by producing exhibitions and programming even on the modern and contemporary will not ease the burden. There are few scholars who have done the kind of homework that is needed to be able to provide the basis of a framework. The deconstruction and re-elaboration of modernity is still in its infancy in regard to these countries. There are beginnings from the West in looking at the influence of the larger Mediterranean, such as North Africa on artists, but this is still far from the Gulf and yet again this is only one side of a story to be told. The danger is to accept the status quo for reasons of expediency and the inexorable pressure of meeting construction deadlines or to counteract those opposed to or skeptical of the endeavor.

It might be said that there is a real need to address some structural changes at the institutional level. This would allow for a means by which to "facilitate" (as distinct from "regulate") a process of decision making that is neither as controlled as a *consultative process* requires nor is overly dictated by marketing imperatives intent on branding or public relations interests overly worried about controlling press and the image, concerns that have been traditionally driven by government interests of self-promotion and by the need to develop a tourist destination that can turn investment into a self-sustaining enterprise, if not a profitable return. In such an environment, perception becomes everything. So how then does a monarchy provide a structure whereby it enables authority to be given to those who can exercise their expertise or experience of what it takes to create a world-class cultural district responsible for the delivery of these projects? Taking up the position meant for me, bringing all to bear in terms of one's experience, as well as thinking outside the box and questioning one's own perspectives, including that of a postcolonial critique and globalization. This needs to be a collaborative process, but you can imagine too how this job is made all the more difficult by those who see their point of view and hence position as threatened by such expertise. But then can the structure of a monarchy allow for such expertise to act in the process of identifying and evaluating proposals to make commitments to opportunities, especially those practices that contain both an affirmative and critical dimension but belong to a different set of values?

NATIONALISM

So, then, one has to ask, with all of this passion for the introduction and development of a globalized Abu Dhabi, where does nationalism lie? There is no doubt that this is a nation-building project concerning the sustainability of the country. Both the Saadiyat project and that of Masdar City in Abu Dhabi, which is to build a planned carbon-neutral environment and develop renewable energy resources, are principal examples of nation-building endeavors. Such projects serve to demonstrate the state as strong, with a clear vision and ability to implement that vision. Sustainability means in this context the need for a massive investment in generating projects that enhance production, wealth, and workforce in the future as well as that protect the environment and peoples, especially Emirati. And it is around this point that it becomes more complex because on the one hand there is a felt need to protect heritage and Muslim values, while, on the other hand, there is a need to enable the UAE to have access to and become part of the larger global information technology network, economy, and culture. This is a delicate balancing act requiring a high degree of tolerance, respect, and understanding. But it also means scrutinizing what is meant by "cultural heritage," which is not simply something fixed to a past or object but rather alive, evolving with time and generations. Moreover, heritage is to be found between peoples who may be of different ethnicities and races, countries, and epochs. The perception of the Emirates as a "tabula rasa" by Western and other commentators is made out of ignorance to be sure, but it is a willful ignorance exacerbated by those in the Emirates who espouse "heritage" talk without a willingness to critically engage with their own history rather than simply use it as a rhetorical instrument of national celebration. All of this requires an openness and transparency insofar as allowing the texture of history as lived to be appreciated for its heterogeneity, modes of being, fault lines, and complex patterns of dispute and negotiation between peoples and cultures.

While the public that is being addressed is principally Emirati, I trust that this will expand to be inclusive of all the nationalities and sectors of a heterogeneous community that is currently working or living in Abu Dhabi. This is a huge challenge insofar as it requires developing a strong educational and public program over the next few years, the period between now and the opening of the Cultural District and subsequent programming of the museum and other cultural organizations. Indeed, I assumed my position precisely because of the extraordinary vision it stood for. For me, the project represented in concept the development of a civic space that provides the means by which the communities of the UAE can experience and engage with the cultural and artistic histories both from the region and internationally. In a society where there is tremendous economic strength and initiative, the opportunity the Saadiyat project offers is to foster creativity and an appreciation of the arts and humanities without being determined by market forces and interests. This, I would hope, then encourages and promotes the development of a nongovernmental sector in the arts, which belongs to the public sphere and is economically sustainable. This would be a civil society in which public intellectuals and those committed to education, creativity, and experimentation in the arts and culture find a sense of belonging within the collective present and a place in which to contribute to its well-being and future.

Art historian, writer, and curator, Dr. Charles Merewether was appointed by the Abu Dhabi Tourism Development and Investment Company as deputy director of the Cultural District on Saadiyat Island in 2007. He resigned his post in Abu Dhabi in 2008. He has just published a book, *Under Construction: Ai Weiwei*, and is currently writing a book on the cultural history of looting.

TWO MUSEUMS, TWO VISIONS OF MEXICAN *ARTES POPULARES* IN THE ERA OF GLOBALIZATION

Shelly Errington

 Two museums in Mexico City officially represent *artes populares* (roughly, "folk arts," but the term is more inclusive). The new Museo de Arte Popular (www.map.df.gob.mx) opened its doors to the public in 2006 in the historic center of Mexico City; the older Museo de Culturas

Populares (www.culturaspopulareseindigenas.gob.mx/museo.html) opened more than twenty years earlier, in 1982. These two museums offer a study in contrasts—in location, in museography, in vision, in their relationships with artisans and producers of popular culture. The newer museum exhibits a vision of folk art as a form of high art suitable for serious collectors—items exquisitely made, isolated in vitrines, with minimal labeling, explanation, or context of use. The collection is large and permanent, based on private collections lent or donated, and new acquisitions are selected from winners of *concursos* (juried competitions, usually government-sponsored but recently with prizes offered by private corporations, which may cull the winners for their collections). The older museum is more informal, more interactive, and often features artisans and cultural events intended to bring the community together with artisans and their arts; it was intended as an exhibition space only, and although it has acquired items over the years, they are not the featured exhibits. The newer museum opened twenty years after Mexico signed onto the General Agreement on Tariffs and Trade (GATT) treaty, and eight years after it signed onto the North American Free Trade Agreement (NAFTA); both had a part in restructuring Mexico's economy, the effects of which are currently being acutely felt. The older museum's opening in 1982 reflected a certain previous stage in the national imagery of folk art and artisans, although its vision and public face has now been updated to promote the idea of multiculturalism, which a few years ago began figuring in official discourse.

In any case, the opening of the newer museum prompts reflection on the contrasts between the two museums and the changing location—both literal and figurative—of *artes populares* in Mexican public culture. These visions are different from each other and even at odds with each other, but neither vision provides space for assessing the economic and political structures that are affecting the production of *artes populares* in Mexico in the early twenty-first century.

The new Museo de Arte Popular opened close to a century after *artes populares* became a visible part Mexico's national imaginary. It was due to the Mexican Revolution (1910–1920) that *artes populares* became fused with the very idea of the newly imagined nation-state. The revolution had overthrown the previous administration of Porfirio Diaz, whose governance was as decidedly nonpopulist as its tastes in art and architecture were oriented toward Europe. In contrast, the new national government's purpose was to recover indigenous civilization as the foundation of Mexican history and to promote *el pueblo mexicano* as a mestizo nation rather than as a European elite ruling the humble indigenous masses. Teotihuacán was excavated in the 1920s under Dr. Manuel Gamio, the chief government archaeologist. Diego Rivera collected pre-Columbian art. Intellectuals and artists (like Frida Kahlo, among many others) decorated their houses with folk art. Folk art had been valorized officially with the publication in 1921 of *Artes Populares,* the catalogue written by "Dr. Atl" as part of La Exposición de Arte Popular del Centenario in celebration of one hundred years of Mexican independence. Dr. Atl included almost anything handmade—jewelry, masks, weaving, laquerware, papier-mâché, tule and palm-leaf arts, ceramics, and many more, few of which had previously been considered worthy of museum exhibition. Dr. Atl's catalogue thus had several effects on the status of *artes populares*. First, it dignified formerly insignificant artifacts and cultural practices, making them visible as national heritage. Second, it included a wide range of practices, not just objects. And third, it effectively set the terms that eventually made them visible to the art market, beginning the trajectory that would eventually turn items used in everyday life and sold in traditional open-air markets *(tianguis)* into autonomous objects worth buying and collecting and placing in grand museums.

During the 1920s and 1930s, which were decades of intense national feeling and nationalist economic policies, the country's warm appreciation for *artesanías* and their expression as the essence of the genius of Mexico continued. Yet in Mexico, as elsewhere, appreciation for folk art was not translated into policies to alleviate the impoverished condition of the people who produced it. Indeed, throughout the world, saving the "culture" of indigenous peoples usually means saving its reified aspects—especially arts, crafts, and monumental architecture—in preference to saving their ways of life, communities, or physical health.

The 1950s, 1960s, and 1970s were in some ways the golden years for Mexican *artesanías* in the national and world market. Establishing museums, promoting fair pricing, creating workshops and competitions that reward excellent materials and workmanship are all ways to help artisans and to valorize the artifacts as worthy objects for collectors not in the avant-garde or with highly specialized tastes. The Mexican government embarked on such enterprises in the 1950s through the early 1980s, helping shape the meanings of *artes populares* in national culture. The Museo Nacional de Antropología opened in its monumental new building in Chapultepec Park. Fondo Nacional para el fomento de las Artesanías (FONART) was established to encourage artisans and market their products in the prestigious venue of Mexico City, asserting their importance for the image of Mexico in the minds of foreign tourists, shoppers, visitors, and Mexican nationals. And national, regional, and local governments established *concursos*—juried competitions and exhibitions with prizes in many categories—of *artes populares*.

The Museo de Culturas Populares reflects the sensibility of this "golden age." Located in the charming and historic district of Coyoacán, its companion museums attractive to tourists in this general area include the privately owned Frida Kahlo Museum, the house where Frida Kahlo and Diego Rivera lived, which is filled with folk art; the Anahuacalli, a somber stone building in a nearby area designed by Rivera to reflect the Aztec cosmos and housing his collection of pre-Columbian artifacts; and Leon Trotsky's house-museum (which is austere and bare of decoration: he was apparently not an art enthusiast). Thus Coyoacán evokes a certain era and sensibility of enthusiasm for popular arts and populism, originating in the Mexican Revolution. Moreover, the Museo de Culturas Populares was the vision of Guillermo Bonfil Batalla, the author of *Mexico Profundo,* a classic on Mexican "national character."

It may be that a new phase for *artesanías* in the Mexican imaginary and its history began with globalization. In 1986 Mexico signed onto GATT and a few years later then-President Salinas y Gotari declared Mexico no longer a third-world country. Since the 1990s, the Internet has globalized communications, providing new venues for marketing and advertising. International tourism, including cultural tourism and eco-tourism, intensified everywhere. In Mexico the web presence of the Ejército Zapatista de Liberación Nacional (the Zapatista Army of National Liberation), which became visible just when Mexico signed NAFTA in 1994, helped gain them international publicity and support, exposing the paradox of an indigenous population living in great poverty yet at the same time economically important for its touristic and artisanal attraction and officially valued for its place in Mexico's past.

The general drift of events worldwide, and certainly in Mexico, in the era of globalization is that more utilitarian and less expensive crafts are disappearing or going down in quality. Artisans of low-end objects cannot compete on price when the market is flooded by foreign imports of cheap and useful items available at the Wal-Marts now covering the land, which threaten to replace the *tianguis* for cheap goods. Imports have also entered the ethnic souvenir market and the religious market; one can buy made-in-China "Aztec calendars" at Palenque (a Mayan pyramid site) and plastic representations of the Virgin of Guadalupe. Other crafts are going down in quality, as Mexicans on the periphery of tourist markets create *manualidades*—"crafts" assembled from premade pieces.

By contrast, luxury versions of handmade items (such as silk rebozos with fabulous fringe and elaborately embroidered *huipiles*—fashionable at cocktail parties and museum openings in Mexico City—and many elaborate pieces made for decoration) are increasing in both quality and price, especially those made from raw materials by one person. One factor in the new prestige is undoubtedly the Banco de Mexico's thick and beautifully printed *Grandes Maestros del Arte Popular Mexicano*, published in both Spanish and English, which accompanied the bank's wildly successful, internationally traveled exhibition by the same name. Another is the *concurso* system, particularly in the last decade or two, in which private corporations began providing large prizes (although the *concursos* are usually sponsored by some level of government or agency) and buying for their collections from winning items. Master artisans who make these items and other highly refined and collectible revival crafts are revered by collectors and museums. In short, *artesanías* are either disappearing, or they are moving toward being collectible high folk art.

Given this turn, the new Museo de Arte Popular not surprisingly is a venue for exhibiting excellent quality pieces, often culled from the prize-winning entries at *concurso*. And, of course, it features a shop stocked with very high-quality crafts at high prices. Attractively renovated at considerable expense, the Art Deco building that houses the Museo de Arte Popular is located in Mexico City's Centro Histórico, the heart of the city's historical and shopping area, where it joins a cluster of nearby major cultural institutions, including the Museo Nacional de Arte, the Palacio de Bellas Artes, and of course the major attractions centered around the Zócalo: the ancient and sinking Catedral, the Templo Mayor (the Aztec temple first discovered in 1978 during efforts to shore up the cathedral), and the Palacio Nacional. Its presence in this cluster of edifices signifying high art and national heritage embodied in objects, both dignifies it (as high art) and diminishes the evocation of life, culture, immaterial heritage, the processes of work, and the live artisans who made it.

Ironically and paradoxically, just when the promotion and revival of high-quality crafts based on traditional methods is encouraging both significant craft prices and even cultural revival in some indigenous communities, extreme poverty exacerbated by unstable violence directed against them has prompted large proportions of men from historically intact *indigena* and other small and poor communities to migrate (or try to migrate) to the United States, leaving some pueblos with fifty percent or fewer of their working-age men.

I would like to see government and museum policies that reward not just individual masters (whose work is indeed admirable), but that also promote and protect small producers of souvenirs and useful items and the ways of life that sustain them. For instance: prohibit imported imitations of locally made crafts to be sold in tourist sites; do not allow major store chains to "clean up" traditional *tianguis* areas, which are also tourist attractions. Those recommendations are a beginning, and they are not prompted by a romantic vision of authenticity; rather, Mexico is a land of tiny businesses that allow a huge number of citizens to sustain a very modest livelihood; street food, tiny stalls of items, ambulatory artisans selling handmade knickknacks all help prevent unemployment and hunger.

Two museums, two locations, two visions of Mexican crafts and the people who produce them. Both are current, and both are attractive and worthy enterprises. At the same time, the unremitting emphasis on quality and on the importance of masterpieces in the Museo de Arte Popular makes it easy to romanticize or remain in ignorance of the larger structural conditions in which artisans work. Acrylic serapes sold in Wal-Marts, plastic Virgins of Guadalupe made in Shenzhen, and Oaxacan carvers now working illegally in California because they could not sustain their families in Mexico are as much a part of the story of *artes populares* as are great masterpieces.

Shelly Errington is professor of anthropology at the University of California at Santa Cruz, where she teaches courses relating to museums, visual media, and multimedia. Indonesia and Mexico are the major sites of her fieldwork and research focus. Errington, a MacArthur Prize Fellow, has been a Fellow at the Institute for Advanced Study in Princeton, New Jersey.

CHAPTER 6

Creativity and Experimentation

> "The things we fear most in organizations—fluctuations, disturbances, and imbalances—are the primary sources of creativity."
>
> *Margaret J. Wheatley*

MUSEUMS ARE living institutions, and they must be able to tolerate some degree of "fluctuations, disturbances, and imbalances" so that they can demonstrate our creativity as they adapt to changing times and contexts. By attuning ourselves, as those with responsibility for museums, to the necessity for creative change (preferably before we enter a crisis), we will be more flexible and be able to plan better in all areas of our museum's work: when our exhibitions or our programming get tired or outdated or if our audiences seem to weary of them, we should be able to reinvent paths leading to fresher interpretations of our collections—one of our core reasons for being. When our financial plan isn't working, we should be able to bring unblinking eyes to it. When our staff is stagnant or intolerant of new approaches, we should be able to reassess and welcome a creative spirit throughout our organizations.

There are so many questions in our museums that must be approached creatively if we are to claim sustainability in today's world. We need to ask: Are there more innovative ways to attract adolescents or seniors or scholars into our museums and to link them to the greater museum project of inclusion? Can we make sure that our museums are relevant to a complicated world by introducing experimental, interdisciplinary programming that stimulates creativity in our visitors? How can we wrestle creatively and innovatively with the challenges posed by globalization and the implications for ownership (or stewardship) of the past that are now rising around issues of cultural patrimony? Is our museum trying to respond creatively to threats to the environment by investigating the possibilities of new alliances? We, as a society, will be requiring creative solutions to a host of problems in our world in the years ahead. Our museums can be models of creativity in the areas of the sciences, the humanities, and the arts. As long as our museums can encourage respect for creativity, innovation, and experimentation in the fields for which they are responsible, they will be able to make the case for their indispensability in society.

There are innovative answers out there for all of us when we ponder the questions. We can invite scientists to work in our art or history museums. Or we can welcome artists into natural history or anthropology museums to suggest experimental interpretations through installation, workshops, or performances. Some of the world's innovative gardens, such as the Oaxaca ethnobotanical museum and the Huntington Children's Garden, have invited sculptors to make pieces that give yet another kind of life to those already special places. Art museums have invited first-year medical students to study the paintings hanging on their walls as part of their introductory classes in clinical medicine. By all accounts the medical students' ability to "read" a patient's condition was sharpened by the exercise of methodically analyzing a painting and trying to stretch to grasp both overt and hidden narratives.

Art museums can shake up the public's expectations by disrupting chronological and geographical art histories as the Getty Museum did in Los Angeles, when it invited the Museum of Contemporary Art (MoCa) across town to send over its great Jackson Pollack, *No. 1, 1949,* to be displayed next to the Getty's own 1890s Monet painting of water lilies to help initiate its Interjections series. Visitors entered the impressionist galleries "knowing" what they would encounter. Instead they were confronted with newly juxtaposed works of art, and over and over again, defied the old museology statistic that repeatedly announces that visitors spend only eight seconds in front of a work of art. Rather, many lingered in front of this nontraditional placement of these artists from different times, places, and points of view, and wondered at their similarities and differences. To move too quickly through any type of museum is to lose a great deal of what it has to offer. Creative displacement can slow our audiences down; our own thinking differently might be models for encouraging fresh thinking in our visitors.

Not that this kind of creativity in art museum display is completely new in itself. It has been a sustaining museum activity that has been going on for centuries. As early as the 1820s, the National Gallery of London daringly reinstalled its collection of contemporary national artists with "old masters" from Spain, France, and Holland. But this kind of creativity and experimentation was not limited to art museums. The National Museum of Anthropology in Mexico City attracted millions of visitors over the last half century because of its groundbreaking presentation of its collections of pre-Columbian objects in 1964. The highly original contemporary architecture for that museum provided a stimulating contrast to the ancient pieces of Maya, Olmec, Zapotec, and Aztec art in the building. This museum effect challenged the traditional view of the "musty" ethnographic museum. The lines between art and anthropology, between mausoleum and museum, have been and must continue to be radically breached. Mexican museums continue to creatively mix the ancient with the contemporary from time to time—always to powerful effect!

Yet as we consider our effectiveness in the realm of creativity and experimentation, we must face the fact that all of our museums are different and have different aspirations and capabilities. Some museums are especially interested in triggering memory related to the most iconic aspects of their collection. Others are determined to inspire their publics by presenting unconventional ideas related to their collections and encouraging discovery of less well-known objects. Increasingly, though, museums are engaging in crossbreeding between memory and inspiration. Indeed, this crossbreeding might go beyond mere interdisciplinarity. As we see it, creativity might actually consist of breaking the boundaries and expectations of what a museum is traditionally seen to be. And each museum has to make the case that it is taking sufficient risk to maintain the sustained interest of its visitors.

The "People's Show" in Walsall, England initiated a phenomenon in the early 1990s when it broke the mold of museums as temples of high art. It did this by encouraging the citizens of a smallish town to take ownership of their local museums and to participate, beginning with showing their own personal collections. From collecting, their focus moved toward interpreting; the People's Show launched a wave of uniquely creative museum involvement throughout England, much of it by people who had not been museum goers before.

For a society to enjoy its full potential it must identify ways to use the past constructively, to present the contemporary winningly, and to stimulate and inspire original ideas and innovative thinking in its audiences. If it were not for the audiences, simply supplying unlimited artists' residencies, scientific laboratories, accessible libraries and greenhouses galore could satisfy the needs of society. Our question, then, is this: what role does your museum play in this transmission of the value of creativity to your own present-day public? If you can answer that question for your own museum and in your own way, you will be participating in making the larger case of justifying the role of your museum as a partner in innovation, a critical need in all societies today. This value must be addressed and answered convincingly at a time when the problems that loom in front of us are so large and so in need of creative solution. Innovation as demonstrable practice needs to be an arrow in the quiver of our successful museums.

Dia:Beacon, that immense showcase of the most ambitious modern and contemporary installations, works unabashedly to ensure that artists themselves come to the site and are comfortable being there so that they might be inspired by the work of other artists. Inspiration is the heart of the matter at Dia:Beacon. Steven Evans writes that Dia:Beacon unabashedly conceives of artists as its primary stakeholders. The artwork is presented generously with the implicit understanding that there is a place in the world where artists can think very big and that their work will speak for itself. Implicitly, the museum communicates the essential, sustaining value of creativity to anyone who takes time to make a visit.

David Wilson, director of the tiny Museum of Jurassic Technology thinks not of what the artists do but of what the museum can do, beginning from the very essence of display. At the Museum of Jurassic Technology, a museum that lives beyond the normal typology of museums, in a kind of parallel universe, Wilson forces us to consider the first element that characterizes a museum, an element beyond the object itself: the casework. He argues that this ostensibly humble foundation for display in a museum is, in the case of the Museum of Jurassic Technology, the tangible point of origin for its own enormous creativity—that the casework can be the opening to "the vast and oftentimes elusive potential of the object on display." Wilson's is a provocative essay that is meant to prod us into looking at the smallest parts of our operations and giving them the respect they deserve as synechdoches of our institutions.

Marco Bassols's transformation of the Natural History Museum in Mexico from a drab conventional museum to a lively laboratory of creativity and experimentation was nothing short of a revolution. Just to enter it after Bassols had invited creativity and experimentation to infuse the institution was to grasp immediately that knowledge should not be contained in mere boxes or silos. It was palpable that learning could be a kind of respectful intellectual free-for-all. During his tenure, the museum became a thrilling destination for learning and playing in the sandbox of possibility.

Nelly Robles García ends this chapter by reminding us that an archaeological site is an open-air museum and can also profit by a dose of creativity. With a mind friendly to innovation in a very staid and bureaucratic part of the museum field, Robles García increased the sense of community ownership of Monte-Alban, a United Nations Educational, Scientific, and Cultural Organization (UNESCO) world heritage site under threat of overuse and encroachment by the neighboring population. Her innovative involvement of the community that was actually potentially threatening the site has resulted in them helping to protect the fragile site.

Creativity and experimentation obviously do not belong solely to the world of art and artists or to our exhibitions in our various types of museums. Whether in education, collections, finance, philanthropy, communication, community relations, staff structure, leadership, or a combination of all of these, the attitude of the museum must be a positive one toward creative examination and practice.

Make the case for innovation. Let it be known that your museum is a key player through the objects it collects and preserves and the connections you make among them, through new interpretation and a sense of infinite possibility it encourages along with traditional inquiry, through its strategic planning, through its new alliances. Every museum needs to be a site of creativity; every museum will have to find its own way to exercise the creative spirit. And every museum must make the case that it is doing so—whether its mission is to celebrate the past or to usher in the future.

IN SERVICE TO ARTISTS. . . .

Steven Evans

During a lecture he recently delivered on his relationship to the work of Andy Warhol, contemporary artist Glenn Ligon spoke of his experience in the Dia:Beacon Riggio Galleries space devoted to Warhol's monumental 1978–1979 work entitled *Shadows*. To prepare for his lecture, Ligon arrived incognito at the museum on a typical day. He spoke of the hours he spent in the daylight-lit gallery under Dia:Beacon's saw-tooth skylights, observing the relationships that blossomed between the public and the work itself.

Shadows, as exhibited at Dia:Beacon, comprises seventy-two silk screen and acrylic-on-canvas panels each measuring 76×52 inches, which line the perimeter of an 8,500-

square-foot room. Warhol repeated two distinct silk-screened shadow images throughout this series, in seventeen colors that range from vibrant hues to a flat gray. While the regular format utilized by Warhol makes the work appear simple to grasp, in his lecture Ligon noted how *Shadows*'s play of color and repetition prolongs the viewers' interest as the work transforms its host gallery into an overtly social sphere: visitors pass through the space, taking in the work, conversing with their companions about its meaning, speculating on the shadow's source object, enjoying the play of color and repetition, pointing, posturing, all the while gazing at the work and at friends and strangers alike.

This was precisely Warhol's intention. In a 1979 *New York Magazine* article, the artist quipped that because the opening would have disco music, the paintings were "disco décor," and further, that while the work may be underappreciated, "the reviews of the party will be terrific." Warhol's *Shadows* brings the audience into the space of the work in a way that explicitly implicates their collaboration in constructing the work's meaning.

Shadows has been shown only in five locations since its creation, and there are scant settings where the intended dynamic between artwork and audience can manifest so animatedly. I would trace that success to Dia Art Foundation and Dia:Beacon's unique expectation that artists are a primary audience. Equally important, our artist-witnesses serve both as gauges—and agents—of the museum's mission and success.

This viewpoint is just one aspect of Dia Art Foundation's mission to be in service to artists. Philippa de Menil, Heiner Friedrich, and Helen Winkler established the foundation in 1974 with this concept in mind. They eventually chose the Greek word *dia*, meaning "through," to represent their belief in the organization as an avenue for artists making work. Ambitious projects that evidence this mission are widely known. Indeed, as Walter De Maria's *Lightning Field* (1977) exemplifies so well, Dia's commissions could be summed up handily: the artist is challenged to think beyond established terms of scale, geography, temporality, or even known feasibility; Dia will find a way to realize the project.

Serving as a conduit for artists extends beyond the act of production. Dia has carefully regarded its artists' intentions for the presentation and display of the work. At Dia:Beacon, for example, a series of Dan Flavin's "monuments" for V. Tatlin are presented on an accordion-shaped, freestanding wall of the artist's design. Furthermore, the fluorescent light sculptures are presented flush with the floor as the artist intended, whereas some other museums have erroneously mounted these works on distancing low pedestals. Dia:Beacon, too, has made a point of not inserting interpretive text. Rather than force a point of view or agenda that may make the viewer self-conscious, our attitude toward presentation is to allow the work to declare for itself rather than to provide a mitigating narration. It is up to the viewer to tease out meaning from an individual artwork. And artists are particularly capable of doing just that.

The direct and simple connection between artist and audience is what attracted me to Dia in the first place in the late 1980s. Freshly graduated from Nova Scotia College of Art and Design's MFA program, I arrived in New York aspiring to get as close as possible to the site of production, and I was aware of Dia's year-long commissions of site-specific works at its Dia Center for the Arts facility in New York's then-quiet Chelsea neighborhood.

Like many artists, including Dia luminaries like Dan Flavin and Robert Ryman, I applied for a job as a museum guard—or more precisely, as a Dia gallery attendant. Artist readers may identify. It is a trumpeted verity that early-career artists often work in galleries or as guards, in part because many of these talents are galvanized by prolonged exposure to other artists' work. As a workplace, Dia quickly became a haven of sorts and has played a quiet role as an employer of young artists over the years; a completely haphazard and incomplete list includes Rachel Harrison, Simon Leung, Julia Loktev, Pieter Schoolwerth, Lincoln Tobier, Meredyth Sparks, Lucky DeBellevue, Patterson Beckwith, Andrea Fraser, Wade Guyton, Haim Steinbach, Isolde Kille, John Miller, Heidie Giannotti, Jeremy Sigler, Jeff Davis, Nancy Shaver, Nate Lowman, Jennifer Bornstein, and Gregg Bordowitz. This tradition continues at Dia today, as many of the gallery attendants and other staff at Dia:Beacon are recent graduates from area BFA and MFA programs, as well as art history and curatorial studies students and graduates. It is this surfeit of creative talent that lends energy to the environment and resiliency to the particular demands of operating an institution like Dia:Beacon or its Chelsea predecessor.

In my days as a gallery attendant, at times it felt like artists (i.e., my artist colleagues and I) were, in fact, Dia's principal audience. Those early days in Chelsea had their quiet moments. Since then, silence has been replaced by a din, and my job has changed correspondingly. In 1999, I relocated to Beacon to help administer the construction of our nearly 300,000-square-foot facility and later became the foundation's assistant director, overseeing the museum and its programs. Today, one of my responsibilities is to create and collect our measurable outcomes for the completed museum: the visitation numbers, revenue spreadsheets, audience feedback reports, and the ever-looming annual economic impact study.

Before Dia:Beacon's opening in May 2003, it was clear that although we anticipated a new, wider audience, it was crucial to preserve the institution's historical tranquility. I am reminded of an early training session during which Dia's curator, Lynne Cooke, explained to our new docents that it was vital to avoid interpreting the work for the viewer, that what was important was to encourage a direct relationship between the viewer and the work, "to be careful not to get in the way," as she phrased it. After all, *dia* means conduit, not filter or obstacle.

Choosing artist Robert Irwin as a project designer for Dia:Beacon emphasized the elimination of barriers between viewer and subject. Working in dialogue with the architects and staff, Irwin subtly heightened viewers' perceptive powers through his treatment of materials and paths. Through a number of devices, including adding windows that carefully alternate between clear and obscure glazing and placing paths that run the length of the building, Irwin quite subtly helps the visitor negotiate the massive space and many galleries. The work is presented, but the act of unpacking its meanings, the operation of actual perception, remains the role of the spectators.

Taking this position vis-à-vis museum education as well as architectural design requires advocating for an interesting and somewhat open situation—or, as Dan Flavin characterized his works, a proposal. While this situation benefits all museum visitors by challenging them intellectually, it is particularly edifying for the artist-witness: they can see, without guidance, how a relationship with architecture might influence perception of an artwork, how a particular context is dealt with, and how viewers succeed or fail at interpretation when that responsibility is placed on their shoulders.

Indeed, consider how the inverse situation could play out at a place like Dia:Beacon. Insert a lengthy explanatory wall text among Fred Sandback's stretched acrylic yarn sculptures, and surely their alchemical spatial effects would dissipate. Juxtaposing an exegesis in vinyl letters to Sol LeWitt's wall drawings would be distracting and redundant, especially considering the artist's use of titles as instructions for creating as well as understanding those works. Through their deceptively simple gestures alone, these artists open a door for the viewer to consider their own creative capacity. An institution may also encourage that capacity, an idea that reaches from the philosophy of Joseph Beuys and resonates particularly loudly in today's "wiki" culture.

Museums attract artists, of course, but considering them as a crucial audience can too easily be lost in an era of spreadsheets and charts. Illustrating the numbers of visitors, their respective zip codes, and the resulting revenues can only tell us so much.

I do not want to dismiss such quantitative measures and how they function with regard to audiences, partners, and regions. But in some quarters there is a sense that museum professionals have moved beyond numbers—that the conversation can return to the possibility of the life-changing effect of an institution's philosophy and programs. Dia personifies this stance, although certainly other like-minded institutions identify with it. The truth is that an institution's creative success cannot be rationalized on an economic basis. Any attempt to evaluate real success must look past established borders, and, equally, museums' programming, partnerships, and acquisition decisions must not play to the numbers but rather to quality. Doing this inspires artists and viewers of all stripes, and inspiration provokes the cultural relevance and individual passion that transforms the audience into ambassadors of the institution.

Steven Evans is Dia Art Foundation's assistant director for Beacon, overseeing Dia:Beacon Riggio Galleries. He has worked extensively with Dia artists and colleagues to realize some of the most impressive contemporary art projects of the last two decades. In addition to his duties at Dia Art Foundation, Evans is a freelance curator, writer, and artist.

MUSEUMS AND CREATIVITY

David Wilson

> "The learner must be led always from familiar objects toward the unfamiliar, guided along as it were, a chain of flowers into the mysteries of life."
>
> *Sir Charles Wilson Peale*

The building in which the Museum of Jurassic Technology (MJT) is and has been housed for nearly two decades was, in the early years of the twentieth century, constructed of redwood, the preferred frame construction material of the era. And while the use of redwood in construction is understandable if only due to the sheer volume of wood a single tree would yield, the true, time-tested benefit of the material lies in its stable and enduring nature. Renowned both in life and as timber for its longevity, redwood is not only impervious to conditions of moisture, to which many other building woods succumb, but, perhaps more importantly in the ecology of Southern California, redwood is also by and large immune to the ravages of termites, the remarkable and admirable white ants who would have long since consumed at the very least great portions of the museum's buildings had they been constructed of a lesser material.

Choice and quality of material are among the most essential considerations in the execution of any task. Materials carry with them not only specific structural qualities and strengths such as sheer, torsion, and compression—the mechanics of deformable solids—but also a multitude of aesthetic and tactile qualities as well, qualities that, over time, have come to be linked to the material in the forms of traditional usage, history, and association.

While exhibitions at the MJT most often begin with a larger and typically more demanding building project, which is the renovation of the physical space in which the exhibition will be housed, the true essence of our construction and shop work consistently revolves around casework.

From the museum's earliest days, the importance of the case, or vitrine, became instantly clear and an appreciation of exhibition casework from museums and related institutions from around the world became an object of intense focus.

In the early days of the museum, the vitrines that came to house the first objects and exhibits from our collections were built primarily of birch and walnut. Relatively affordable and workable with what was then a modest array of tools, these woods, with sufficient finishing, produce a beautiful surface and even depth when extra time and care is taken. Over the years, however, we found ourselves employing more exotic woods with names like padauk, purple heart, zebrawood, coco bolo, kevazinga, and wenge. These woods, sharing great richness in both color and pattern, have, however, very individualized characters or natures—natures that become especially manifest during the process of fabrication. Purple heart burns easily if the cutting blade or router knife is not meticulously sharp, leaving a black scar that can only be removed with a great deal of effort. Coco bolo will almost self-finish to a warm luster due to the natural internal oil of its fiber. For an early exhibit entitled Purification by Sublimation, we employed a luminous orange African wood known in the west as padauk. With careful choice of boards, the natural coloration of padauk is of such intensity that it appears to be unnaturally stained. We were excited by the prospect of working with the material; however, after our first cut, it became apparent that the wood released an unexpected and strong toxin that sent both my partner and me into serious respiratory distress. Wearing OSHA C9 respirators to protect our lungs, we finished in padauk the project of the construction of the frames for the small windows that today peer into a dark distance displaying the scientific instruments of purification by sublimation.

With the passage of time, the improvement of our skill, and the acquisition of more refined fabrication tools, casework at the MJT has been able to expand not only in terms of material but design as well. For our microscopy hall, we constructed a pair of long cases (again of padauk and glass), which stand on a single decoratively routed plank. Constructed specifically to hold its eight Swift microscopes, the cases offer equal protection from the hazards of hostile dust and particulate matter, as well as exuberant young museum patrons. Visitors, accordingly, have the choice of looking at the case, into the case, or ever deeper into the microscopic world of Henry (Harold) Dalton's astonishing and astonishingly beautiful micromosaics created entirely from diatoms and the scales from the wings of butterflies.

Since its inception, the MJT has drawn inspiration from the history of the institution of the museum and most especially from the museums of the seventeenth, eighteenth, and nineteenth centuries. These earlier institutions have been deeply important to the formation of the MJT for many reasons, but among the perhaps more obvious influences, these early museums have inspired us by the careful craftsmanship and exquisite design of their casework. Designed with an elegance of proportion and meticulous craft, it would be less than forthcoming not to acknowledge that often the case, rather than its contents, has most thoroughly commanded my attention.

Within the exhibits of the MJT, a careful observer might notice quotes from or homages to certain of these historical institutions that have so inspired our work. From the skylight in our Library for the Diffusion of Useful Information, which reflects the exquisite lanterns of Sir John Soane's Museum on Lincoln Fields Inn, or the vitrines in our exhibition of vulgar beliefs entitled Tell the Bees: Belief Knowledge and Hypersymbolic Cognition, which are markedly reminiscent of the distinctive casework in an earlier incarnation of the illuminated manuscript halls of the J. Paul Getty Villa, to the Henry Dalton microscope cases that were directly inspired by the numismatic displays of the Museum of the City of St. Petersburg at Peter Paul Fortress, our casework at the MJT has in many, if not most, cases an historical precedent.

Very much allowing ourselves to be guided by these precedents, these sources of our collective inspiration, the museum, in building practice and especially in its casework, finds itself inextricably aligned with an ideal of humble service to not only the extraordinary potential of the natural and human-made materials at our service, but also to the vast and oftentimes elusive potential of the object on display. Fully recognizing that the avenue to intellectual and spiritual expansion can be found by way of any number of worldly entrances, the object itself may be only the starting point. Expanding through the case-work and beyond, the object is given the opportunity to extend itself into a larger con-text, potentially revealing formerly latent facets of its unique character and hinting at its role in the infinitely complex and magnificent universe.

David Wilson is the founding director of the Museum of Jurassic Technology, which he opened in 1988 at its current Culver City, California, location. The MJT has exhibited internationally and Mr. Wilson has lectured throughout North America and Europe. He has produced six independ-ent films. In 2001 the MacArthur Foundation granted David Wilson a fellowship in recognition of his accomplishments at the Museum of Jurassic Technology.

ART AND SCIENCE, NATURE AND ART IN A NATURAL HISTORY MUSEUM

Marco Barrera Bassols

Translated by Francisca González Arias

In memoriam, Stephen J. Gould

According to Stephen J. Gould and Rosamond Wolff Purcell, museo-logical tendencies that accentuate the process of democratization include fomenting creativity and creating spaces for experimentation, as well as developing transdisciplinary viewpoints that confer on the museum an important role in the coming of the society of knowledge.

The museum is no longer just a space for reflection and wonder. It is beginning to take on the appearance of a laboratory. As such, it goes beyond a strictly educational scope and embraces other forms of participation by specialists as well as by artists and the pub-lic, all of whom find in it a place in which to share experience and knowledge. All this enhances the museum experience and takes it to a whole new level. By fomenting creativ-ity, the museum also becomes a creator of new forms of interaction and experimenta-tion, while opening up multiple viewpoints. The end of an era is beginning—an era based on a nineteenth-century matrix that envisioned the museum as a set of disconnected boxes. Many people are hoping this is so.

In *Crossing Over: Where Art and Science Meet*, Gould establishes that, although they use different languages to communicate, art and science reflect and embrace each other when juxtaposed. For example, during the International Symposium "The Museum as Medium," organized by Pablo Helguera for the Guggenheim Museum in 2002, I spoke about the program Residencias Creativas (Creative Residencies), which was developed by the Natural History Museum of Mexico City in 1999. I will go into more detail about this program in this text. This program, which will now be called Arte y Naturaleza (Art and Nature), has been redesigned as part of the new natural history museum, which will open its doors in 2012.

The original Residencias Creativas program consisted of a space for the exchange of ideas among scientists, artists, science educators, and the public through the development of artistic projects related to the museum's goals: science, nature, the environment, and art. In 1997 when I became director, the museum was neglected, mired in bureaucracy, and at an impasse. Its contents had not been updated in thirty years. Residencias Creativas was part of a revitalization strategy to achieve the museum's renovation. The idea was to turn the museum into a dynamic place that would permit the coexistence of seemingly different disciplines. For this purpose, museum personnel designed a space of eight hundred square meters divided in half to house an experimental laboratory and an exhibition area for the projects in progress. The models for this design were the Exploratorium of San Francisco, California, the Banff Centre for the Arts in Canada, and the Zentrum fur Kunst und Media (ZKM) in Germany, although this trend was also reflected in other museums such as the Natural History Museum of Los Angeles County and its temporary exhibition entitled Conversations.

Elías Levin, the Residencias Creativas curator, organized the program along three axes: science (technological development and distribution), art (visual and dramatic arts and literature), and media (distribution, interaction, and creation). This combination was intended to develop short-, medium-, and long-term projects, in situ or in collaboration, overseen by a cross-disciplinary advisory committee. The museum designed major temporary exhibitions to display the results to reaffirm its long-term commitment to the program. In just two years, projects by five artists were developed in different fields.

For example, in the field of electromagnetic resonance, the artist Ariel Guzik created *Resonador Espectral Armónico, Ojo de Ortóptero* and *The Art Ensemble of la Araña (Spider) o La Banda Nerviosa Automática.* The latter was exhibited at Spain's international art fair, ARCO, in Madrid in 2006. Guzik also developed the *Espejo Plasmath* and edited two CDs. In the area of sculptural robotization, insects and humanoids were constructed from scrap iron by the sculptor Pablo Castillo. Instrumental innovation was represented by Gibrán Cervantes' Urkúngulo with a collection of berimbaus suspended from a structure that allowed them to be played by four hands and by the Mitote Orchestra directed by percussionist Daniel Sánchez. This orchestra, composed of homeless children whose instruments were crafted out of recycled trash, espoused the concept that "one person's garbage is another person's wealth." Finally, in the area of photography Francisco Mata based the creation of the museum's new visual identity on its collections.

In barely one year, twenty-five artists applied to be accepted into the program, including Gabriel Orozco, Manuel Rocha, César Martínez, Marianna Dellekamp, and Minerva Cuevas, among others. The topics that they wished to explore included:

- The artistic intervention of items that were no longer part of the museum's collection
- The qualities of trees and amate paper
- The ordering of genetic codes for the development of abstract paintings
- Hydraulic processes (coexistence of liquid and solid materials)
- Ecological deterioration
- Mechatronics and robotics
- Creation of aromatic grasses
- Video-art installations and computer animation
- Theories related to networks and art on the Internet
- The human body, nature, and society
- Auditory installations
- Magnetic properties of objects
- Social behavior of humans and animals
- Health, illness, and hospital iconography
- Video games and mechanics
- Humboldt and the rainforests of Latin America
- Animal tracks
- The museum's boundaries: inside and the outside
- Vision and ocular structures
- Two-dimensional creation through the use of TNT and gunpowder
- Hypnosis

The diverse range of the these themes reflects the motivations and interests of contemporary artists. The program also enabled artists to become closer to a museum that many of them had visited when they were children, and it increased the museum's appeal, enabling the museum to steer away from the "captive audience" of children who are taken to the museum on school visits. Finally, Residencias Creativas generated conditions that reintroduced the participation of artists in projects characteristic of classic Mexican museography such as those initiated by Fernando Gamboa in the 1930s with individuals like Miguel El Chamaco Covarrubias, Iker Larrauri, and Rufino Tamayo and his murals in the Museo Nacional de Antropología.

In this same tenor, I would like to highlight the temporary exhibit Estridencias de la Selva, Los insectos de las selvas húmedas de México (Stridencies of the Jungle: The Insects of Mexico's Rainforests). It consisted of fifty photographic portraits of a representative variety taken by Claudio Contreras, with ambient sound conceived by Ariel Guzik. It was a double project that permitted the creation of an environment where images, suspended like drops of water from the center of one of the vaulted galleries, zoomed in on the insects, while the ambient sound explored their language with the *Ojo de ortóptero* system, which imitated the stridencies or screeching of crickets and cicadas (ortópteros and homópteros). While the portraits were being viewed, a wrap-around sound was produced and one was engulfed by the jungle stridencies generated by variations in intensity, saturation, scarcity of light (day/night), or humidity, just as in nature. Sounds were produced through dozens of microchips to which quartz crystals were added, hidden, and dispersed in the semicircular interior of the vault. As Ariel Guzik mentioned, an incomparable atmosphere was produced by the simple audiotape made in the field of the sound of these insects and its amplification and reproduction through loudspeakers. This is due to the fact that *Ojo de ortóptero* re-creates the phenomenon synthetically and in a short time so that the public has the opportunity to comprehend the daily cycle in just a few seconds: "At dawn," says Ariel, "you hear the murmur of the crickets, which is replaced by the noise of an ensemble of cicadas at noon, and with the approach of evening both species coexist in resonant harmony." The subtlety of Ariel's work is only a sample of the results that the museum and the artists were able to generate through this dialogue.

The museum and its residents transformed the space through their unwavering spirit of collaboration and enthusiasm that permitted the scientists to submerge themselves in the minds of the artists and these, in turn, explored the other field of knowledge. The winners were, above all, the public, as well as the museum. This pilot laboratory, which encouraged experimentation, allowed all to gradually come together to achieve the metamorphosis of natural history and contemporary art. What happened, no more and no less, was that the languishing natural history museum began to transform itself into a dynamic museum of knowledge.

Marco Barrera Bassols is a museologist, museographer, and historian. He is founding president of the Mexican Association of Museum Professionals, former director of the Natural History Museum of Mexico City, former assistant director of the National Museum of Popular Cultures, and associate partner in Museográfica, S.C.

CREATIVITY AND EXPERIMENTATION IN THE WORLD OF ARCHAEOLOGY

Nelly M. Robles García
Translated by Jack Corbett

 The science of archaeology, with its empirical nature and dependence on material objects, defines those fixed parameters and practices governing the ways archaeological sites, the objects found therein, and the relationship between site and object are to be understood. At the same time, however, these very parameters and practices can become insuperable barriers to bridging the distance separating the scientist, the empirical archaeological world, and the general public.

Starting from the reality that archaeology has a specific place in education and leisure in contemporary society, it confronts challenges such as:

- Ensuring the clarity of the historical message and the significance of archaeology to the recipient
- Transmitting the need to conserve archaeological heritage
- Reducing the gap between those who control scientific knowledge and members of diverse publics seeking clarity and satisfaction from the scientific community

The field of archaeological heritage management offers possible answers, opening as it does enormous possibilities for creativity and experimentation with different systems and methods for understanding, interpreting, and disseminating heritage values. In itself it constitutes a flexible form for approaching knowledge as well as the physical components (sites and objects), making them accessible to diverse publics for their collective enjoyment. In this sense, without deprecating or abandoning archaeology's basic values, it permits us to emphasize those important points that via imaginative strategies and creative experimentation permit the attainment of valued objectives. Here I summarize some strategies.

ARCHAEOLOGICAL SITES ARE OPEN-AIR MUSEUMS

Those of us responsible for archaeological site management constantly complain about the often-undisciplined behavior of the public. We have all suffered efforts to convert archaeological plazas into impromptu soccer fields or youthful competitions to climb and descend stairways in record time, to scale fragile walls or paint or scratch the original stones, or to sit on delicate sculptures to rest or to take a photo. Another common practice is to convert archaeological sites into large picnic areas, campgrounds, or places to celebrate family gatherings.

In the face of these diverse threats we have chosen to manage Monte Alban, a World Heritage Site, as if it were actually an outdoor museum. That is, fully aware that the behavior of visitors is dramatically different when entering a museum rather than an archaeological site, we try to give the latter a museum-like character, which in fact it truly deserves. In this way we seek to evoke behavior associated with a museum visit. That is, the message we project to the public once they enter the site is that it is not a place to play games, to treat as a public park, to destroy or enjoy in individualized pursuits. Instead it is a place to experience learning, reflection, creativity, exchange, sensory perception, and creative sharing.

How do we accomplish this? From the moment the visitor enters there is a conscious construction of an environment fostering such values, beginning with the staff itself. Monte Alban includes in its professional ranks not only archaeologists, but teachers, artists, and conservation biologists. The site prepares for public access through sufficient oversight, interpretation, and education. Personnel explain clearly both the opportunities and constraints related to site visitation. In this respect they are both prepared for and comfortable with interaction with a broad spectrum of visitors precisely because they have trained for the experience.

In addition, site personnel create a variety of programs that help visitors derive greater benefit from their stay. They learn to see the site from different perspectives; it is not simply a collection of old stones but a tribute to the hands and minds that made such construction possible.

Archaeologists don't bite! They might even be friendly! Most site visitors have never seen an archaeologist at work. And this is because most archaeological projects try to separate their work from the daily activity at the site. Nevertheless, by integrating a quick visit to an ongoing project, visitors to an outdoor museum will be able to understand important aspects of archaeology (e.g., the rhythm, discipline, and sense of responsibility the archaeologist brings to each task). In turn the site benefits by promoting a positive outlook toward this or other projects addressing archaeological heritage. And we do not forget that one picture, or in this case one clear view, may explain more than a thousand words, and a brief explanation from an archaeologist may produce a lifelong change of attitude.

When the visitor to the site/museum encounters an archaeologist who, besides posing for a picture, is inclined to answer a few questions, it promotes a sense of connection between the visitor and the site. Taking advantage of the photographic and mental image of the archaeologist is an excellent way to promote a respectful attitude and a deep interest in archaeological heritage. In addition, to the extent a project member explains to a visitor what lies below the surface, showing some emerging finds and sharing the emotions of archaeological discovery, we have the best strategy to generate curiosity and respect for the discipline, something I call defending archaeology with archaeology.

CREATING ACTIVITIES ON THE BASIS OF ARCHAEOLOGICAL EVIDENCE

Archaeological data are an inexhaustible source of inspiration for enjoyable games. For many children the novelty of participation in prehistoric games or using imagination to re-create rituals, clothing, sounds, narratives, and communication with nature sparks creativity and curiosity. Even when archaeology is unable to discover these elements in their cultural totality, it can offer insights into activities, games, ritual, and daily practices, and into the representation of some of the people who inhabited that space and time.

On the basis of even fragmentary evidence it can be a highly creative exercise to try to interpret, in small groups, the complete version of a game, an offering, a ceremony, a family activity, or even a funeral ritual. This becomes even more powerful and engaging when, as is the case at Monte Alban, contemporary ethnographic information underscores the continuity of ancestral practice.

CREATING A COMMUNITY MUSEUM

Over the last several years, site personnel at Monte Alban have participated in the promotion of community museums. A community museum, geared to the scale of small rural communities, serves as a center of identity and pride. The entire community participates, with occasional support from experts in fields such as archaeology, restorations, and other specialties as needed. Effectively the concept rests on the organizational capacity of communities to create small centers of cultural dissemination, a classic example of grassroots mobilization of imagination and resources. The scale and formal structure, of course, differ markedly from grand institutional museums.

A community museum represents a great collective effort, drawn from extensive identification and discussion of representative themes of local culture by the community population itself. Such discussions may last months, if not longer, until a consensus emerges on the significant themes to be represented in the museum. Then there is a second great effort as the community creates a base collection of those elements of community culture it wishes to display. Local families capture local knowledge and objects (prehistoric and historic), thereby legitimating their contributions to a collective understanding of their past and traditions. In this fashion community museums draw their existence from collective work and experience. Personnel from Monte Alban contribute their specialized knowledge or technical skills, gaining in return powerful lessons on the value and opportunities created through collective effort.

Beyond the reaffirmation of community identity, the process of museum formation serves to emphasize the value of sites, objects, themes, and heritage. That is, the process serves to energize the community as a guardian of its heritage, mobilizing a community conscience against looting and vandalism of archaeological remains. Communities that form their own museums even adopt their own sanctions against those caught destroying community heritage, thereby attaching their own value to it. And they are more likely to regard outside experts as allies in a shared effort rather than as unwanted intruders.

These are just a few examples drawn from the many possibilities associated with the management of an archaeological site such as Monte Alban and others around it. Along with the archaeological finds themselves, the process of managing values and knowledge become important elements to share with diverse publics. But doing so effectively means infusing our traditional notions of archaeology with a strong sense of curiosity, of innovation, of surprise and discovery, and above all with a very heavy dose of imagination.

Dr. Nelly Robles García is director of the archaeological zone at Monte Alban, part of the UNESCO World Heritage Site with the nearby city of Oaxaca. She is author and editor of eight books on Oaxaca archaeology and cultural resources management, and has been awarded numerous prestigious prizes for her pioneering work in archaeological site management.

CHAPTER 7

New Alliances

ONE CAN IMAGINE that there was a time when museums did not have to be forever seeking out alliances, when the mere fact of their existence was enough to allow them to thrive. Of course, we know that museums always did need alliances, but they did seem to be more organically tied to their missions: to the academy, to public and private schools, to collectors, to foundations, to funding government agencies, or even to corporations underwriting their exhibitions. Now, all of us need to make the case that we have a vital and ongoing strategy that combines the nurturing and protection of traditional and organic alliances with the building of new alliances. It is this combination of the tried and the new that is rapidly becoming essential to the dynamic and sustainable advancement of our core missions.

Every museum needs to be able to convince its supporters that it works ethically, consistently, productively, and appropriately with the traditional network of educators, collectors, interpreters, creators, vendors, and donors of objects. Every museum also needs to show that it functions as a vital link in the world of informal education, including the world of the Internet, which has proven so valuable to those who cannot physically cross the thresholds of our museums, to the creation of a variety of social and professional networks, or even those who just want to "check us out." With the new technologies that are emerging daily, it is easy for everyone to learn about museums and what they do. New though these technologies may be, they really constitute traditional alliances in new clothing. How, though, and to what extent can we reach out and encourage other kinds of alliances? Museums today need to consider becoming partners with nongovernmental organizations, with environmental groups, with health services both official and holistic, with museums with which they might not be typologically aligned, with unexpected government agencies, with nations, private foundations, and superficially unrelated philanthropies if they are to further link their work to the concerns of our time. The essays in this chapter discuss but a few of these options.

Alliances with other museums both like and unlike our own, both local and foreign, are being explored more and more since the period of the pioneering partnerships of the Guggenheim Museum in New York City with Bilbao, Spain, and the Boston Museum of Fine Arts with Nagoya, Japan, at the end of the last century. More recently the Palace Museum in Beijing instituted an unprecedented alliance with the Peabody Essex Museum in Massachusetts so that they could restore together the Juanquinshai studio in the Forbidden City. According to Wang Shiwei, senior engineer of the Palace Museum's historical architecture department, as reported in the 11 November 2008, *Los Angeles Times,* this represented the first time that "the Palace Museum is cooperating with a foreign organization to repair its facilities comprehensively."

To some extent, art museums are being pushed along this path of unexpected alliances by artists and by their own curiosity about new horizons. Lita Albuquerque, an adventurous and well-established contemporary artist, describes her increasing connection to astronomy and astrophysics. Albuquerque's involvement with and support from NASA in her creative explorations of the outer limit of space and of artistic practice provide a sense of other possibilities for creativity that can occur when we ally ourselves beyond our own discipline. Naturally, any museums that wish to show Albuquerque's art resulting from this alliance also become involved with those relationships.

María Isabel Grañén Porrúa explains the philanthropic work that she and her husband, Alfredo Harp, undertake responsibility for in Mexico. For them, museums are a part of a web of interests. Reading Grañén Porrúa's text reveals a growing complexity in the world of philanthropy. It also reveals a growing interest on the part of philanthropists to be involved in the decision making about how exactly their money is spent. So we are informed that although the Alfredo Harp Foundation is less likely to build an art museum per se than it is to weave art in, intrinsically, with their other projects. With that in mind, we read that this foundation, a primary purpose of which is to inspire a love of reading, contracts artists to create exciting, engaging projects to create and sharpen aesthetic awareness and artistic engagement for children visiting the library, which the foundation both funded and built. When this foundation funded and commissioned a textile museum, their larger consideration was to reinvigorate artisanal work in local villages. It encourages the Casa de la Ciudad to display exhibitions by artists and performers in spite of the fact that the Casa is essentially an archival institution. Relationships with sponsors (or potential supporters) should, perhaps, now be viewed as creative and innovative opportunities crafted to link their interests more holistically to our museum work—in ways that they and we may not have imagined appropriate in the past.

The formation of new alliances is a shifting landscape that overlaps in many ways with globalization and, as such, sometimes has an ambiguous character. Ramiro Martínez affirms the importance of global alliances today—even as he warns that community must still come first: the linkages to one's immediate community in "all pertinent aspects of a community's life and their contemporary cultural moment" cannot be sacrificed to international alliance making. The challenge, then, is to seek out new alliances while maintaining a profound respect for our own core constituencies, collections, and missions. Martínez's essay serves as affirmation and warning. We must be careful not to get so carried away by the alliances made possible by interdisciplinarity and globalization and opportunism that we ignore or alienate our principal supporters: those nearest and dearest to us and our mission.

Sometimes new alliances can pave the way for future stages in a museum's path. As Carrie Przybilla remembers, the enormous Louvre Project with Abu Dhabi (which Charles Merewether discussed in chapter 5's analysis of globalization) took its first baby steps in an earlier collaboration between the Louvre and Atlanta's High Museum. Przybilla writes that, from the perspective of Atlanta and the High Museum, the alliances with the Louvre and the Museum of Modern Art (MoMA) helped the High make the case for a much-needed larger facility and thus validated the Atlanta museum's own evolving expansion strategy. So alliances that were evidently worthwhile for their own sake also had unintended positive consequences.

Spain, as a country with a Ministry of Culture that consistently supports the arts (albeit with alternating partisan policies), has been employing alliance building as a way of engaging in soft diplomacy. Santiago Palomero's Spanish position represents a kind of manifesto proclaiming Spain's desire to build a system of webs and networks throughout Latin America. Spain is betting that museums can function as bridges to countries and regions—in this case mostly but not exclusively ex-colonies—where relationships have been frayed over the centuries as a result of the trajectory from conquest to independence.

Soft diplomacy is a means of promoting a country's larger strategic relationships. Indeed, a number of European countries, with their powerful government support for museums and culture, understand their museums as major diplomatic tools. As Anthony Appiah pointed out in chapter 5, the British Museum often allies itself with third-world countries, generously encouraging them in their own versions of the museum enterprise. These alliances can also help in ethical collection building, as is the case in Sudan where, as we pointed out in chapter 2, that museum is assisting in saving Sudan's rapidly disappearing rock art. France is an ever-more aggressive promoter of its culture through its museums and has been from Napoleon's day to the present. By thus allying itself with Abu Dhabi, France both underlines its image as a cultural powerhouse and lines its coffers to help sustain the Louvre's activities and growth.

Alliances with similar expectations are occurring all over the world. One has only to look at, for example, the website for the Intercontinental Museum Network's first African-Swedish Museum Network (SAMP), which states the intention "to promote north-south museum collaborations." SAMP is the result of a number of alliances ranging from the Swedish International Development Cooperation Agency, to an elaborate set of museums in Asian, Latin American, and African countries. Thus, an alliance of museums themselves, and artisans, governmental organizations, and supragovernmental organizations function to further the protection and promotion of the tangible and intangible heritages of participating parties in ways none of these museums could dream of doing on their own.

Artists, museum professionals, governments, funders, and even the general public (if we listen well to them) are all able to help museums imagine and forge new alliances. Museums themselves need to be creative, inclusive, relevant, and open to the world for these alliances to have real impact. They can be invaluable if embarked upon with great thought and care, energy, and clarity. Every museum advocate needs to be able to discuss the possibilities of new and productive relationships. We need to be able to make the case, with respect to our own museums, that what we have already achieved takes advantage of new alliances. Then we need to demonstrate how we are planning to ally ourselves creatively, dynamically, productively, and sustainably with new and old partners in the future.

Healthy alliances that both respect a museum's core mission and authentically expand its reach will bring the rewards that always, ultimately, accompany open, generous minds and creative spirits.

SETTING PRECEDENT

Carrie Przybilla

 The series of exhibitions assembled from the permanent collection of the Musée du Louvre in Paris specifically for display at the High Museum of Art in Atlanta from 2006 through 2009 was promoted as "an unprecedented partnership" by the High. Certainly, it was a novel relationship for the Louvre, which had never before made such extensive loans to a single institution: cuts in France's once-generous funding for the arts have obliged the Louvre to establish new, entrepreneurial alliances. For the High, on the other hand, this sort of multiyear collaboration with a single institution was quite familiar: for three consecutive years in the late 1990s it partnered with MoMA in New York for a series of exhibitions, and the arrangement served both institutions well, at least in the short-term. It also set the stage for the High's partnership with the Louvre.

The MoMA partnership was spawned by the 1996 Summer Olympics, hosted by Atlanta. For this event the High mounted the largest exhibition in its history, Rings: Five Passions in World Art, comprising objects from museums around the world. Ned Rifkin, then the director of the High, intended to use the momentum generated by Rings to attract equally significant exhibitions to follow it and marshaled his staff and board to approach other institutions regarding potential exhibitions. At MoMA, they hit pay dirt.

MoMA, then in the early phases of an expansion campaign, was looking for ways to generate revenue. It was also wrestling with what to do with its permanent collection: most of it would have to be put into storage during the construction. Aside from being costly, this meant that various partial and promised gifts would languish in the possession of their owner-donors, who might start having second thoughts about the planned disposition of these works. And at the same time, MoMA wanted to keep its professional staff occupied despite the coming lull in its exhibition schedule. A partnership with the High offered at least partial solutions to these quandaries. The two institutions quickly agreed on a series of exhibitions to be organized by MoMA, drawing from areas of particular strength in its permanent collection and accompanied by full-color catalogues. The first was Henri Matisse: Masterworks from the Museum of Modern Art, which opened 2 November 1996 and ran through 19 January 1997. It was followed almost exactly a year later by Picasso: Masterworks from the Museum of Modern Art (8 November 1997 through 15 February 1998). The final exhibition in the collaboration, again filling the late-autumn/early-winter slot of 1998 and 1999, was Pop Art: Selections from the Museum of Modern Art (24 October 1998 through 17 January 1999).

The first two exhibitions were essentially prefabricated. Matisse was curated by John Elderfield, who in a footnote in the catalogue for the High acknowledges that its texts are largely revisions of what he had written for MoMA's 1978 publication Matisse in the Collection of the Museum of Modern Art or for the catalogue for Henri Matisse: A Retrospective, which MoMA had mounted in 1992. Similarly, MoMA has a long history of Picasso exhibitions and publications that Kirk Varnedoe and Pepe Karmel were able to marshal when assembling the exhibition and catalogue for the High. MoMA was also able to expand the reach of the Picasso exhibit, and the income it generated, by sending it on to the National Gallery of Canada after it closed in Atlanta. And both exhibitions were rousing successes for the High, setting records for daily attendance, selling hundreds of High memberships as well as lots of catalogues and associated merchandise, and garnering favorable media attention.

Pop Art did not fare as well, for reasons that are not clear. It was certainly a strong exhibition, filled with exceptional works by Warhol, Lichtenstein, Oldenburg, Rosenquist, Dine, and more than a dozen additional artists. Perhaps the number of artists included in the show stymied visitors. Potential visitors may also have noted that the title of the exhibition did not promise "masterworks" from MoMA's collection, as was the case for Matisse and Picasso, but rather simply "selections." In any case, the show placed new demands on MoMA's staff. Aside from its 1989 Warhol retrospective, MoMA had not organized a major Pop exhibition in more than a decade. Curator Anne Umland required three assistants to research and write individual catalogue entries for the objects in the show because so little had been done with most of these objects. Perhaps any show from MoMA was bound to seem lackluster after the stellar success of Picasso, which set records at the High. It is only in comparison that the attendance figures for Pop Art seemed disappointing. In any case, the collaboration concluded on a less-than-jubilant note, at least from the High's perspective.

MoMA's interest in collaborating with the High basically came down to money. The High paid a rental fee for the three shows, plus the cost for producing the catalogues as well as for round-trip shipping and insurance for the objects. Just as it was able to add Toronto as a venue for the Picasso exhibit, once each of the shows was assembled, MoMA could, and did, send them to additional venues abroad, further increasing the income each generated.

The benefits to the High are not as easily quantified. The revenue from sales of tickets and memberships is hardly incidental but represents only one aspect of what the museum gained. The High was also nursing expansion aspirations at the time, and the success of the MoMA shows served as proof of its need for a larger facility. The High's Renzo Piano–designed expansion, which opened in November 2005, can thus be viewed as validation of this strategy. But the High's collaboration with MoMA might also portend an ongoing need for these partnerships, such as its current arrangement with the Louvre, to fill the new space and maintain its membership base.

Dare one hope that partnerships with other museums might supplant blockbusters?

Carrie Przybilla was a curator of modern and contemporary art at the High Museum of Art in Atlanta from 1988 through 2007. She received her graduate degree in art history and museum studies at the University of Southern California. She has also been on the curatorial staff at the university museums at Illinois State University and at the Museum of Contemporary Art, Chicago.

ALLIANCES, NEW AND RENEWED

Santiago Palomero
Translated by Francisca González Arias

 It was a great honor to sign the Declaration of San Salvador de Bahía while assistant director general of state museums of the Ministry of Culture of the Spanish government. For this reason alone the challenging adventure of working for Spain's museums, on which I eagerly embarked, would have been well worthwhile. I advise all those who work, or want to work, for a museum to read this declaration carefully. It is the first document clearly illustrating the role of museums as strategic tools of sustainable development and intercultural dialogue that has been formulated since the Declaration of Santiago de Chile in 1972, when museums opened themselves up to society and to development.

The famous "avenues of liberty," which were the goal of Salvador Allende, were laid down in Chile and bore their first fruit three decades later in Brazil, another Ibero-American country that has fought hard for its autonomy and democratic development. Signing this document marks a special cultural commitment among twenty-two Ibero-American countries and a promising start because something like this has never occurred before. We hope, to paraphrase the famous line from the ending of the memorable film *Casablanca*, that it marks the beginning of a long museum friendship.

Due to its geographical and historical positions, Spain has offered itself as a "bridge" between European and American museums. The European experience in management, online technologies, financing, marketing, evaluations, consumer studies, computerized documentation, research, and dissemination can be useful for Ibero-America. Problems with European museums that have closed because of bad planning, privatization, and the "theme park" idea can foster mutual reflection. Specifically, Spain has contributed its experience in the Ministry of Culture's complex development of museological plans that have been well received in Ibero-America.

Spain has offered itself as a reverse "bridge" toward Europe by virtue of the American experience and what it can teach Europe: imagination, diversity, the empowering of indigenous communities, social interaction, participatory management, multicultural-ism, and transversality. We in Spain are trying to call attention to Ibero-America's bold and confident use of museums as tools for sustainability and development and as insti-tutional examples of freedom, restoring the old civic virtue of the first "Museion." These American initiatives are models that serve as lessons to our adequately financed and tech-nologically equipped European museums, reminding us never to forget their responsi-bility toward the public.

Those of us who travel the Atlantic between Spain and Europe and Ibero-America are aware that our Spanish museum policy should begin with a gesture: allowing free admission to Ibero-American citizens who wish to visit Spanish museums. The Depart-ment of Fine Arts of the Ministry of Culture must take measures to ensure that this ges-ture becomes a reality that will hopefully continue in the future. Not in vain, César Antonio Molina, the present minister of culture, was formerly the director of the Insti-tuto Cervantes, which has numerous centers in Ibero-America. It is no coincidence that one of these new centers, inaugurated just a few days after Molina's appointment, is in San Salvador de Bahía.

Alliances, for better or worse, are almost certainly unpredictable. We cannot know if they will occur among great national museums or between small local museums, whether they will be thematic, whether they will be good or bad, predictable or extraordinary. What matters to us is having nurtured the circumstances that permit the development of new alliances in the museum world.

In Spain we are also developing our own networks internally. The Ministry of Cul-ture is trying to create a new museum network with a national and international stan-dard of quality that presents a constitutional, plural, and coordinated vision of Spain that will also facilitate interregional development and exchange among the museums and museologists of the various regions, or autonomous communities, of Spain.

Of course, my personal and professional experience in the Sephardic Museum (Museo Sefardí) of Toledo, Spain, has been based on the historical importance of Jewish alliances and solidarities. The Association of European Jewish Museums, which was conceived in the Joods Historische Museum of Amsterdam and was enlarged at meetings in Prague and Paris, together with the Museum of Israel (Jerusalem) and the various Holocaust Museums of Europe and America, or the "Bet Hatefussot" or Museum of the Diaspora of Tel Aviv, are established entities that played an important role making possible a reinter-pretation of the Jewish presence in Spain. This personal and professional history has encouraged my current interest in the larger sphere of "alliances."

I am certain that the trend of creating museum franchises is little more than a pass-ing fashion and as such it changes very fast. As both a professional and a visitor, I per-sonally prefer small museums as opposed to the large "museosaurs" because they are easier to visit and manage. In addition, I believe that despite the great beauty and appeal of dinosaurs, they became extinct too easily due to their lack of adaptation, something that did not happen to the small mammals that have remained. Although these large museums do not interest me very much, I wish them all the best, because there are many people who want to visit them, and all those who go to a museum, whether the museum is large or small, are worthy of respect.

In conclusion, I would like to quote a passage from Miguel de Cervantes's *Don Quixote*, which I offered at the first Ibero-American Meeting of Museums as part of the presentation of the charter of San Salvador de Bahía. Museums should resemble "the Knight Errant who travels through barren, desolate places, through crossroads, forests and mountains, seeking dangerous adventures with the intention of bringing them to a happy and fortunate conclusion, to achieve his sole desire of lasting and glorious fame" (II, xvii). Like the Knight Errant, the museum must "search the far corners of the earth, enter into the most intricate labyrinths, attempt the impossible at every step, and in the solitary uninhabited wilderness withstand the sun's hot rays in the middle of summer, and in winter the harsh rigors of icy winds" (II, xvii).

Herewith are a few of the closing proposals and recommendations from the Declaration of San Salvador de Bahía, produced at the 2007 Meeting of Ibero-American Museums, from which this essay evolved:

- Creation of the Ibero-American Museums Network, with the purpose of promoting the development and articulation of institutions public and private—and promoting professionals of the Ibero-American museological sector, as well as the optimization of the protection and management of heritage and the interchange of produced practices, experiences, and knowledge
- Promotion of a wide program of professional formation and technical qualification for museums, offering courses in the different areas of museology and making possible the accomplishment of traineeships and interchange between museological institutions of the different countries
- Institution of the Ibermuseus/Ibermuseos website to present and publicize, in a virtual network, information about Ibero-American museums and other issues of interest for the area
- Implementation of a program of circulation of expositions and goods, aiming to amplify the access to the cultural goods of the Ibero-American countries
- Stimulation of the development, by Ibero-American museums, of classification systems that facilitate dialogue and the circulation of information.

Santiago Palomero is the deputy director of the National Museums in Spain. He was formerly the associate director of the Sephardic Museum, Toledo, Spain, where he was responsible for creating alliances all over the world in order to make that museum a truly international expression of the Spanish Jewish diaspora. He has written and published widely on museums.

THE CROSSING OF ART AND SCIENCE: EXPANDING THE FIELD

Lita Albuquerque

I came to alliances through the back door. I didn't know I was creating alliances, but something in me knew that allying myself with others was the only way to create an expanded field of inventiveness.

I grew up in a fishing village on the Mediterranean, in a big stone house by the sea. I still remember the fishermen throwing out their nets in larger and larger circles. These circles created expanded fields of influence, similar to the spiraling arms of galaxies, forming the kinds of images we can now see through the Hubble telescope. Back then, I felt in my heart that there was an important image we all had forgotten. I saw each of us as little blades of grass, digging deep into our own roots to emerge with a mirrored blade, reflecting the sky. In the collective vision of all the blades of grass reflecting the sky, we would actually see the forgotten image.

Today, it seems to me that our technology is paralleling and birthing our spirituality. Thanks to our current Internet advances, even a nomadic tribesman can connect to the world at large; my childhood image of unity is coming to fruition. It is as if our technology is showing us that we are all one mind, and the information is there for the taking. We are forming a tangible collective intelligence that was unparalleled in the past, perhaps only experienced by a few privileged, enlightened beings. Today, this intelligence is accessible to all of us if we are interested in participating.

As a child, I believed that our creative energy paralleled the biological model. In other words, I knew that one plus one did not necessarily equal two, but rather three, since the collective of two together formed an entity of its own, an alliance. I inherently understood that each creative effort, like the creation of life itself, is not an isolated act. This was not evident in my family life growing up. The idea of forming alliances was nonexistent, and my life was fraught with conflicts that came from making the "other" the enemy. To make the "other" my ally has been a great revelation, but something that came to me not through revelation, but as a natural process.

What brought me to forge alliances in my work was my love for space and movement. I also wanted the body of the viewer to be involved in the experience of space. I wanted to create works that were phenomenological, and to do that I needed a large space and many people to participate to create the scale I needed. That shift started small, with my ephemeral works out in the desert that involved students performing the work under my direction. My love for space and movement also led me to the performing arts, which require an ensemble of people to make an event happen, whether it is a dance, a musical piece, a theater piece, a filmic work, or simply a set or an installation.

I started working with making sets for choreographer Lesli Linka Glatter and vocalist Joan La Barbara. In *Abhasa-Image Bearing Light,* a multimedia installation for the Fisher Museum at the University of Southern California, I collaborated with architect Robert Kramer and composer Harold Budd, receiving an National Endowment for the

Arts grant for interdisciplinary art. This spirit of working in ever-widening circles was reflected in an exhibition at the Los Angeles Natural History Museum. Working with the many thousands of items in the collection was thrilling. Even more thrilling was meeting the research scientists. It was as if a door had opened to a world I didn't know existed. Another project that largely expanded my field was *Sol Star,* done for the Sixth International Cairo Biennale, where I found myself creating alliances with both the American and Egyptian governments, including a large team of people on both sides to produce the piece.

My works increased in scale, and this year I created a global project that encompasses the entire planet, *Stellar Axis: Antarctica,* executed on the Ross Ice Shelf at McMurdo Sound, Antarctica. I formed alliances with the National Science Foundation, astronomers, filmmakers, a photographer, and two production teams, one in California and the other with the National Science Foundation (NSF) in Antarctica. *Stellar Axis: Antarctica* has been by far my largest project in terms of scale, production, logistics, budget, fund-raising, and the number of people required to make it happen. Currently, I am working on the conceptual aspect, which will require a great deal of collaboration. I will create animations in which we will see the Earth from space, surrounded in stars that rotate in opposite spiraling motion at both poles and through the axis of the Earth. This resembles the doubled strand of DNA, but connected to the stars. It is my goal to bring it to fruition where it can be exhibited as a museum installation.

On my team was Simon Balm, an astronomer who spent one year at the South Pole with the National Science Foundation. His expertise and experience were extremely comforting not only because we were going into unknown and uncharted territory, but also because he was the link to the politics and inner workings of the NSF on site. Two more integral collaborators were Sophie Pegrum, documentary filmmaker, and still photographer Jean de Pomereu, whose work will be extremely important in bringing the project to a greater audience.

Working with world-renowned scientists at the Crary Lab at McMurdo Station, Antarctica, has expanded the field for both sides. Just being in the lab made me feel like I was a part of NASA. We all were elated to be at the crest of scientific research concerning the future of our planet. Simon Balm states that working closely with *Stellar Axis: Antarctica* altered him so much that he now defends the artistic perspective to scientists. My work with him and the scientific community created a fever in me to participate in even greater conversations. Once we are expanded, our field emits ripples and touches other expanded fields all over the world. Allying myself with the NSF expanded my world exponentially. I was in a realm of research, rationality, and experimentation, all a part of the creative process.

Although over the years I have worked on many large and expansive projects that involved many people, my experiences in Antarctica clinched my understanding of our interconnectedness and interdependency and therefore our need for alliances. Spending five weeks in an extreme environment where the severe weather can and does change on a dime, we all understood very quickly how interdependent we were. Creating alliances in this kind of situation was a matter of survival, but it is also symbolic of our lives in less extreme environments. Alliances in any environment are a must, and are primal, elemental, and profoundly human, the model that we are beginning to follow.

So while I came to alliances through the back door, joining with a greater circle of people in a variety of disciplines has become an integral part of my work today. My massive projects can only be achieved in their entirety through opening dialogue in ever-widening circles. Yesterday, for example, I sat in a room in the Spitzer Science Center at the California Institute of Technology with thirty or so international astrophysicists. As I listened to each describe his or her particular field of expertise, I could not help but feel we were all working toward a common goal. True, we were coming at it from different angles and expressing different aspects in a myriad of ways, but we were working together to manifest that magnificent unified image I had as a child. Imagine the ripple effect as artists make alliances with astrophysicists to create a bridge between all of our respective fields.

As an artist, I have not been afraid to break through barriers or go where the work calls me, whether it is out in the desert, at the opposing poles of the Earth, or climbing up the side of a building. I have enthusiastically embraced other artists, scientists, and experts to manifest the current vision. What is important is stretching the boundaries, pushing the envelope, and following the momentum of vision. They are spearheads for gathering momentum to fuel my projects. This will create ripples of alliances. A favorite Hubble image is of two galaxies merging, their spiraling arms wrapping around each other as if one were going to fuse into the other, forming new galaxies. Galactic alliance. I think we have reached that moment in time.

Lita Albuquerque is an internationally known installation and environmental artist, painter, and sculptor. Albuquerque has been the recipient of numerous grants and awards, including the Cairo Biennale Prize and several National Endowment for the Arts awards. Her art has been collected by the Whitney Museum of Art, the Getty Trust, the Frederick Weisman Foundation, and the Los Angeles County Museum of Art.

MUSEUMS AND ALLIANCES/ALLIES

Ramiro Martínez

 Museums and alliances/allies appear as an obvious combination of terms, especially since the first is a service provider to society in general. This obviousness is possibly the same reason why alliances between museums and cultural institutions and other organizations are most often taken for granted and not always creatively explored.

Alliances must be viewed from a broader perspective than just from that between museums and contributors or funders, or the public in general. Museums, whether private or public, are a fundamental part of the educational system, either as collectors and keepers of objects, researchers, and generators of information or as educators and others. As such, their mission is to reach as many segments of the general public as possible in a directed and effective manner. Schools and students, of all types and levels, are important targets, not only as passive museum visitors, but also as active collaborators. Our cultural institutions must work both inside and outside our facilities and search to become partners with organizations (defined as any group of people) to further interest and interactivity. Relationships with sponsors must be viewed productively and creatively beyond financial or marketing considerations and include them as evident potential audiences and cultural promoters.

The social contract of museums with their public means that museums must always look to those audiences that have a more difficult access to their programs and are sometimes left outside the obvious publics. Therefore museums must act as mediators, aiding and encouraging our visitors to engage new information and experiences. Within less-organized cultural contexts, this may take on increasingly complex methods to promote participation in museum programming and an increased investment in various strategies of public transport to the museum, as well as new publicity and interpretation methods.

In some instances, museums act as agents of inter-institutional and international relations. In the last twenty years, the exchange of exhibition and research projects between cities and countries has increased the flow of artists, curators, critics, and audiences. Globalization is nowhere as present as in our institutions. One side of this has become an important issue with regard to cultural tourism, and both the new economic developments and intellectual possibilities such travel creates. Institutions must search to become integral parts of a city or country's assets and be regarded as allies by local, state, and federal authorities, specifically with matters related to obtaining financial resources.

Museums must actively seek to participate and become embedded in all pertinent aspects of a community's life and their contemporary cultural moment. They can no longer risk being looked upon as distant depositories of knowledge and must instead become indispensable players in an increasingly complicated web of relationships, both locally and internationally. The way of succeeding at this is to expand its network of alliances and to view them as fundamental parts of their objectives and operations. This expansion is to be thought of in different directions, international and local, public and private, large and small scale, each with its own specific value to be explored and exploited.

It is this vital alliance with various communities that must be always kept in mind when analyzing an institution's operation both on the long-term and the daily basis. Museums, whether art, science, history, natural history, and so on, are most probably global organizations by definition (defined as institutions with a lot of mobility and exchange of people, objects, knowledge, and capital). A museum is always generating and presenting narratives of "others": other cultures, other people, other discoveries, other creativities. Inherent to this investigation of the "global other" must also be the sense of the local. Because it is these institutions' main objective to link this "otherness" to a local community and aid in the creation of a network that feeds and develops those who participate in its programming on both a personal or institutional level or a local or global one.

Museums must take on the ever-changing and complex challenge of facilitating the understanding of a different perspective or point of view in a usually traditional milieu. In a theoretically extremely well-communicated and informed world, understanding has not developed at a parallel rate. Also and unfortunately, the preoccupation with this issue seems to have decreased as it seems that the efficiency of communication has automatically increased our level of comprehension.

Based on this premise, that comprehension has not necessarily been enhanced by the technologically more-effective modes of communication, we must try to develop more realistic links with our audiences, through programs based on mid- and long-range terms and parallel activities that complement it. Museums must look to develop spaces of communication or sites of information that additionally foster reflection and deeper understanding. They must foster real communication across latitudes, cultures, and various ways of seeing and thinking.

Speaking from my own experience in an international contemporary arts museum located in a city with an extremely strong and traditional cultural background, many of our goals have been to foster contemporary perspectives on the global culture in which we live. We pursue this through the specific kinds of exhibitions we present and through the ideas they address. We have been particularly interested in making links between contemporary art practices and cultures seemingly quite different from that of Mexico, be it the present cultural context of Berlin or of Beijing. We have sought to not only present artwork from these contexts and describe these foreign sites of cultural production, but also have additionally looked to identify connections and common ground between the lived experience in the foreign sites and that of Mexico. These points of convergence are stressed through how our exhibitions are presented textually and visually and through the discursive strategies designed for our public and education programming.

The objective is at once to show both the unique cultural difference that globalization allows us to be exposed to, while also stressing our common links, as all cultures deal with an increasingly connected and interdependent world. Our goal is continually to make the foreign or international clearly relevant to the local. It is only through identifying these connections and through looking to develop new ways of seeing one's local and global context that we feel we are truly offering our publics a valuable, contemporary museum experience.

Alliances must be thought of and developed parallel to the museum's program as part of its core. In this sense, their design must consider all levels of participation in order for institutions to have an active role as agents for critical revisions on the ever-changing culture of today. Alliances—engaged commitments between partners—developed by museums with their local and international publics will increasingly take on complex and multifaceted forms, as our institutions seek to reflect the worlds in which we live and within which we seek to continue to play a vital role.

Graduate from the Wharton School of Business (University of Pennsylvania), Ramiro Martínez was the director of the Museo Tamayo from 2002 until 2009 and was previously a part of the leadership of the influential Museo de Arte Contemporáneo de Monterrey. Some exhibition highlights include Louise Bourgeois, Isamu Noguchi, Pierre Alechinsky, Jesús Rafael Soto, Manuel Álvarez Bravo, and Henri Cartier-Bresson.

NEW ALLIANCES/NEW PHILANTHROPIES: THE ALFREDO HARP FOUNDATION

María Isabel Grañén Porrúa

Translated by Francisca González Arias

 In recent years, the city of Oaxaca has become the center of a cultural movement fomented largely by civil society. We residents decided to join together, combine our efforts, and participate in the economic and cultural life of our beautiful city.

The Alfredo Harp Helú Foundation (Fundación Alfredo Harp Helú [FAHH]) is one of the best examples of community involvement: it promotes various educational, recreational, cultural, antipoverty, environmental, and health programs. With the passage of time, these programs have become more ambitious. It is the intention of the founder, Alfredo Harp Helú, to be a vital part of these projects, deciding on where to invest resources and to build on the benefits generated by the foundation's goals. For this reason the museums and cultural institutions that have been created through the foundation are active, not only for the tourists who visit the city of Oaxaca but also for its residents.

The foundation's challenge has been to shape healthy human beings who think independently with their own constructive opinions. We are interested in creating spaces that foment reading, entertainment, research, and reflection, as well as promote recreation. Our foundation is working toward a more sensitive world that rejects violence.

It is the aspiration of the Alfredo Harp Helú Foundation that many partners will join its projects, thus making the projects part of the community and of daily life, and that these projects will play a vital educational role for the public. In some cases, the federal and state governments have taken part in these projects; in others, municipal governments and, to a large extent, numerous artists have been encouraged to contribute toward the humanistic process we promote, improving the quality of social life.

Concerned about environmental deterioration in the state of Oaxaca, the foundation is sponsoring the creation of fifteen greenhouses, each with a million plants. This program sought the best technology and was able to purchase equipment from a Swedish company at a reasonable price. For its part, the state government, enthused about the program's results, contributed staff to tend to the plants' growth and development. In turn, the towns that benefit will watch over tree growth and be responsible for the maintenance of the greenhouses. This combination of efforts is the only way to ensure that fifteen million plants are planted annually in the state, in addition to the ten million that the state government has agreed to plant on its own. The idea is for these greenhouses to become productive projects for the people.

A cultural circuit that fosters art and art appreciation in society has been created through recuperation of spaces in the historical center of Oaxaca. Among these projects, the Casa de la Ciudad (House of the City) stands out. It is a center devoted to the dissemination of the importance of historical architecture and it seeks citizens' participation in the protection of this cultural heritage. For this purpose, a beautiful large residence belonging to the city and dating from the time of the viceroyalty was restored; in it, exhibitions, seminars, and lectures about how to make the city more livable are organized. The operation and expenses of the Casa de la Ciudad are provided by the foundation, and the city of Oaxaca benefits from the building's restoration and appropriate use, as well as from the research and proposals produced by this cultural center.

Mexico preserves a rich documentary and bibliographical legacy. Because of this, the protection of archives and libraries in Mexico is a priority for the AHH Foundation. A civil association called the Support for the Development of Archives and Libraries in Mexico (Apoyo al Desarrollo de Archivos y Bibliotecas en México [ADABI]) was formed for this purpose; it promotes projects in support of institutions that take care of both public and private archives, since all of these constitute the national patrimony. A financial allotment is offered; in addition, requirements that are specific to each project must be outlined so that all projects initiated are brought to a conclusion. ADABI also publishes inventories, guidebooks, and catalogues. The results of ADABI are manifest: in just three years we have sponsored almost 240 projects and 113 publications in twenty states of the Mexican Republic. The Harp Helú Foundation has invested approximately five million dollars in ADABI since its creation. It is important to note that this figure complements the proportional parts contributed by each of the sponsored institutions. That is, ADABI requires that the owners of the archive also contribute to the project. In some cases, meals and lodging have been provided for the staff organizing the archive; at other times the foundation has managed to match about fifty percent of the cost. Whereas before ADABI's existence these institutions had no intention of investing in their documentary and bibliographical reserves, now they are ready to do so.

The foundation supports education in Mexico with a wide-ranging program of grants for institutions of higher learning, as well as for Mexican universities and schools with limited resources, and it has also started a program to encourage reading. We would like to nurture readers by instilling in children the custom of reading. For this purpose we created a children's library in Oaxaca in which several area artists participate, among them Francisco Toledo, José Luis García, Margorie Theabault, and Demián Flores. The Children's Library seeks to make children aware of beauty and of aesthetic spaces in which caring for nature is a priority.

The project called for reading rooms, a playroom, an auditorium, spaces for temporary exhibitions, and a computer room with the most modern technological equipment in order for the children of Oaxaca to be up-to-date in this area. Of course, the services and events we organize are free. The BS Children's Library has been a success in the community. A large number of children accompanied by their parents come frequently to read. It is moving to see the rooms crowded with people and to know that enrollment in our courses is full, that storytellers, puppets, marionettes, dance groups, and teachers are often present, and that every event is well attended.

The cultural projects promoted by the Alfredo Harp Helú Foundation are novel because they arise from local needs, are adapted to the environment, and include and educate society. The sum of our efforts and the alliances forged with the community through our programs will help us to advance firmly in the creation of a more humane world.

María Isabel Grañén Porrúa is president of the Alfredo Harp Helú Foundation. She is also president of the Biblioteca Francisco De Burgoa in Oaxaca, where she has built that library into one of the most important in Latin America. The Biblioteca Francisco De Burgoa is a resource for scholars, notable for its valuable incunabula and books in the local indigenous languages. She holds a doctorate in history and is an expert on colonial documents and printing.

CHAPTER 8

Authentic Experience

THE "AUTHENTIC EXPERIENCE" in a museum, though essential as a sustainable value, is one that we will not be able to define absolutely. We will certainly not reach a unanimous decision about what the authentic experience is. Still, we can perhaps agree that museums allow for an encounter with the real, with an art object or artifact or specimen, a living thing, a historical document, or a moving image that imparts a special knowledge and value through its collection and preservation, through its interpretation, and through the subsequent imprinting on memory by means of its display or educational project. Each museum should be able to articulate for itself what "authentic experience" is and how it differs from reading a book or looking at a copy of the object in reproduction or online.

Authentic experiences can also speak of being authentic or "true" to one's own mission. It is undeniable, though, that many of our museums have been pressured, over the last twenty-five years or so, to revamp themselves to accommodate the demands of mass culture and to be competitive in the face of the plethora of leisure-time choices. That means that we often don't know which way to turn so as to honor our commitment to the authentic: that it is difficult to simultaneously fulfill the requirement to serve as a "destination" providing not only entertainment and knowledge, but shopping and fine eating experiences as well. Nevertheless, we must still make the effort to distinguish between what we can do as museums and how we differ from mass entertainment—while still appealing to our various constituencies. If we can do that, we will be able to argue successfully for the uniqueness of our offerings and clarify why society should value them in the form of their museums.

It seems impossible to be a person of our time and not to grasp that authenticity is a malleable concept. We are constantly reminded that what was authentic "then" is inauthentic "now." What is an authentic experience to some in our audience is a waste of time to others. What is authentic here is a parody there. Nevertheless, it is incumbent upon us, if we believe in our museums, to be able to ask and answer how our own museum (whether it is dedicated to the scope of world art, the teaching of science, the explication of history, gardens, dolls, fish, bells, or natural history) differs from schools, libraries, theme parks, playgrounds, and even books. How does what we do touch a critical mass of people in inimitable ways so that they leave our premises enriched? And if our museum does not do that, what (we have to ask) can we do about solving that problem?

There are so many temptations today that subvert authenticity. There are serious professionals who suggest that museums send high-tech images back to countries claiming restitution of their patrimony rather than the objects themselves. (How quickly the call for an "authentic experience" for one museum public devolves into a justification for another public making do with copies!) There are sculptures that, despite a museum's best efforts, cannot be attributable as genuine or real. Note, for example, the famous Kouros, the Archaic-style Greek boy in the Getty Museum, that, despite the open debates of scientists and connoisseurs, defies a decision about its authenticity. Or, in the matter of conservation of works of art: how much restoration remains authentic at a later time when restoration standards have taken a different road? How does video art fit into the question of authenticity, with its constant looping and its eternal reproducibility? And where in a natural history, anthropology, or science museum are reproductions appropriate to supplement authentic material?

In all of these cases and more, the museum has historically played an authoritative role that allows for the determination of authenticity. Its expert curators make the determinations and its educators usually have the obligation to communicate those decisions to the public. The research that a museum undertakes behind the scenes provides the infrastructure that allows for the intellectual authority that becomes the foundation of exhibition and collection. But ours is a time that is asking more and more for transparency in all areas of the institution of the museum. Inevitably, one of the next stages of what constitutes an authentic experience in our museums might be the communication directly to the public of how these decisions about authenticity are reached. This is already happening in some museums and is a good sign that we are responding to the needs of our public to be privy to more of what we do.

Our writers in this chapter offer some examples of how they each approach the issues surrounding the "authentic experience." They can inspire us to think about how we might be able to provide more and better such experiences to our own visitors. We will also see that authenticity of experience is, in some ways, related to the reminder that we raised in chapter 4 on inclusion by Vanda Vitali, in that there are also limits to what museums can do themselves to communicate authenticity. In the end, it revolves around a willing partnership with the public.

Art museums should be able to ask themselves if, as contemporary sculptor Mark di Suvero once said to me, they are providing an aesthetic rather than an anesthetic experience. This is not an easy matter for art museums today. Alan Shestack points out, referring to old-master art museums, that today's audiences are generally less aware of the religions, mythologies, and histories that inform and unlock the keys to understanding the art on display. The "old art" might just put our audiences to sleep unless it is accompanied with contextualization that helps the visitor approach that art. For contemporary art there is often a resistance on the part of the viewer to enter into the mind of today's artist. At the same time, far too many contemporary curators insist that the visitor simply has to do the work of "getting the art" by him- or herself. We talk about how we want to bring in the public and be inclusive and relevant to their lives, but our museums are often quite snooty about helping them get close to a difficult work of art. Shestack asks that we do more to help ease the access for the largest possible body of visitors, so that they can have an authentic experience in the museum they are visiting.

James Elkins, on the other hand, poses other solutions. He puts the burden of access to an authentic experience heavily on the visitor and offers an in-depth set of instructions how, by actually eschewing context, by spending a great deal of time with a given work of art, and by accepting the absence of mediation, the visitor might most intensely approach any given work.

Shestack therefore worries about authenticity in museums and what that means for the greater society, while Elkins worries about the individual visitor or patron. Each of us—museum professionals, museum supporters, and museum goers—needs to wrestle with the philosophy of our own museum and the museums we choose to attend. We need to question how much mediation we should be offering to allow for an authentic experience. How much mediation is too much? How dangerous is it to our museums if we offer too little?

Gardens are living museums and raise other questions with respect to authenticity. Francisco Toledo, the celebrated artist and civic genius of the state of Oaxaca in southern Mexico created, along with botanist, linguist, and philosopher Alejandro de Ávila Blomberg, a beautiful and resonant ethnobotanical garden in the center of the city of Oaxaca. Although Ávila in this garden follows all of the conventions of a museum (in that he collects, preserves, and exhibits plants), he forcefully reminds us in his essay that the meaning of a garden is not just restricted to the plants on display. Rather, it is also about the real human connection to the land. Ávila is moved by the spirit of his garden's ancient past and the links it represents in the chain of humanity that nourished it. He not only makes reference to those links, but also refers to the thousands of collaborators who helped reconstruct that garden with their hands and tools. Reading about the spirit of this garden causes us to wonder how every botanical garden, and by extension all of our institutions, might also be able to communicate the spirit behind it—and not just to colleagues committed to museums, but to the visiting public for whom we ultimately exist.

Jorge Wagensberg, writing from Barcelona, muses about science museums and how they must be connected to the real, the tangible, and the tactile so that they can inspire and arouse curiosity about the physical world. He sees the authenticity of a science museum as tied to societal change because, as he writes, if it does its job the individual visitors to a science museum will "move from indifference to wanting to learn." Wagensberg ends his essay by reminding us that "reality stimulates more than any of its representations."

Mari-Tere Álvarez's meditation on *Guernica,* Picasso's rage against the unprovoked attack by the Germans on that eponymous Basque city, also underlines the power of the real, the original object. In the case of *Guernica,* the painting exercises a power that has proven to extend far beyond the artist's original intention. It has become a cry against all the pain and suffering wrought by war.

It is with the Wagensberg and Álvarez essays that we are brought forcefully back to the defining point that all museums are authentic inasmuch as they are founded on reality. When they are watered down to being mere reflections of reality, they lose their own sustainable value and begin to approach theme-park and mass-entertainment status.

Whether a children's museum, where all of the seemingly raucous play connects the kids, albeit it unconsciously, to principles of water flow or magnetism or color theory, or a science or history or art museum or a zoo, the sustainable success of any museum depends upon providing an encounter that begins with the things themselves. It is our job to be able to be convincing that authenticity is more important now than ever before to society. It is our job to help our viewers to be able to distinguish the real from the manipulated. We need even to be able to communicate to them how *we* manipulate reality by our presentations—by our juxtapositions, by our hierarchies, by our own opinions being represented as fact. Our museums should be major players in the realm of the authentic experience. We are privileged that we work in the realm of real materials, and we need to make a compelling case that to distinguish the real from the bogus is an obligation of every citizen. Museums should be there to help.

WHEN I WAS A YOUNGSTER

Alan Shestack

 When I was a youngster, I frequently visited the Memorial Art Gallery in Rochester, New York, my hometown art museum. Admission was free and the place was filled with plaster casts of famous antiquities, some real Greek and Roman sculpture, a few medieval objects, paintings, and assorted treasures from all times and places. There were no special loan exhibitions, nothing to distract one from the richness of the permanent collections. The collection itself provided enticing visual stimulation and the individual objects were adequate historical touchstones. One could contemplate the art without the distraction of crowds. Even as a boy, I appreciated the serenity, the opportunity for undisturbed communion with the objects, and the intimacy that space and time afford the contemplation of a given work of art. Sadly, I have to say that such life-changing museum experiences—requiring the time to become familiar with a work of art and to savor the visual experience—are much rarer today, and in any case are probably not what most people seek when they come to the museum. For me, even though I have had the good fortune to see hundreds of museums around the world and many spectacular special exhibitions, those early moments when I was free to discover a special world that had opened up to me has remained the ideal I carry in my head. The best museum experiences happen when the visitor can study a work of art at leisure and gradually come to understand it. The downside, of course, is that quiet galleries are quiet because they remain relatively empty, and while that might be good for the individual visitor, it is hardly a defensible use of public resources in a democracy.

Museum people concerned about their museums' sparse attendance turned to the special exhibition model—showcasing treasures from other museums or other countries, or selecting items from their own holdings to make a point. Although we continue to pay lip service to our old mission statements (collecting, preserving, interpreting works of art that have been vetted by those who have specialized visual experience and knowledge) we are no longer satisfied by focusing primarily on our permanent collections—and have instead moved our resources, talents, and commitments to short-term special exhibitions. It is ironic that many of the same curators who consider the preservation of the objects in their care as their primary mandate will, at the same time, agree to lend or borrow fragile, irreplaceable objects for a temporary show. Despite new art-packing techniques, works of art in transit are subjected to risk and are occasionally damaged or even lost. This is not to say that all such exchanges are irresponsible or inherently a violation of the public trust. Some exhibitions bring together objects under one roof to permit comparisons or otherwise-impossible juxtapositions. Many of these shows are instructive and deepen understanding.

The important thing, however, is that we recognize this to be a paradigm shift from focusing on permanent holdings to using art as a lure to the public or to create media events. Several decades ago, when museum professionals met, the conversation was usually about the works of art that each museum had recently acquired. And for a few years at Association of Art Museum Directors' (AAMD) meetings, several of the country's top directors always presented short, informative talks on their own most spectacular acquisitions. Now the talk is almost exclusively about special exhibitions. The real question is what or who is driving this phenomenon? On the one hand, curators enjoy masterminding special exhibitions because it is one of the few ways in which they can demonstrate their scholarly knowledge, publish their findings in handsome catalogues, and be for a while in the institution's spotlight. On the other hand, trustees, especially businesspeople, are accustomed to thinking in quantitative terms to define success: increases in attendance and the increased revenue at the door, the amount of media coverage, or sales in the museum shop. Even relatively small museums feel compelled to present a program of special exhibitions. Since they have very little to lend, they have very little borrowing power. In response to the need, an entirely new field of exhibition lending services has emerged and burgeoned. These businesses arrange prepackaged shows, which do not depend on the expertise of the curators or the strength of the museum's collection or its traditions, to say nothing of serious, scholarly interest, but solely on the presumed popularity of the subject matter.

The special exhibition "frenzy" is also a response to a much deeper sea change in the way we understand the world around us. Special exhibitions are self-contained, coherent groupings of objects supported by audio tours, explanatory wall labels, and brochures. The implication is that the public is not expected to know about the works of art beforehand but that there is something special about the topic. The fact that these exhibitions are temporary adds to their cachet and attractiveness. Another reason for the popularity of temporary exhibitions is that permanent collections are much more difficult to navigate and to digest. To make the most of a visit to the permanent collection, one must have some sense of when, where, and how these objects fit into their cultural and historical contexts. Importantly, the museum audience is no longer the same as it once was; there was a time when visitors understood biblical and mythological allusions, literary interpretations and historical references, geography, poetry, and philosophy. At some point it became apparent that what was once common knowledge was no longer so. In response, museum educators throughout the world have worked hard in recent years to provide contextual and interpretive information to demystify works of art so that the untutored museum patron can have access to them. But the problem has certainly not yet been solved and we still need to undertake a major reconsideration of how museums present their holdings.

The special exhibition now seems totally entrenched in museum life and is broadly employed because it brings in crowds (to say nothing of money) and justifies the museum's existence to political bodies, the art press, and trustees. The *Art Newspaper* now lists each year the special exhibitions held all over the world: they are presented according to attendance figures, the most heavily attended first, like major league batting averages. During the short period of my professional lifetime, there has been a major shift in emphasis from displaying collections to preparing special exhibitions. Everyone from every corner has contributed to this reordering of priorities: the "public," curators, the media, trustees, art critics, foundations, and corporate funders. Needless to say, some of the great exhibitions have been aesthetically spectacular and have provided great contributions to our understanding of an artist's work, of aesthetic questions that an artistic movement sought to solve, or of a moment in the history of art. One thinks of the English Country House show and 1492 at the National Gallery, or the recent Renaissance and Baroque tapestry exhibitions or the Vollard show at the Metropolitan. But, just as often, the kinds of shows that spring forth respond to the need to entice the public (Monet is summoned more than any other artist). In the world of museum experience, one sad result is that, as the galleries fill with people seeking the benefits of the new exhibition, the quality of the experience is diluted (if that quiet moment with the art remains the Platonic ideal). Indeed, if a special exhibition is successful by business standards, each visitor has to jockey for position in front of each work and sees more of the backs of other people's heads than of the works of art! It is hard to be contemplative in a crowd. Somewhere in the hurly-burly, the role of the museum as a shrine for personal interaction with works of art has been lost—or at least greatly diminished.

During the past half-century, museums have undergone such profound changes that one is compelled to ask whether things are truly better today and if we are still living up to our widely accepted, time-honored mission to protect and conserve works of art for future generations and serving our audiences in appropriate ways. Indeed, those of us who thought we knew with certainty how to define our mission are now questioning whether we need to acknowledge a new paradigm.

What should we do now? First and foremost, we must face the repercussions of our failed educational system, which only tangentially has to do with schools. Now we expect the museum-going public to appreciate art, even though many museum goers have had no exposure to the cultural context out of which the objects spring. It is something like teaching literature to people who can neither read nor write. So the museum's first mandate might be to work harder to provide an understanding of the historical context for the art on display and basic instruction in "reading" works of art. This may require producing a body of handout literature with timelines, definitions of the various schools of art, literary and historical influences, crosscurrents of aesthetic influence, and so forth. If we can make our permanent offerings as coherently packaged as we make our special exhibitions (to reduce the haphazard character of the permanent collections, which is limited to whatever the museum happens to own), then the sideshow will become less attractive than the main act. We need to support educators of the first order to lead our audience back to the original touchstones of our culture (or the culture at issue: Islamic, Buddhist, "primitive," etc.) and to use new technologies to enhance this effort. We must start acting as if we really care about the visitors' experience. A lecture series on how to look at art would bring in throngs.

Second, we should not throw out the baby with the bath water. Special exhibitions have earned an honorable place at the table. Keeping in mind the wear and tear on objects being crated and re-crated for travel both at home and abroad, as well as the expenditure of curatorial effort and other staff time that goes into these special productions, no special exhibition should be mounted unless there is considerable scholarly value or unless bringing together a body of material will make it possible to make telling comparisons. We can agree that works of great significance, critical to the message of an exhibition, should travel if they are in stable condition. But we can also agree that these precious works should not be subjected to the stress of travel for exhibitions of questionable value. That means the "bartering" system, which forms the underpinning of current inter-museum relations and which greatly influences exhibition planning (to get what we want to borrow, we have to be willing to lend), has to be rethought.

And finally, the museum-going public needs to be trained in how to visit a museum. For example, no one explains to new visitors that they are not required to see the whole museum in one visit or that they will have a much richer experience if they limit their tour to a manageable amount of time and an equally manageable number of galleries. A museum visit should not be a forced march, but an opportunity to become conversant with a slice of visual or cultural history: the work of one artist, an art movement, or the work of a well-defined time or place. The lesson for museums might well be to treat the permanent collection galleries as if they were special collections, perhaps augmenting the permanent holdings with a loan or two to bring the material together into a cohesive whole.

In the end, it is the responsibility of the museum staff, led by its director, to set goals for limiting the number of special exhibitions, approving only those that live up to the highest values, which the public has a right to expect from its experts in the field to ensure that the works of art are not put at undue risk, that the exhibitions are of extremely high quality, and that they make a sound contribution to scholarly inquiry.

Alan Shestack was born in New York City in 1938. He studied at Wesleyan University, Harvard, the Courtauld, and the Zentralinstitut fur Kunstgeschichte in Munich. He has been director of the Yale University Art Gallery, the Minneapolis Institute of Art, and the Museum of Fine Arts, Boston, before joining the National Gallery of Art as chief curator and deputy director. Dr. Shestack retired in 2009.

AUTHENTIC EXPERIENCES

James Elkins

 What is an authentic experience? Let me define it provisionally, roughly, and pragmatically: it is an experience that the viewer feels is unmediated by the context. It feels as if the work is speaking directly to the viewer, as if there is no coercion, inappropriate didacticism, curatorial manipulation, irrelevant historical information, or other ideological interventions. It feels genuine, as if the work is speaking directly to the viewer, and it feels irreproachable, because the experience of the work is the viewer's own experience and not given from some outside source.

I am not saying there is no such thing as authentic experience: that would be in line with a common misreading of first-generation poststructural critiques by Barthes, Foucault, Derrida, and others. I am saying that the idea of authentic experience, the hope that there might be authentic experience, and the conviction that one can have an authentic experience (or that one has had authentic experiences) are themselves historically conditioned. They depend entirely on what is understood as authentic and on the value that has been given to authenticity.

So in what follows I describe, very sincerely, strategies for creating authentic experiences. I do not in any way think that these are misguided. Much of the art-viewing public wishes to have such experiences, and there are ways to make such experiences happen. But I am also not claiming that authentic experiences are the best way to experience art. Sometimes a deeply inauthentic experience—a visit to a gallery with an audio guide, with children screaming, tourists gaping, and friends pontificating—can be exactly appropriate. Sometimes deeply mediated experiences can be optimal (for example, going to a museum after having read several hundred pages about the artwork you're about to see). Sometimes manipulated experiences (driven by dramatic lighting, mood music, advertising hyperbole) can be necessary for any productive encounter with the work. Sometimes it can be important to believe that you are encountering the artwork outside of politics and culture, in line with Kant's aesthetics, so that it is just you, the artwork, and the nonconceptual "aah!" that accompanies the experience of pure beauty.

But still, because we value authentic experiences, here is a little guide to some of the issues that are involved.

First, I think it is helpful to divide the field of experiences into *immersive* and *self-reflexive*. The former means the work is experienced as if it had no context; the latter means the work is experienced as a part of historical, critical, and comparative contexts. (Again, these are not truths, because we do not approach artworks without a half-cognized background of historical and critical concepts; this is more a measure of how we feel or what we hope to feel.)

Immersion is seductive, and it can be argued that any strong emotional response to an artwork depends on the feeling of an immersive experience. I argue this in a book on the history of people who have cried in front of paintings (*Pictures and Tears*). In that book I suggest some strategies for museum directors and curators; these strategies help increase the probability that an encounter will be immersive:

1. Avoid the ordinary wall labels. Depending on the museum or gallery, labels can be informative, but they are always distracting; they provide parts of the context that changes immersive experience into self-reflexive experience. At their worst, labels can be condescending, unctuous, and opaque.
2. Spend time (an hour, more) in front of just one object. People don't often do that, but it helps a great deal, because gradually, whatever contexts you already know (the history of the artwork, its reputation, the artist's personality, etc.) will fade away. It will seem that you are beginning to encounter the work itself.
3. Don't go to the museum with friends. If you do go with friends, don't talk to them. Go around in silence: look, absorb, think, meditate. Don't talk, because talking substitutes a whole range of distractions—you'll be thinking about whether your opinion was as clever as your friend's or about whether you agree with what your friend says.
4. Don't go intending to see more than one object. One object is plenty. If an artwork like the *Mona Lisa* really is as important to western culture and identity as it is said to be, then surely it deserves an hour of your time. How much time does it take to read *War and Peace* or even a Harry Potter novel?
5. Find low-lit galleries and go during off-peak hours. This is to avoid the distractions of other people. Whenever you see yourself being seen or think you might be seen, you will be attending—no matter how little—to your own appearance. All that kind of interaction is distraction: it makes you self-conscious and initiates the stream of consciousness that leads to self-reflexivity in front of the artwork.
6. Promise yourself to return. Once is not enough. If the *Mona Lisa* is as important as, say, *War and Peace*, then surely it should be something that occupies an important place in your imagination, and therefore something that you should want to see again.

These are strategies for having immersive experiences. But it is also important to prepare yourself for times and places when immersion just is not historically correct or critically appropriate. For example, work done in the last thirty years, under the general influence of poststructuralism, is rarely aimed at immersive experiences. There are many exceptions, but after the 1950s artworks have not always been made with the intention of eliciting immersive experiences or strong emotional reactions. In my book, *Pictures and Tears*, the touchstone example is Rothko: he wanted viewers to cry, or at least to feel tragedy, pain, and ecstasy.

So, by way of brief conclusion to this brief essay:

1. Authentic experience is crucial to some artworks.
2. Authentic experience is demanded by a large portion of the museum-going public.
3. Authentic experience is something we are historically determined to value. Authenticity hasn't always existed in art theory, nor has immersion, absorption, presence, or even aesthetics.

James Elkins is E. C. Chadbourne Professor in the University of Chicago Extension, Department of Art History, Theory, and Criticism, School of the Art Institute of Chicago. He writes on art and non-art images; his recent books include *On the Strange Place of Religion in Contemporary Art, Visual Studies: A Skeptical Introduction, What Happened to Art Criticism?* and *Master Narratives and Their Discontents.*

MEZCAL FOR THE EARTH

Alejandro de Ávila Blomberg

In July of 1998 we began to plant trees on a piece of land in the city of Oaxaca that had housed a garrison for over one hundred years. Before it was occupied by the military, the property had been part of the orchard of Santo Domingo, the most splendid colonial monastery in southern Mexico. After the barracks and training courts were torn down, in the space that was emptied out between the building where the friars had lived and the enclosing wall built later by the soldiers, we set ourselves to create an ethnobotanical garden, a landscape designed to link the human trajectory along ten millennia with the natural history of the region. A year earlier we had begun to plow the crusty ground and to dig out the rubble, sowing beans to enrich the soil. At the same time, we had started to gather like busy ants hundreds of plants in the surrounding mountains and ravines: agaves, barrel cacti, incense trees, oaks, and a long etcetera. We were finally ready to plant the first tree that sunny morning. Gathered together around the pit, all of a sudden a bottle appeared, which was opened in silence. Without a word, our collaborators poured a shot of mezcal in the earth and blessed our first plant.

I was moved deeply by the sensitivity of a group of men, almost all of them youths between eighteen and twenty-five years of age, who had come to work with us in a more or less fortuitous way, some of them having been raised in the countryside while others had made their living building houses in the city. It was a surprise to me that they should express so much reverence for the earth. Looking at their fashionable t-shirts made in China and listening to their trendy music, I never imagined the spontaneous ritual they would conduct that morning with such feeling and dignity. That's how the garden was born, imagined by nationalistic intellectuals and materialized by persons who experience scraps of tradition and spasms of mass globalization every day. Who are the "authentic" creators here? Is the authenticity of our joint labor something that concerns our skillful gardeners as much as it worries our world-famous artists?

It took time for me to understand that the question could be answered in symbolic terms. Several months after the blessing, when the garden was finally beginning to look like a tract of scrubby forest rather than a dust bowl, a family from a distant village knocked on our gate as it grew dark. Behind them came a young man with a big smile. They explained to me that some years back he had lived as a soldier in the space where the plants were now growing. He had been frightened badly at the garrison (they never explained why), and to recover his spiritual health, they asked permission for him to light a candle and pray to the earth at the site where it had happened. Of course I had read anthropological studies about the perils of the soul for the indigenous people and about the complex ceremonies to bring it back when it has fled in shock, but the arrival of that family took me again by surprise. I did not expect an authentic case of "animism" at the garden. It made me reflect on what it could mean for that repentant soldier that we should be planting trees where there had been weapons. Quite a bit of time had gone by since the soul of the young man had been harmed; why hadn't he come sooner to cure himself? I would like to think that the creation of the garden allowed him to heal in peace.

I recalled that incident two years later, when I was in Madrid in December 2001. The reason for my trip was to represent Maestro Francisco Toledo, our patron archangel, at the award ceremony of the Queen Sophia prize for the conservation of cultural heritage. Santo Domingo in Oaxaca had been chosen among scores of candidacies from all over Latin America and Spain to receive the first edition of the prize. The jury emphasized that the fundamental criteria in making the award had been the participation of non-governmental organizations in the project, the breadth of vision that had allowed the different components of the cultural center to be integrated, and the interdisciplinary nature of the work teams that made such integration possible. These explicit remarks of the jury notwithstanding, our cultural authorities took the Queen Sophia prize as an exclusive recognition for the restoration architect, and the rest of us were dismissed from the ceremony. At that moment I saw again in my mind over one thousand bricklayers and stoneworkers rebuilding the walls of Santo Domingo. I heard again a hundred chisels beating on the surface of the stones in unison, the muffled steps of dozens of men carrying bricks on their shoulders, and the loud, high-pitched voice of the foreman giving out orders in Spanish, then translated softly into the language of each work squad. I remembered also the confrontations with the state politicians, when Toledo and we, his followers, fought against the official proposal to convert Santo Domingo into a five-star hotel, convention center, and big parking lot. Where were the architect and his friends the government officials back then? The authenticity of our effort acquired deeper significance after that prize.

Three days ago, Florentina de Jesús, a textile artist who has also received recognition by the queen in Madrid, visited us at the garden. She spins her cotton finely with a spindle and weaves marvelous huipils on her backstrap loom. Doña Tina speaks Amuzgo and a little Spanish; to get to her town from Oaxaca you have to travel the whole day. She had never come to the garden before. For five hours we walked among the plants. She observed carefully the leaves and the flowers of each species. She listened attentively to my long-winded explanations about plant dyes and about maize domestication, translated patiently by her partner. Seated on a rock next to the reflection pool, she told Don Agapito in Amuzgo that she would like to come weave in the garden. When she said goodbye, she told me in her broken Spanish, "Thank you, I liked and made me think." When I was a teenager, the film *Love Story* was a big hit with its slogan, "Love is never having to say you're sorry." In true LA fashion, for a long time we heard in Mexico thousands of phrases defining "love is. . . ." Thirty-five years later, I still run the risk of sounding tacky if I say that for me, authenticity is getting such a compliment from Doña Tina for your work.

Alejandro de Ávila Blomberg graduated with degrees in anthropology and physiological psychology from Tulane University and a master's degree in psychobiology from the University of California at Berkeley, where he is presently completing his doctorate. He was field representative in Mexico for the World Wildlife Fund (WWF) from 1990 to 1993, where he established the Fund's first office in the country. He is currently conducting fieldwork to conclude his doctoral dissertation on biological classification and nomenclature in the Mixtec languages. He was the founding director of the Oaxaca Ethnobotanical Garden at the Santo Domingo Cultural Center and is a curator at Oaxaca's recently inaugurated textile museum.

THE "TOTAL" MUSEUM: A TOOL FOR SOCIAL CHANGE

Jorge Wagensberg

 A science museum is a space dedicated to providing a stimulus to scientific knowledge, the scientific method, and scientific opinion. This is the upfront definition that distills the unspoken working hypotheses of over twenty years' envisioning Barcelona's Museo de la Ciencia de la Fundación "la Caixa," and the definition that today explicitly sums up the ideas of the new museum opened on 23 September 2004. This, if you will, is a real mission statement of what I would call total museology.

It is something that is already in the air as a tendency at some present-day museums, but neither the science museums of the past nor most of today's are in line with it. In principle, to follow through with this definition and to consolidate these tendencies, perhaps a new museography needs to be invented. The first science museums were natural history museums or museums of machines and instruments that exhibited real items in glass cases to the public, but with a clear mission to build up and conserve collections for scientific researchers. The latest science museums are ones, generally physics museums, where visitors may interact with real phenomena, but with an absence of real items and a certain degree of abuse of audiovisual and information technology resources. However, it so happens that science seeks to understand reality. And it so happens that reality is made up of both objects and phenomena. Objects are made of matter that takes up space. And phenomena are the changes experienced by objects, so that the latter, above all, take up time. Furthermore, neither objects nor phenomena are in any way to blame for the scientific disciplines laid down in school and university curricula. The interdisciplinary approach only makes sense if first there are disciplines. This is true. But once the disciplines are there thanks to formal research and teaching institutions, the museum may tackle any portion of reality using any kind of knowledge. This means that a science museum may deal with any subject from a quark or a bacterium to Shakespeare or an issue of sociology or city planning.

And it also means that reality, whether objects or phenomena, is an irreplaceable aspect of a museum, a must-have. Reality is even "the museological word." I would go even further: a museum is concentrated reality. Perhaps this is the only thing that distinguishes museology from any other form of scientific communication. The lecturer and the teacher have the spoken word as the basic element of transmission, even though they enlist the aid of the written word, still or moving images, models, simulations, computer programs, and so on. A lecture can be given without slides, without diagrams, and without demonstrations of any kind, without reading any text, but a lecture cannot be given without speaking. In fact, a lecture cannot even be given just by reading a text. Books, newspapers, and magazines have the written word as their basic element of transmission, even though they use diagrams, drawings, maps, and photos. But books or magazines without written words do not exist. They would be something else, an album perhaps. Silent films exist, but films without images do not exist, nor radio without sound. In a museum, there is no ban on using simulations, models, graphic images, or new technologies, but only as accessories of reality, not to take its place.

At a science museum there is no ban on teaching, informing, instructing, and entertaining. It cannot even be avoided, but none of this is a priority. In fact, for any of these goals there is another medium that does it far better. A good teacher and a good talk with colleagues teaches more and better than a visit to a museum. A good Internet search engine informs better. Life itself is the great instructor, and each individual has his or her own favorite pastime for entertainment (for some people, of course, this can be the museum itself). But what is the museum's very own job? What is its ideal function? What does it do better than any other system? The answer lies in the definition I started with: stimulation. Creating a difference between before and after. At a good museum or a good exhibition, you have many more questions when you come out than when you went in. The museum is a tool for change, for individual changes, and, therefore, for social change too. The museum is irreplaceable in the most important stage of the cognitive process: the beginning. Moving from indifference to wanting to learn. And there's nothing like reality to provide the stimulus. Reality stimulates more than any of its representations. And it is with this, just this, where a science museum acquires, perhaps, its meaning, its raison d'être in the twenty-first century.

> Physicist Jorge Wagensberg has become one of the most popular science communicators in Spain. Wagensberg is a professor in the theory of irreversible process and also leads a bio-physics research group at the Universitat de Barcelona. He is the author of numerous scientific works that have appeared in international publications and of an extensive range of work spreading popular science toward other realms of culture. He is director of "La Caixa" Foundation's Science Museum, known today as CosmoCaixa, Barcelona. Wagensberg is a professor of physics at the Universitat de Barcelona.

Reprinted with permission of Prof. Jorge Wagensberg.
With permission from *El Museo "Total," Una Herramienta de Cambio Social,* Hojas de Ciencia para alumnos de Secundaria Programa Ciencia Viva, No. 25, Febrero 2006 Fundación La Caixa © Ciencia Viva/Museo de la Ciencia de Barcelona.

GUERNICA GERNIKARA

Mari-Tere Álvarez

Picasso's *Guernica,* considered by some to be the greatest masterpiece of the twentieth century, hangs in the *Museo Nacional Centro de Arte Reina Sofía,* Madrid. It is displayed in a gallery that accommodates its incredible size, over twenty-six feet wide and eleven feet high. Depending on the day of the week, you may have the gallery to yourself or more likely you will be avoiding bumping into people as you try to take it all in. You might hear some awed comments or just loud silences all around you.

What constitutes the authentic experience in art has been argued by the greatest of thinkers since Plato to Walter Benjamin. For Benjamin, an authentic experience was that unique, unmediated, direct experience that one could only have with the real physical objects, an experience that cannot be replicated with a reproduction. "Even the most perfect reproduction of a work of art is lacking in one element: its presence in time and space, its unique existence at the place where it happens to be" (Walter Benjamin, *The Work of Art in the Age of the Mechanical Reproduction,* 1936, 2). To see the *Guernica* reproduced in a catalogue or on a monitor is nothing like experiencing it in person.

"GUERNICA, MOST ANCIENT TOWN OF THE BASQUES. . . ."

Pablo Picasso, living in Paris at the time, learned about the bombing of the city of Guernica almost immediately after it happened. The *London Times* headlined the story the next day; correspondent George Lowther Steer wrote,

Guernica, the most ancient town of the Basques and the centre of their cultural tradition, was completely destroyed yesterday. . . . The bombardment of the open town . . . occupied precisely three hours and a quarter during which a powerful fleet of aeroplanes . . . did not cease unloading on the town bombs . . . more than 3,000 two-pounder aluminum incendiary projectiles. The fighters, meanwhile, plunged low . . . to machine-gun those of the civilian population who had taken refuge in the fields. (*London Times*, 27 April 1937)

The Spanish Republic had, three months before, commissioned Picasso to paint a large mural for the Spanish Pavilion's Exhibition at the Paris International Exhibition (World's Fair) in 1937. Picasso had yet to choose a subject. This violent assault changed that immediately. Horrified by the destruction, Picasso found his subject, completing the giant canvas in just twenty-four days.

"THEY JUST LOOKED AT IT IN SILENCE. . . ."

With the bombing of Guernica still fresh in everyone's minds, visitors entering the Spanish Pavilion had an almost surreal experience, encountering the painting for the first time. Josep Lluis Sert, architect of the Spanish Pavilion, wrote,

It was curious to observe in the months that followed . . . in reviewing the exhibits in the Pavilion, to see the reaction of the people. The people came there, they looked at the thing and they didn't understand it. The majority didn't understand what it meant. But they felt that there was something in it. They did not laugh at *Guernica*. They just looked at it in silence. (Sert, "The Architect Remembers [1947]," in *Picasso's Guernica*, ed. Ellen Oppler [New York: W. W. Norton, 1988], 199–200.)

French Painter, Amadee Ozenfant recorded other unmediated responses from the period: "Some lady goes past my table. . . . She looks at *Guernica* and says to her child: 'I don't understand what is going on there, but it makes me feel awful. It's strange, it really makes me feel as if I were being chopped to pieces'" (Ozenfant, "A Visitor's Journal [1937]," in *Picasso's Guernica*, ed. Ellen Oppler [New York: W. W. Norton, 1988], 214–215).

"I WAS BLOWN AWAY AND TRANSFIXED. . . ."

After the World's Fair, the painting journeyed from location to location. First, *Guernica* traveled to Scandinavia, then on to Great Britain; at Whitechapel Art Gallery, 15,000 Londoners visited the painting in the first week. In 1939 it arrived in the United States, touring North America to raise support for the Spanish Refugee Committee. Then from 1944 until 1981, *Guernica* was housed in the Museum of Modern Art (MoMA), New York, transforming the painting from political protest (Spanish Pavilion and the Spanish

Refugee Tour) to one encouraging a more aesthetic response, accompanied as it was by studies and photographs chronicling the history of the creation of the work.

Nevertheless, despite some inevitable domestication that came from transforming *Guernica* into an art object in an art museum, it would never lose its aura and authority. Furthermore, it took on another layer of political import when it became a painting emblematic of another era filled with heinous war acts. Nonviolent protests and vigils during the Vietnam era took place in *Guernica*'s gallery in MoMA. In 1974, protesting then–U.S. President Nixon's pardon of Lieutenant William Calley, one of the leaders of Vietnam's My Lai massacre, which killed three hundred to five hundred women, children, and elderly, artist Tony Shafrazi spray-painted "KILL LIES ALL" in red directly onto *Guernica*.

"THE WAR HAS ENDED"

By 1968, Franco, Spain's long-time dictator, was making overtures for *Guernica*'s return to Spain. Picasso rejected the suggestion and would not entertain any proposals until the republic was restored. Such was the power of the actual painting that it was even acknowledged by Franco. He perceived that the power of the actual piece, should it arrive on Spanish soil during his own time, would be perceived by some as a blessing by Picasso on that dictatorship. Such was the aura of *Guernica*. No reproduction could offer a blessing!

It was not until Franco's death in 1975 that optimism began to grow about the work coming home to Spain. King Juan Carlos I, Franco's successor, immediately converted Spain into a constitutional monarchy, meeting one of Picasso's modified conditions, and Spain began its appeal for the painting. Although Picasso's heirs and MoMA challenged the request, finally the parties approved *Guernica*'s journey to the Prado Museum, another of Picasso's conditions.

On 10 September 1981, under the heavy guard of the Guardia Civil, *Guernica* arrived at Barajas Airport and was transferred to its new home at the Prado Museum. The painting was greeted by applause and tears as it entered the Prado. The next day the newspaper *El Pais*'s lead headline repeated the famous words of victory given by Franco on 1 April 1939, "The War Has Ended," but this time this infamous phrase had a positive meaning describing the arrival of the painting as Spain's victory over the dictatorship; an era had come to a close.

The painting was installed in an adjacent annex of the Prado Museum, El Casón del Buen Retiro. Segregated from other works of art, it was exhibited in seclusion, with the painting encased in a sort of postmodern altar comprised of a thick layer of bulletproof glass. This postapocalyptic vision came complete with the Guardia Civil associated with the repression during Franco's regime. The Guardia stood on each side of the painting holding machine guns. After passing through a metal detector, visitors entered the gallery and got to view for the first time Picasso's *Guernica* on Spanish soil. Visitors walked in reverently and saw the potent symbol of a newly found democracy under protection of the Guardia Civil. Art critic Christopher Knight, visiting the installation, wrote,

> In 1984 I was at the Museo del Prado in Madrid, where Picasso's 1939 antiwar masterpiece, *Guernica,* had been installed inside a separate fortified building. . . . Not only were some guards heavily armed—helmeted soldiers with machine guns, in fact— but *Guernica* was also behind a thick wall of bulletproof glass. Like travelers at airports today, the carefully controlled queue of visitors had to pass through a metal detector before entering the austere gallery. (*Los Angeles Times,* 4 June 2008)

Notwithstanding the military surround, the painting inspired an almost sacred sense of awe in those who visited it. In retrospect, *Guernica*'s period in the Casón was a product of the transition to democracy, rather than representative of the full democracy that was to come.

In 1991 a controversial decision was made, transferring all of the Prado's modern collections to other buildings for reasons of space. Consequently, although Picasso's will and the MoMA transfer agreement stipulated otherwise, *Guernica* moved literally down the street to the Museo Nacional Centro de Arte Reina Sofía. Today, in the Reina Sofía, the painting is no longer in its bulletproof shrine. Rather it appears to be as protected as any other work in the collection. Here *Guernica* is besieged by visitors of all ages, nationalities, and walks of life, all having unique experiences. On the seventieth anniversary of the Guernica bombing, the surviving members of the Abraham Lincoln Brigade came to visit the painting; well into their 90s, they all arrived wearing mementos and insignias to pay homage to the painting, which, for them, recorded it all.

Guernica, in the Reina Sofía National Museum of Modern and Contemporary Art in Madrid, is the touchpoint for many experiences ranging from the purely aesthetic to the profoundly political. *Guernica* may be the icon of the Reina Sofía, but its authenticity does not depend on any single mode of display. A recent re-hang allows visitors to see it better than ever before, but it also is presented in yet another context. Surrounded by Calder's *Mercury Fountain* and films by Luis Buñuel, it becomes apparent that Picasso was not alone in his powerful artistic response to the bombing of Guernica.

GUERNICA GERNIKARA?

In Basque, *Gernikara* translates as "to Gernika." Certainly, if the painting *Guernica* were to be sent to the city of Gernika in the Basque Country for display (and for another further recontextualization), it would touch its citizens perhaps more intimately, but not necessarily more authentically than it does in Madrid, or than it did in Paris, São Paolo, or New York City. This is a painting, the authenticity of which reaches out in an infinite number of ways to an infinite number of people—from those whose story it most immediately tells, to anyone else who recognizes, through great art, the pain and loss of war.

But it will probably remain in its place at the Reina Sofía, telling its profound story to the largest possible audience—at least for the indefinite future.

Mari-Tere Álvarez, of the J. Paul Getty Museum, received her PhD from the University of Southern California (USC). Her dissertation examined art markets and fairs in Renaissance Spain. She directs an international project on the Renaissance patron and intellectual Mencía de Mendoza. Álvarez has worked extensively on seventeenth-century Spanish art, particularly the work of Sculptor Luisa Roldán (+1706), as well as the painters Juan de Valdés Leal (+1690) and Bartolomé Esteban Murillo (+1682). Her interests also lie in the area of museum studies, and she serves as associate director of the International Museum Institute at USC.

CHAPTER 9

Generation and Dissemination of Knowledge

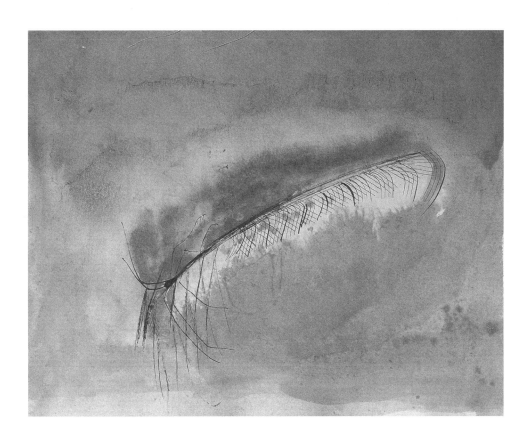

THERE WAS a time when the museum was considered to be one of society's most authoritative institutions. In varying degrees, as a revered protector and interpreter of culture, museums of all types generated, organized, and disseminated knowledge for both specialists and the public as a whole. That magisterial museum stance was hardly questioned, even as museums reflected and affected the changing nature of knowledge itself. Over the centuries they evolved from being strange and alluring private cabinets of wonder to playing a role as one of the essential public containers of knowledge, organized in the Enlightenment's clear intellectual categories, and now in large part evolving into more openly interpretive, often experimental, and increasingly contextualizing institutions. Today's museums have become more tenuous in their assertions of truth, reflecting the shifting state of the definitions of knowledge itself. Indeed, Eileen Hooper-Greenhill's stunning writings have convincingly credited museums with the "shaping of knowledge."

Certainly, during the late nineteenth and early twentieth centuries, museums were the authoritative, often-dogmatic, stages for art and history, science and botanical gardens, as well as innumerable other specialized fields of knowledge. By the end of the twentieth century matters were becoming complicated. The function of museums as temples protecting the material knowledge base of society had expanded to include a role as a kind of town hall, a safe place for airing competing claims about the nature of reality. At the same time the public began to demand that their museums represent demonstrable and sustainable relevance and inclusiveness. Furthermore, the 1960s and 1970s brought about a revolution in academia that affected museums. Even as researchers in universities began to question the nature of many traditional fields of study, they also began to question museums and the nature of the authority vested in them. Anthropologists, archaeologists, and historians challenged the objectivity of museum displays. And by the 1970s and 1980s the field of art history had veered away from connoisseurship and reverence for the object. The ultimate result of so many radical repositionings was a fundamental metamorphosis in the formerly uniform idea and ideal of the museum itself.

Some of our museums began to present (or at least acknowledge or aspire to presenting) varied interpretive voices. More contextualized narratives became common in exhibition; we generally tried to be more transparent in revealing how we reached a particular point of view.

Most stunningly, in the last half of the twentieth century, museum architecture began to evolve in ways that reflected the changes taking place in the understanding of knowledge: museums that were traditionally built to look like Greek or Beaux Art temples, the containers of eternal truths in their hallowed walls, were now being built in renovated warehouses, railroad terminals, and power stations, altogether more contingent structural communicators. Architects were commissioned to design museums that were works of art in themselves that invited critique and public opinion. Indeed, everybody did have an opinion about the newly built museums. Since architects imagined them, they represented an individual perspective on a particular museum, not a Platonic ideal of "museumness." Just as the contents of museums were being questioned as to their implications, the profound change in architectural expectations would conspire to underline an alteration of the public's views and expectations of the museum itself. "Magisterial" may not have been totally abandoned as a core value of museums as the twentieth century moved into the twenty-first, but, clearly, the authoritative stance had softened and a new aspiration entered the conversation. When the Victoria and Albert Museum in London won the "2007 Visitor Attraction of the Year Award," it was pleased to announce, on its own website, that the magazine *Time Out* had described the Victoria and Albert Museum as the "magisterial yet accessible one we take visitors to when we want to show off what London is made of." We believe that this shift reflects a welcome change, but we all must also be aware of the challenges, with respect to our responsibility to the dissemination and the origination of knowledge, that accompany this change to a less authoritative stance.

As a result of this "softening" about where our museums stand as authoritative institutional figures today, we are faced with new problems regarding the various publics we serve and our less clearly determined roles in the generation, organization, and dissemination of knowledge, and even information. We know that we must work harder to clearly express our peculiar relationship and responsibilities to knowledge management if we are to continue to enrich and better the lives of our constituents. And this enrichment is in respect to whether the visitors actually enter our doors, use our publications, or have a virtual connection to our work.

Today's questions emanate from the complexity of representing knowledge in the first place. Some of the questions facing us are: How does our museum communicate knowledge laden, as we believe it to be, with multiple perspectives? How does each museum fulfill its role as a guardian of knowledge? How do we encourage interdisciplinary research and representation without losing focus on the genre for which we are responsible? How do we encourage critical thinking, based on the encounter with the real object that we museums stand by? What is the relation of the academy and the museum? How do we fulfill the responsibility to transmit an inheritance of knowledge while at the same time generating curiosity, creativity, and critical thinking?

Each museum, naturally, needs to deal with the challenges it faces with respect to generating and disseminating knowledge in its own way. But confronting this issue in a transparent manner is the key to our ability to advocate for ourselves and for our research role in the future. Another of the principal questions we will have to answer, inevitably, is about the numbers of people we serve and how we serve them. If we accept that bringing great numbers of schoolchildren on once-in-a-lifetime field trips through our museums serves to increase their ability to learn through contact with our collections and exhibitions, we must also be able to advocate for our successes with those children in qualitative ways. Or we need to argue that we must approach education through the schools differently. If the children can't come to us more frequently, perhaps we need to go to them more regularly for, at least, visit preparation and follow-up. We need to argue that we are part of the creation of human beings who, because of their contact with museums, will be more innovative, informed citizens of the world. We need to be able to prove that we are enhancing what our visitors are learning and how they live their lives. We need to argue that the nature of the experience we provide to our communities with respect to knowledge is unique and irreplaceable. And ultimately, of course, we must be able to articulate exactly why and how the dissemination of the knowledge in our possession matters at all.

By strengthening the case for our education departments at all of the levels at which they operate, we believe that we will all be better able to fight for bettering the means by which we can connect with youth, with the general public, with special interest groups, and with academics. A wide range of obligations to all of our publics must be fulfilled whether we are in history museums, natural history museums, science museums, botanical gardens, aquaria, or zoos. We know that there are many approaches to museum education and that the particular style that any museum espouses will be a reflection of what it is. This chapter provides several perspectives on how we might, on our own terms, think about achieving this essential goal sustainably.

Steven Seidel writes that one of the principal challenges that a museum can address for society today and in the foreseeable future is whether or not it can help its audience develop a larger and more open sense of the world. He advocates for us to learn to listen to our visitors better in order to gauge our success in achieving that goal. Fred Hiebert speaks directly to that challenge in his meditations on the Afghanistan exhibition he curated for National Geographic. Obviously the conception and execution of this Afghanistan exhibition is one that could only have been accomplished with the prestige and resources of National Geographic and the major museums to which the show traveled, but we believe that the ideas Seidel and Hiebert set forth are adaptable on any scale, for any of our museums, if we focus on the principles behind them.

But what about the knowledge generated in the back rooms, the archives, and the restoration labs? The public is demonstrably interested in "behind-the-scenes" knowledge as well the normal display of precious objects, fully restored and analyzed. Many museums have long answered the call of generating knowledge, whether studying the migratory paths of birds, the creation of indigenous rugs, or the study of minerals, with big expenditures of manpower and financial resources. In the past decade, however, we have begun to see ways in which that research is being used directly as exhibition resource material. David Bomford offers the example of the National Gallery in London, where he initiated a groundbreaking exhibition program entitled Art in the Making that brought "technical art history" to the public and at the same time spoke eloquently to specialists in the field. Graciela de la Torre, long a trailblazing museum director in Mexico, examines the theme of interdisciplinarity in our museums—passionately promoting it, while recognizing the threat it might also pose to traditional museum power structures and their own brand of knowledge management.

In arguing for our sustainable value to society as unique guardians and protectors of a certain kind of knowledge, we will need to ask and answer many questions about how we, through the means by which we manage that knowledge, actually succeed in educating our publics. Nor will we all have similar answers to those questions. Some of us might insist on hewing to the dissemination of age-old bodies of knowledge; others will and should want to break new ground. But all of us need to be able to articulate our stances and to argue forcefully why what we do and how we do it is important to bettering the world in which we live by educating at all of the levels for which we are responsible. We will need to present both questions and answers to our boards, our ministries, our heads of departments, our foundations, and our individual patrons. If we frame our approaches compellingly, and we do so by taking into consideration all of the other sustainable values presented in this book, the chances are greater that they will want to work with us, to support our efforts, and to help us consider how we might grow and develop over time.

MINDS IN MUSEUMS—KNOWLEDGE EVOLVING

Steven Seidel

 For any single object in any museum in the world—whether a fish in formaldehyde, a pen-and-ink sketch on paper, a butter mold from a nineteenth-century farm in rural New York, or a Balinese shadow puppet—there is both a "current understanding" of the significance and meaning of that object and a history of ideas, interpretations, and knowledge about it. It is impossible to either truly understand that object or the nature of knowledge—specifically, how we come as individuals, groups, and fields to know what we know—without engaging with that history. What we understand about this object today will change in five, ten, twenty, or fifty years. It could change next week.

In the context of a history of evolving ideas about particular objects, it is likely that, in a sense, today's experts are "wrong" in their understanding of any object in the museum. They may declare themselves wrong and proclaim a new interpretation of the object, or others may declare them wrong. Given this, how we orient ourselves to the evolving nature of our knowledge and, perhaps even more significantly, to our ignorance, may be the most defining quality of our individual and institutional character. Our orientation to what we feel we do and don't know may also be the most fertile meeting ground for all those who coexist (though don't usually actually interact) in a museum, including museum professionals, field experts, and both highly knowledgeable and less informed museum-goers. In other words, when we stop thinking of experts as having definitive answers and novices as having little or nothing to contribute to collective understandings and see both more as people uniquely prepared to contribute and evaluate new ideas, insights, and possible interpretations, we have engaged a far more flexible understanding of knowledge and understanding.

In this regard, it is possible to conceive of the museum not only as a place for presenting objects, but also for presenting the history of how those objects have been thought about and understood and a place for documenting new ideas and interpretations as they emerge in the exhibit rooms. New or old ideas about the significance of particular objects, then, could be placed in the context of our evolving understanding of them.

ASSESSING IMMEASURABLES

If one thinks of a museum as a child—not a vague, generic child, not children in a general sense, but a child one knows well and loves—we might gain useful insight into the problem of assessing a museum's "success." The child we know and love is a complex and marvelous human being in whom we see, at any moment, tremendous achievements and even greater potential. As a child grows older, of course, we may begin to question whether her achievements match the potential we saw in her younger days. So, too, with museums. In a sense, sensitive assessment, while demanding and rigorous, is an attempt to relate what has been realized to perceptions of potential. Only in relation to potential does assessment demonstrate a commitment to growth, development, and a feeling of love, and certainly those who care enough to seriously undertake to evaluate a museum are motivated by love.

It would be so pleasing if we could turn to our public schools for models of assessments and evaluation that capture and reveal the fullness of a child's experience and her achievements in relation to her potential. Unfortunately, the dominant educational practice in the United States today is unidimensional, standardized, and has interest only in very particular aspects of children's lives, experiences, and knowledge. This narrowing of focus in educational assessment, while it may well serve to ensure that certain "bottom-line" results are achieved, such as all children achieving basic levels of literacy, also has the effect of primarily, even exclusively, valuing that "bottom line." Many have noted that "you assess what you value" and that, in turn, assessment "drives" the curriculum. In short, what you assess is a powerful predictor of what you are likely to get. Narrow assessments, whether in schools or museums, tend to narrow ambitions for the nature and quality of the experience people have in these settings. "Turnstile metrics" count bodies but provide no useful information at all about minds.

Insofar as the mission of the museum is to contribute to the generation and dissemination of knowledge, evaluation and assessment in museums must provide insight into what happens in the minds of those who enter through the turnstile at the front door or the security desk at the back door. But this requires a shift from measurement, which provides numbers, to true assessment, which provides descriptions and insights. Assessment, in this regard, draws meaning from the root *assesoir,* which suggests sitting next to or beside someone or something. In this way, assessment involves getting close enough to someone to see from the perspective of that person or to observe her or him "up close." In the attempt to understand how a museum experience affects a human mind, there seems no alternative to getting up close and personal and trying to see from another's perspective.

AN INVITATION INTO A CONVERSATION

Certainly many people both in and out of museums are actively engaged in reconsidering the nature of knowledge and how it is generated, but little evidence of that conversation or those evolving ideas is visible in most museums today. This visibility is essential if the conversation is to open and include everyone who comes to the museum, whether as a professional or a visitor.

The most uncertain yet significant feature of our evolving understanding of the nature of knowledge, the role of the museum, and any objects in our museums is what future generations will make of them or, more urgently, whether they will care to join in and contribute to this evolution. Insofar as the study of objects is an important human enterprise, a critical way to understand the past, the museum must be a place where young people are invited into these conversations. To make an invitation into a conversation genuine, one has to demonstrate that one is truly listening. The ideas and thoughts of the museum visitor—whether five, fifteen, or seventy-five years old—must be listened to, heard, documented, and reported, just as the thoughts of experts might be treated at a seminar or symposium.

Steven Seidel, EdD, holds the Bauman and Bryant Chair in Arts in Education at the Harvard Graduate School of Education. At Harvard, he is the director of the Arts in Education Program. From 2000 through 2009 Seidel was director of Harvard's Graduate School of Education Project Zero. In addition, Seidel has worked as a professional actor, stage director, and high school teacher.

AFGHANISTAN: HIDDEN TREASURES FROM THE NATIONAL MUSEUM, KABUL, AND THE GENERATION AND DIFFUSION OF KNOWLEDGE

Fredrik T. Hiebert

Afghanistan: Hidden Treasures from the National Museum, Kabul, is an exhibition that explores the art and cultural themes of Afghanistan—a critical area of the ancient and modern world virtually unknown to the American public. Today, Europe and the United States see Afghanistan in the news fairly often, but for reasons having to do with modern-day conflict. Afghanistan continues to struggle in its emergence from the conflict with the former Soviet Union, Taliban rule, the U.S.-led invasion following September 11th, and subsequent efforts to stabilize the country. The country's problems are omnipresent in our social consciousness, but there has been little or no focus on the contemporary culture of Afghanistan and the nation's rich, ancient heritage. Young Americans today struggle to even identify the country; a recent Roper Public Affairs survey revealed that nine out of ten young adults could not locate Afghanistan on a map of Asia. With 228 artifacts drawn from four archaeological collections of the Kabul Museum and extensive interpretation, this exhibition makes the art and culture of ancient Afghanistan come alive—for a wide variety of audiences—in a way that only a museum experience can do. Hidden Treasures addresses two major themes for its viewers: (1) the exhibition's significance for understanding the past and how Afghanistan's ancient cultures fit into a conceptualization of historical cultural development, and (2) the implications of this exhibition for understanding Afghanistan's modern history. The most important take-away message is in generating a new perspective on Afghanistan's role in ancient civilization and trade. Archaeological research in Afghanistan has been active for more than one hundred years, yet it is one of the least well-known regions of ancient civilization. Scholarship has been severely hampered by the war and political chaos there over the last twenty-five years, and the study of ancient Afghanistan as an active player in exchange and a center of cultural production has been limited by the lack of physical or visual access to its archaeological heritage. This exhibition literally places objects from the center of the Silk Road before the American public, creating an opportunity for significant scholarship and study through witnessing the artifacts and organizing panel discussions and educational programming around this event.

The public learned about the region's rich natural resources and elaborate cultural traditions and witnessed concrete evidence of trade centers and an original, sophisticated local artistic tradition. One of the most provocative issues the exhibition raises is whether Afghanistan, a country whose modern borders were summarily drawn by Western powers, has an ancient identity. By focusing on the period in history from the third century BC to the first century AD, the exhibition aims to document the development of a diverse art and culture that absorbed elements of the traders and raiders who passed through Afghanistan, creating a rich, ancient identity. It is perhaps only fortuitous that the ancient provinces known as Aria, Bactria, and Arachosia are today the modern land of Afghanistan. But this fortune is particularly important for modern Afghanistan as it struggles to establish itself as a modern nation-state. Afghans can be proud of their ancient identity—particularly since it is a nontribal, nonethnic, ancient identity.

The collections presented in Hidden Treasures provide an unparalleled opportunity to allow the U.S. public to examine, with new information, issues of the relationship between local cultures and foreigners at the center of the Eurasian cultural exchange network in northern Afghanistan and how historical artifacts can become elements of competing historical world views. This exhibition challenged audiences with new information on how cultural identity is maintained even thousands of miles from a homeland. It presents new evidence of an active center of long-distance trade that affected the cultural development of surrounding peoples. This new information helped audiences to better understand the origins and influences of both Western civilization and Asian civilizations, and that cultures east and west did not develop in isolation.

As a secondary take-away, Hidden Treasures underscores the present-day significance of these collections' survival in a nation plagued for decades by conflict. The heroic efforts of individual Afghan citizens to hide their country's most precious treasures and artifacts from the Taliban marauders is a miraculous story. Through interpretive materials, including text panels and film, Hidden Treasures illustrates how Afghans heroically guarded their cultural heritage during invasion, civil war, and intense factional fighting that led to the destruction of the National Museum of Afghanistan. The exhibition, its films, and interpretive materials tell the full story of the hidden treasures of Afghanistan: why they were hidden, how they were found, what their significance is culturally and historically. The interpretive plan of the exhibition is to present the artifacts approximately in the groupings and positions in which they were found, so that even subliminally, the visitor is brought to understand the context of the beautiful and rare art objects on display.

A central component of the communications strategy of the co-organizers, the National Geographic Society and the National Gallery of Art, is to encourage provocative and engaging press coverage of the exhibition and to develop public programming in the regions featuring the exhibition, working with local organizations in each venue to highlight the artistic and cultural significance of these collections, as well as the fascinating story of their discovery and rediscovery. One of the principal criteria for venue selection was a demonstrated commitment to educational programming and outreach. Each partner museum for this project—the Asian Art Museum of San Francisco, the Museum of Fine Arts of Houston, and the Metropolitan Museum of Art in New York— represents large and culturally diverse populations, and each venue varies the exhibition to make this project accessible to the broadest possible audience in their region. For example, the San Francisco Bay area includes the largest Afghan American population in the United States. The visitor experience in Hidden Treasures is also complemented by media components—short films providing context for recent Afghan history and daily life, closer examinations of certain objects, and the story of the collections' rediscovery. An audio tour provided rich contextual information on many of the individual objects. An exhibition catalogue with essays from some of the world's most renowned Silk Road scholars, photojournalists who have covered the country for decades, and others presented photo essays and explored major themes through personal words. In addition, comprehensive background on the exhibit is available online from both the National Gallery of Art (www.nga.gov/exhibitions/afghanistaninfo.shtm) as well as from the National Geographic Society (www.nationalgeographic.com/mission/afghanistan-treasures). In each city, lecture and concert series extend the message of the exhibition to include updates on archaeological research, Afghan music, and culture. These resources, which are continually being added to and developed over the course of the fifteen-month exhibition tour, provide a new perspective on this critical area of the world, challenging audiences to reconsider how they understand Afghanistan in our modern world.

Dr. Fredrik T. Hiebert, Archaeology Fellow at the National Geographic Society, was curator of the exhibition Afghanistan: Hidden Treasures from the National Museum, Kabul. Beginning in 2004, he participated in the re-inventory of the hidden collections from the National Museum in Afghanistan that forms the basis of the exhibition.

ART IN THE MAKING: ANOTHER VIEW OF ART HISTORY

David Bomford

I want here to circle around the notion of what has come to be known as "technical art history," a rather broad field of inquiry that centers on the primacy of the physical work of art—an inquiry into intention and creation, constructing narratives of imagining and making. Technical art history—which is a relatively modern name for something previously undefined that has been going on for a long time—concerns itself with all the processes for making art and the technical and documentary means by which we throw light on those processes. It is principally concerned with the physical materials and structures of works of art and how they are prepared, used, combined, and manipulated, but (and this is what makes technical art history so intellectually satisfying) it also interests itself in how an artist arrived at the finished or, indeed, unfinished work. It charts the stages of invention, development, realization, elaboration, and revision: in short, it is a route into the heart of the artist's intentions and changing ambitions.

The purpose of technical art history is to clarify, to reconstruct long-ago sequences of creation and evolution or, later, of change and decay. Every observation made of a work of art has the potential to displace the narrative in a different direction. Much of the evidence is straightforward—descriptions of materials used and patterns of working—but sometimes conclusions based on technical findings can be ambiguous and we have to test conflicting hypotheses to explain what we observe. Tantalizingly, the evidence may never be conclusive enough to arrive at a definitive answer, but we may be certain that there is a right answer, if only our skills and imaginations are perceptive enough. The work of art, the object, exists after all: some sequence of actions (what Degas called a "series of events" in connection with his own extraordinarily innovative methods) resulted in this work of art looking the way it does. And it is the work of the technical art historian to try to decipher what happened, to apply forensic analysis (in scientific, art historical, and critical terms) to determine the processes that created this work in this place at this time and by this artist's hand.

Twenty-one years ago, Neil MacGregor took over as director of the National Gallery in London and immediately began a series of conversations about the directions of current and future scholarship at the National Gallery. I and my colleagues in the conservation and scientific departments there had a huge amount of unpublished research on the materials and methods of paintings in the collection, and we were keen that this should somehow be presented to a wider audience in an intelligent and intelligible way. Thus came about the idea of a series of exhibitions and publication that we called *Art in the Making*. Three subjects were proposed initially: Rembrandt, Italian trecento painting, and Impressionism. We immediately launched the series and went on to do those three *Art in the Making* catalogues and exhibitions in three consecutive years. Most importantly, each catalogue was jointly (and equally) written by an art historian, a conservator, and a scientist—and they were the happiest and most fruitful of collaborations.

The catalogues have become standard student texts in many university courses, but striking the right balance between scholarly rigor and popular accessibility (they were, after all, primarily intended for the general public) was, as always with exhibition catalogues, a fine calculation. Our approach was twofold: to piece together as much documentary and anecdotal evidence from the periods and contexts in question as we could find and then to match it with technical observations from individual works of art. This twin-track method—following different pathways (the documentary and the technical) and trying to arrive at the same destination—is a fundamental basis of technical art history. A very clear demonstration of this formed the core of our catalogue *Italian Painting before 1400,* in which we studied the late-fourteenth-century treatise of Cennino Cennini and exactly matched its detailed descriptions of technique with trecento paintings in the National Gallery collection. It has been done so often since that such an approach now seems commonplace, but documentary and technical comparisons had never been done in that precise way before.

At the same time, we tried to place these exquisite gold-ground paintings in their wider context by reconstructing dismembered altarpieces whose individual panels had been dispersed to collections all around the world. One particularly satisfying case was of seven panels by Giotto, showing the life of Christ and ending with the Pentecost, the single panel of the series in the National Gallery collection. The other six panels were scattered in collections across Europe and the United States. The panels were clearly linked by style and technique and clearly belonged together in an obvious sequence following the chronology of Christ's life. But were any scenes missing? And how were they originally arranged and fastened together? To try to solve the puzzle, we asked each museum who owned one of the panels to make an X ray of it and send it to us. It took a month or two for them all to arrive, but when they did, and we arranged them this way and that in patchworks on the floor of my studio high above Trafalgar Square, the solution became obvious. The seven panels had all been part of one great plank of poplar wood, and when the x-rays from across the world were placed end to end there was the beautiful continuous wood-grain rippling along the entire length, still intact and clear after six and a half centuries. So we were able to confirm that the seven scenes were painted on a single plank that was subsequently sawed into pieces and dispersed, and we even identified a seven-arched fourteenth-century altar block still in situ in a Tuscan church on which this long horizontal altarpiece may originally have stood.

What this example illustrates is that the altarpiece builders of fourteenth-century Italy tried to use the largest, simplest structural elements they could find and that the huge vertical and horizontal registers of those great complex altarpieces that still dominate many Italian churches almost always consist of massive single planks painted with separate scenes separated by attached moldings. In the course of our research we clambered over countless altar rails and squeezed into the dusty spaces behind many an altar table to examine these monumental structures.

For the different Art in the Making subjects, different priorities emerged. For Rembrandt, the great questions over the last few decades have centered on attribution. At the beginning of the twentieth century, almost one thousand paintings were attributed to him—reduced in successive standard catalogues to around six hundred, and then four hundred. The figure now generally accepted by the Rembrandt Research Project—whose work adds up to the most sustained exercise in technical art history yet undertaken—is just over three hundred. How do we account for this? In recent decades, it was assumed that many of the paintings optimistically attributed to Rembrandt in the nineteenth and early twentieth centuries couldn't possibly be by him—but the idea that large numbers of them were fakes or later pastiches turned out not to be true. The obvious fakes were easily eliminated, still leaving many authentic seventeenth-century paintings clearly in the orbit of Rembrandt, but of questionable authorship.

The explanation is that many painters in the Rembrandt workshop consciously imitated his style—in fact, guild regulations demanded that they emulate their master's work—and since they were using essentially the same materials, scientific analysis couldn't distinguish between his work and theirs. And so the Rembrandt Research Project, and those of us in the London National Gallery who worked with them, developed a specialized form of connoisseurship based not only on close examination of brushstrokes and paint surfaces, but also of technical images such as X rays. We built up a body of detailed observations from undisputed Rembrandts and used inductive reasoning to confirm or reject other works.

One celebrated case investigated by colleagues in the Netherlands was of the 1629 Rembrandt self-portrait in the Mauritshuis—long admired as perhaps the most exquisite of all the early self-portraits. There also happened to be a rather rough, neglected copy of the Mauritshuis painting in the gallery at Nuremberg, which nobody took much notice of. Well, you can probably guess what happened. In their systematic examination of both pictures, the Rembrandt Research Project discovered that the beautiful Mauritshuis version had a completely uncharacteristic drawn outline underneath the paint, which accurate measurements showed to have been traced from the Nuremberg picture. Dramatically, the attributions of the two paintings were reversed—the rough, neglected one was confirmed as the original; the exquisite, admired one was a contemporaneous copy. And this opened up a whole new idea of what was going on in the Rembrandt workshop: pupils routinely copied their master's work—including the self-portraits—and Rembrandt would even sign pupils' copies if a paying client (who probably couldn't tell the difference anyway) demanded it. There are also examples of copies, made by pupils of Rembrandt, of works in progress that include features subsequently suppressed by Rembrandt and now visible only in X rays. In his great 1640 self-portrait, Rembrandt originally included his left hand resting on the ledge in front of him but then painted it out. In a contemporaneous copy by Ferdinand Bol, the hand is still there.

If the great uncertainty about Rembrandt has been that of authorship, the great questions that hang over the Impressionists concern the truth or mythology of their spontaneity, their use of color, and their rejection of academic tradition. Our *Art in the Making: Impressionism* catalogue looked at their paintings more closely than had ever been done before and addressed a whole range of issues about their working practices, concluding, for example, that their paintings are rarely as spontaneous as they appear or were intended to appear. The vast majority of Impressionist paintings are the result of careful calculation and repeated, layered working over several sessions. Monet's series paintings are a wonderful illustration of his planned "spontaneity." In his garden at Giverny or on his famous painting boat, he would keep grooved boxes with many numbered canvases. As the light changed throughout the day, he could pull out one canvas after another and work on it for no more than half an hour—or sometimes for just a few minutes, perhaps until the sun hit a particular leaf on a tree—then he would put that canvas away and pull out the next. And so it would be repeated for days or weeks on end, until he had finished the series.

In one celebrated series, *The Valley of the Creuse*, which he began in early spring, leaves and blossoms started to grow on a tree that he had begun to paint weeks before without leaves. He hired workers with ladders—so the legend goes—to strip the tree of its leaves so he could finish the series as he started it. So much for "truth to nature" or "record naively the scene as it appears before you," as Monet was given to telling his ardent admirers. And of course Monet also worked tirelessly indoors in his studio, layering and retouching those seemingly carefree works begun out-of-doors—but in his carefully constructed mythology he always denied it: "A studio?" he would say furiously, "A studio? How can any painter shut himself up in a room?" And he would sweep his arm expansively around the landscape and cry, "This is my studio!"

In our first three *Art in the Making* catalogues, we tried to examine not only the minutiae of painters' working methods, but also the broad contexts in which they operated, ranging from the late medieval pigment trade through the transport of Baltic oak in seventeenth-century northern Europe to the rise of artists' colormen in eighteenth- and nineteenth-century Paris. The pleasure of technical art history is the sheer variety of the territory in which it is conducted, beginning with a tightly focused view of a single object and moving outward into esoteric and unexpected avenues of inquiry, which could lead anywhere and everywhere.

The preoccupations of technical art history are very much those of the great traditional mainstream of art history—attribution, dating, style and technique, authenticity and the detection of forgery, and reconstruction of original intentions. But if its targets are traditional, its methods certainly are not. It is a strange hybrid: excitingly old fashioned in its aims and thrillingly modern in its methods. If the old art history was based on looking, technical art history is based on looking very closely indeed. And what about the name? I have been writing throughout as if it was a universally agreed title for this type of research. Many of us now use it to describe what we do, but others would deny that it is anything other than a familiar support system for regular art historical inquiry. My own view is that it is a discrete area of study—and, happily, the name seems to be becoming commonly accepted by museum and university colleagues alike.

David Bomford, associate director for collections at the J. Paul Getty Museum, was senior restorer of paintings at the National Gallery, London (1968-2007). He served as secretary-general of the International Institute for Conservation from 1994 to 2003. Bomford was editor of the international journal *Studies in Conservation* for ten years and author of numerous books and papers on conservation and art history.

INTERDISCIPLINARY WORK AND KNOWLEDGE MANAGEMENT: A DYNAMIC FOR THE CONTEMPORARY MUSEUM

Graciela de la Torre

Translated by Francisca González Arias

 When it began life as an institution, the museum emphasized the particular discipline of its specialization: for example, science, art, anthropology, or history. But as the spectrum of its activities and services has increased, the need to fully articulate functions deriving from several other branches of knowledge intensified as well: communications, psychology, education, museology, and philosophy combined with the discipline that gives the museum its uniqueness, and, indeed, with techniques derived from contemporary administration. This need could be seen as a way of maximizing the museum's potential as a cultural space: theory linked to practice, scientific disciplines in dialogue with the humanistic, academics and educators looking for common terms. But what ultimately underlies all these issues is the museum's potential for finding new models of knowledge management.

We could argue that the future of the museum does not depend now, as it did in the last century, on the degree of specialization of regular activities; rather, without abandoning these, the capacity of synergy among interdisciplinary groups should be considered crucial in the future. The dynamics of future museums reside not so much in specialized processes as in interdisciplinary projects that define the contemporaneity, versatility, and originality with which the museum (as institution) will cultivate the development of its social role and with which it will sustain its cultural offerings.

The museum of the future should know how to detect, increase, exploit, and even measure its "collective brainpower" to succeed in its area of expertise and give added value to its goods and services. Given that intellectual capital becomes the institution's most important resource, perhaps the greatest challenge for the director will be the ability to detect individual talent and instigate collaborative networks among interdisciplinary teams within the museum.

A model for museum administration based on knowledge management and interdisciplinary work will call for the casting aside of pyramidal (and even horizontal) patterns of authority in favor of multidimensional, rhizoidal, inclusive, and responsible lines of action, the composition of which will require not only clear objectives but also straightforward agendas to produce a balance between autonomy and collaboration.

In this nonhierarchical structure, the museum director will become the architect of the surrounding, interrelating organizational functions through task forces or nexus points, depending on the project, and assuming responsibility for the results. Each human component of a task force should channel his or her area of expertise creatively—knowledge, experiences, and abilities—but at the same time should be capable of sharing the information for the sake of a common project whose mission is, as its ultimate goal, getting through to society.

Nevertheless, it should be recognized that some museum directors who are unwilling to relinquish their power could see a model of the kind we contemplate as a threat. In this situation, knowledge management as an organizational model based on interdisciplinary nexus points could also present a challenge to the museum's communication with other traditional structures and agents with which it is supposed to interact and which are accustomed to a one-dimensional view of the museum task.

However, we should realize that in our century the speed with which new knowledge is generated can render uncompetitive those cultural institutions that have not managed to assume a new environment, new strategies, and new work tools to incorporate, interpret, and use individual, as well as the institution's own, information and knowledge. To accept the challenge will not only contribute to an ongoing learning process, but also exponentially increase institutional expertise, and thus the contemporary museum's potential for success.

Graciela de la Torre was director of the Museo Nacional de San Carlos and the Museo Nacional de Arte (MUNAL). She is currently director of visual arts at the National Autonomous University of México (UNAM) and is founding director and responsible for creating the Museo Universitario de Arte Contemporaneo (MUAC) in Mexico, where she is developing an important collection of Mexican contemporary art and presenting groundbreaking exhibitions. De la Torre serves as the Mexican representative to the IMI.

CHAPTER 10

Communication

COMMUNICATION, the means by which we "get the word out" about our work, is one of our critical sustainable values because it is, first, the way we register what we are doing in the society at large. Communication needs to be a key element of what everyone on the staff does in a museum with respect to the public. But not everyone has to communicate in the same way for the institution to be able to make the case for its efficacy. The director's office and its public relations and marketing apparatus communicate to the public in a role analogous to that of an embassy or a corporation. Educators create programs that mediate between the director's and curators' content and the public, including students, local organizations, discrete groups, and academic institutions. Curators communicate with their peers by means of journals, conferences, and catalogues, and with the public by virtue of how they present their collections and conceive of their exhibitions. Guards and reception staff are essential communicators: as the first people who interact with visitors, they communicate with them by how they answer questions, how they stand, and how they treat those visitors. And finally, the docents and volunteers communicate the essence of our museums in their jobs at the museum but also in their conversation with their peers. Any communication emanating out of our museums needs to emblematize the message and the mission of the museum. And all of our communications contribute to the web of meaning woven by the museum. What is communicated by our museum and all those related to it needs to be a part of an indisputable demonstration of our creativity, our openness, our relevance, the authenticity of what we offer, our support for curiosity, our tolerance, and the vitality of the knowledge we are disseminating.

We must also be aware, secondly, that communication is not limited to the ways in which we interact with the public. Internal communication needs to be carefully attended to as well, so that everyone on the museum staff is aware of and has the opportunity to buy into the larger goals of the leadership. We must strive to find a demonstrable way to communicate with the staff not only the goals of the institution, but their own roles in achieving them. Curators, registrars, educators, administrators, researchers, volunteers, docents, guards, and interns need to be a party to communicating the attitudes, the ideals, and the very soul of the museum, not just to the public, but to each other.

In his essay, Tom Freudenheim examines and challenges the closed, elitist messages we can transmit to our public through such seemingly innocent elements as signage and entrance fees. He challenges us to listen to our visitors, asserting that, with all of our surveys, we still know very little about what they think about us or, even more poignantly, why there are so many people who do not think about museums at all! As Freudenheim's title suggests, we ought to have a "reality check" from time to time to find out what exactly we are communicating and to whom.

Gary Vikan brings a very up-to-date and pragmatic notion of communication to his job as director of one of the world's fine art collections. He straightforwardly claims the desire to empower his visitors to enjoy themselves while they are discovering and learning. He employs technology, not to water down the authentic experience of engaging with art, but rather to entice visitors into his museum. Vikan communicates the liveliness of his museum by experimenting with music in the galleries, as well as through the massively popular Internet sites, Wikipedia and YouTube, and of course through social networking. With his battle for free admission, he truly puts up a welcome sign to his local constituency. Indeed, museums are now using social networking to communicate, as well—especially with students at university and college museums.

Sometimes, though, communication is what literally emanates from the office of public relations. Writing from Canada where she heads a cultural center, Lori Starr reminds us that the best museum programs in the world would be meaningless without our ability to communicate them to the publics who might be interested in experiencing them. It is our job to make that awareness happen. At the same time, this is a kind of communication that needs to be carefully monitored from within, probably more often than we do, to be sure that it retains a spirit of openness and inclusion. Communicating properly is another facet of the public trust. After all, the ways in which a museum presents itself will be scrutinized when there are financial problems or issues around acquisitions or de-accessioning.

At the Thyssen-Bornemisza Museum in Madrid, the founding director, Thomas Llorens, decided he wanted to better communicate that the collections were accessible to a larger public than would normally enter the museum. Javier Arnaldo describes this effort as a kind of hors d'oeuvre, a sample of the museum's permanent collection, "in context," free of charge. Since, like so many of our museums, the Thyssen Museum is required to earn revenues through the turnstile, it cannot, practically, have a policy of free admissions. But by means of this small but free show, this particular Spanish museum is able to have it both ways: it communicates inclusiveness by having a no-charge exhibition, and then, after having successfully enticed the public by offering a unique, in-depth experience, finds that visitors will often buy a ticket to experience the whole museum.

Finally, Elliot Bostwick Davis, at the Boston Museum of Fine Art, tells the story of a particularly difficult challenge from the perspective of a curator. Davis was charged with communicating a relatively radical notion of American history through display, one that incorporated ideas and objects that ran counter to the traditional histories supported by the Boston Museum. Through the development of Davis's new exhibition she sought to shift the weight from the Anglo-centric view of American history common in New England to a potentially controversial one (controversial only in New England!) that gave much more weight to pre-Columbian and Spanish colonial stories. Davis's communication challenge incorporated many of the values espoused by this book: she had to disseminate new knowledge, do so creatively, and make it inclusive of her immediate community but also relevant to the more current ideas about history. The experience needed to be authentic, not just trendy, and it needed to recognize the more global realities that truly shaped American history—beyond just those of the British empire. We know that change is difficult and potentially controversial, but Davis met her challenge because she saw it as not just an intellectual problem, but one in which communication was as central to the solution as the content.

Notwithstanding the need to communicate about our activities, policies or deep programmatic changes, the value of "communication" has still deeper implications. After 11 September 2001 in New York, the city's great museums became sites of solace. Somehow it was communicated (without press releases or announcements) that those institutional protectors of the DNA of our shared civilization and civility were places where people could gather for comfort. At a moment of communal despair, it was not the creative and relevant and innovative exhibitions and programs that those museums had initiated over the years that attracted the streams of visitors; rather, it was what these museums had communicated over the decades about the continuity of humankind through their stewardship of precious paintings and documents, specimens and artifacts. The museums of New York City bore indisputable witness to and communicated material proof of the persistence of humanity and its great and ordinary achievements. They proved themselves to be among the affirming and sustaining institutions we most need in moments of existential doubt.

REALITY CHECK

Tom Freudenheim

I confess to having done my share of bread-and-circus museum entertainment. In the early 1970s a belly dancer contorted around the Baltimore Museum of Art's Family Day in connection with an exhibition of Persian manuscript illumination; the kiddie lure nearby was a less sensational turban-winding demonstration. The satellite galleries that I established in downtown Baltimore and at nearby Columbia Mall were viewed as successful outreach efforts in their day, although neither proved viable for the long term. No visitor studies were done. What I'd really like to know now, thirty-plus years later, is whether anyone remembers these efforts and whether they still resonate with whatever visitors might have participated.

When I arrived as director of the Worcester Art Museum in 1982, my very first executive order (museum directors have a way of using self-important language) was to zap the admissions fee and to take down the "members only" sign at the side entrance. The sign seemed so "country club" in tone. The way I calculated it, the gate revenues cost only slightly less to collect and manage than they brought in; the net gain was minimal. As the new director, I wagered that both of these actions, taken without trustee approval (I wasn't about to wait for a meeting!), would somehow make the museum feel more accessible. By marketing the museum as free to everyone, I was able to increase membership levels, despite the fears that free admissions would lose us members. (Postscript: the admissions fee was reinstituted by my successor and remains in place.)

These are not presented as self-congratulatory anecdotes. Rather they describe my own learning curve on the way to asking questions that museum folks are generally afraid to pose. Despite advances in theories about different learning styles, we know pitifully little about what really happens in the course of a museum visit. Happily, the field of visitor inquiry has grown over the past few years, and I was instrumental in setting up a visitor research system at the Smithsonian in the late 1980s; its many published studies have greatly enriched the field. And yet is anyone asking the questions that really intrigue me? What about the non-museum-visiting segment of the population, which is presumably considerable? What are the long-term resonances of museum visits? And of course there's the related question of why museum leaders make so little effort to get answers to basic questions. Are they afraid of what they might find out? Is the survey polling for cultural endeavors really reliable, or is it fixed the way political polling is? If it's true that "more people go to museums (or cultural presentations) than attend . . . [you add the rest: sports events, movies, etc.]," then how do we explain the fiscal woes under which most cultural organizations labor? One answer, which I reject, is that "we just don't charge enough." That's certainly the rationale by which New York's Museum of Modern Art (MoMA) argued its twenty-dollar admissions fee. I've often heard the excuse, "After all, they pay high prices to go to a rock concert," without the understanding that a museum visit isn't anything like a rock concert (my belly dancer notwithstanding).

In the early 1960s, when I was a graduate art history student in New York, MoMA's gate price was seventy-five cents; nevertheless, I had to make a conscious decision as to whether I would make that museum visit: did I have enough time to warrant the expense and get my money's worth? In those days, the Met, Frick, and other museums were all free, so I used them casually, moving in and out with comfort, making them my own— no less than Central Park. As a member of the first generation of museum workers who could actually make a decent living at our trade (previous generations either had private incomes or survived as impoverished country mice), I have taken pride in those advances in our field. But now that many museum directors receive salaries that are meant to reflect the corporate pay levels of their trustees, one has the increasing sense of removal from reality: broad access to what the museum purveys isn't fully understood by folks who can move in and out freely—by going to invitation-only events or using their American Association of Museums and International Council of Museums cards for free admission (just as I do). Don't they know anyone for whom the museum admissions fee is a stretch? I do.

Which returns me to the fundamental question posed previously: what do we know about people who *don't* visit our museums, and might we learn something from them? Polling is a very costly venture—even polling the people already on the premises—so it's easy to shrug off the question with excuses. But I'm actually interested in the person who isn't a museum visitor. Is she or he uncomfortable? Is there a fear of not knowing enough or not knowing how to behave or how to react? Is it simply lack of interest in art or natural history or science? Is there even an awareness that the museum exists and of what a museum visit is like? Those questions interest me because, as a non–sports fan, I'm quite comfortable admitting my lack of interest in sports events. Yet I have attended them (albeit infrequently) and I know the modes of behavior (but perhaps not enough to feel completely comfortable with all of them) and the rules of whatever the game is. More significantly, I am always subliminally aware of whichever sports season is on: Major League Baseball, NFL football, NBA basketball, and so on. The TV and radio newscasts (even on my local National Public Radio station) make sure my awareness level is properly tuned to sports seasons—not just to the World Series or the Super Bowl, but the entire season. I'm not uncomfortable with that because it's a healthy reflection of what's going on in the community in which I live. But so is the normality of a museum exhibition or the local orchestra's concert, although generally they are only worthy of attention for whatever sensational or celebrity value they may bring to newscasts.

When I was director of the Museum Program at the National Endowment for the Arts (1978–1982), I tried to address this issue: is there a way to raise subliminal awareness levels for cultural presentations by according them the same *regular* and *daily* attention that we associate with sports news? I solicited a variety of commercial TV stations in medium-sized cities around the country, offering to provide funds for such an experiment. There were no takers. So we still don't have any answers, other than the self-fulfilling prophesies that we feed our public relations departments, that then make their way into the increasingly lazy media (why be creative and thoughtful when you can get the information in predigested form?). Would I get in trouble for telling people outside the Metropolitan Museum of Art that the twenty-dollar admission fee is only "suggested"? Or for surveying MoMA visitors as to whether they received their money's worth from the visit? That people "vote with their feet" to produce record museum visitor numbers is not unlike believing that our electoral system works properly although we know that a huge proportion of the population never votes.

Finally, admitting that my life as a museum junkie has provided innumerable joyful as well as instructive moments, I would hope that eventually we find ways of measuring the resonance of a museum visit. The best we can do now is via exit polling: asking a visitor questions on the way out of the museum or the exhibition. But don't we really want to know whether that museum visit was meaningful for the long term? Did it generate other museum visits or more interest in a specific subject or simply some raised sensibilities? Was it instrumental in making a career choice? (It was for me.) I can still remember my first blockbuster exhibition (Treasures from the Vienna Museums, in Toronto, shortly after World War II), and the ways in which I have rethought endless issues of interest to me because of what I've seen in permanent collections and special exhibitions. Rather than assuming ourselves to be purveyors of transformative experiences (which we surely are), museum leaders need to develop their self-critical facilities and to re-enter the less exotic worlds they presumably once inhabited prior to their museum service. Everyone can use a regular reality check!

> Tom Freudenheim has served the international museum world in many capacities. His positions have included the director of the Baltimore Museum of Art, the director of the Worcester Art Museum, the deputy director of the Jewish Museum in Berlin, and the director of the Gilbert Collection in London. Dr. Freudenheim was also assistant secretary for museums at Washington's Smithsonian Institution and director of the Museum Program at the National Endowment for the Arts in Washington. He has published and lectured widely in the field of museum policy and the arts.

COMMUNICATION: ONE MISSION, ONE BLOG

Gary Vikan

 The mission of the Walters Art Museum is a simple one:

> The Walters Art Museum brings art and people together, for enjoyment, discovery, and learning.

This brief but powerful statement is posted in every office and is printed on every one of our business cards. It can be recited by every member of our staff. We live with it because we believe in it.

In October 2006, we eliminated our general admission fee. In the first eleven months of free admission, our attendance grew by more than fifty percent. This dramatic step was taken with the shared conviction of Walters trustees and staff that our collections are not private assets to control and impart as we see fit; they are public assets to which we are obliged to provide physical, intellectual, and emotional access in the creation of individual and societal value.

The act of "going free" gave powerful expression to the Walters mission statement. At the sixty-thousand-foot level, from above, this is nothing more than the inevitable consequence of the gradual shift in emphasis among public museums from what they have (collections) to what they do (create public value). At the Walters, we no longer understand our role as that of gatekeeper and revered authority, but rather as that of enabler and facilitator. Our visitors, both real and potential, are not our students, or even our guests, but rather our partners in fulfillment of our mission.

And this sense of partnership is growing inside the Walters as well. Our major fall 2007 exhibition, Déjà Vu? Revealing Repetition in French Masterpieces, was accompanied by our first ever self-guided cell phone tour. Its main narrator was a member of the Walters maintenance staff who is blessed with a deep, rich voice. Our visitors also got to hear from our chief installer and our chief registrar, who talked about what it's like to open a crate with a Corot painting inside and hang it on the wall. And after the exhibition opened, we added additional comments on the show as experienced by some of our visitors and by our teen guides, the Walters Wonderkids. By extending the "circle of ownership," we built a sense of broad-based partnership from inside to out, and from outside to in.

As an extension of this dialogue, in February 2007 I began a weekly "director's blog" which is, as of this writing, still unique among American fine arts museums. Every Wednesday, through the Walters website, I pose a question and express an opinion about a cultural issue that is, at that moment, part of the national conversation. Often, the topic springs from something I've just read in the *New York Times*; always, there is a personal flavor to my comments.

Many of my blogs receive posted comments. That of 8 August 2007 grew out of a recent visit to Lascaux II in Perigord, coupled with the fact that our museum owns a good, early copy of the *Mona Lisa*. Entitled "Lascaux II Works, So Why Not Mona Lisa II?" it engendered an extended cyber conversation about the meaning of the word "authentic" as it applies to works of art and to the art experience.

I frequently incorporate information from Wikipedia, and in July, I posted a video on YouTube describing a recent Walters experiment that introduced newly commissioned music in the galleries of our fall 2006 exhibition, Courbet and the Modern Landscape. Later, this video was added to a page on our website devoted to the Courbet show in which we presented our experimental rationale, our successes, our failures, and what we learned from them. This page debuted in one of my weekly blogs (27 July 2007) with the provocative title "A Surprisingly Effective Innovation . . . Or a Curator's Egotistical Interference."

My director's blog, my use of and contribution to collectively created content on the Internet, our museum's act of "going free," and the multiple voices now speaking for and with the Walters all converge in the values that underlay our mission and in the definition of communication implicit in it—not in the old-fashioned sense of a voice of authority imparting special wisdom to the uninformed, but rather in the new sense of someone in a position of privileged access inviting the public into meaningful conversation.

Together, as collaborating partners, we create the public value that is the only vindication for the continuing existence of the Walters Art Museum—or any like institution—and for the role of people like me in such institutions.

Gary Vikan has directed the Walters Art Museum since 1985. Under his leadership, the Walters has achieved record attendance levels, has secured three major collections, and has significantly increased the endowment, operating budget, and museum membership. Dr. Vikan, a native of the state of Minnesota, received his PhD from Princeton University.

THE POLISHED EDGE

Lori Starr

"Even bad publicity is good publicity, as long as they spell your name correctly," the saying goes. Nothing truer could be said about museums today, where celebrity and fashion, design and the ultra-cool converge. One museum might look familiar from a car commercial; you might know it because you "friended" it on MySpace. "Back-of-house" exhibitions reveal the historically unseen and unrecognized aspects of museums and are democratizing previously rarified inner sanctums. Museums are regaled and reviled. They make headlines. It wasn't always so.

Working on my masters in art history in the 1970s at I. M. Pei's new East Wing of the National Gallery of Art in Washington, I stared at the acute angle of pale red, Indian limestone of the facade and saw that after only a few weeks, it had been polished by thousands of hands. So euphoric were the crowds, so spellbinding was the escalator ride among the Calder mobiles, so pleasing were the exhibitions that people climbed the grass outside determined to touch that edge—a spontaneous ritual. *The Art Museum as Educator,* thick as the New York City phone book, had just been published. There were resources—federal grants, corporations, and foundations. I wasted no time and moved to San Francisco as a Rockefeller Fellow in Museum Education and Community Arts.

In San Francisco I worked in the new Downtown Center at Embarcadero Plaza—a youthful business hub—and it was easy to get the crowds the old-fashioned way. Mailing lists, word of mouth, and a loyal network of artists, collectors, and friends turned out. There was little to no advertising. Public relations then meant "spokespeople." They made announcements and published membership magazines. "Marketing" was a forbidden word. The term "audience development" was the euphemism.

We educators were the grassroots, "get-it-in-the-hands-of-regular-people" marketers, distributing flyers on the street, calling the news stations, long before the e-blast was invented.

The fellowship ended and I moved to Los Angeles, preferring its rawness, its boulevards of strip mall ugliness, the low horizon, the light, and the "you-can-get-here-in-twenty-minutes" optimism. Lush gardens were the promise behind every bungalow. Artists could afford to live in lofts downtown. I found work at the Los Angeles County Museum of Art in the education department. Blockbusters came and went. Curators, educators, and money managers occupied different states of mind. While the head of operations was calculating how many people per minute could pass through The Bronze Age of China, the educators were figuring out how to bring the large Chinese population to the museum for the first time. Curators anguished that our free brochures would undermine catalogue sales. Why were so few families coming, why was everyone so old, why can't we bring in new voices to interpret what we're showing? Those of us in direct contact with visitors wanted to break new ground and we did. We created music, dance, and film programs, brought contemporary artists in to talk about the most ancient material in the collections, and invited many communities into the "temple" for their first time to engage in dialogue around the collections and exhibitions.

The Getty was another story. I started working at the old Villa in 1986 with the title head of public information. As a museum educator, I figured I could reach more people by working in the most primary way—through stories in the media. I didn't flinch when it became obvious that my job would be about keeping the Getty out of the press, so shrill had the stories been up until then about the Getty's fortune and the danger it posed of running art prices too high. It didn't take long to get plenty of stories, but not the good kind.

The Getty Kouros story broke ("It's a fake!") and the Aphrodite story soon followed ("It's stolen!"). News helicopters circled over Malibu. At the Getty I learned that media crisis management appealed intensely to me—the pressure of questions and deadlines, the high propensity for failure, the anxious waiting for the newspapers to hit my driveway at 4 a.m. Good news was better. Superb exhibitions and some remarkable acquisitions of paintings, drawings, and photographs fueled a media hungry for Getty news. The 1997 Getty Center opening was a huge success—for which it was not prepared. Soon we were making radio commercials suggesting people wait a little longer before visiting. More was, suddenly, less!

I had been in my new job at the Skirball Cultural Center for only three months. The institution had a healthy appetite for marketing but lacked a coherent communications infrastructure and needed to grow its multidisciplinary approach to programming. The building project attracted media attention and from that the programming evolved; the Internet presence grew exponentially and, in turn, the audiences. Evidently, and perhaps surprisingly, it became evident that Jewish institutions could be for everybody if done in community collaboration. I was given greater responsibilities to ensure collaborative projects between departments and ultimately appointed museum director. With Einstein (which opened in Los Angeles in 2004 and was co-organized by the Skirball, the American Museum of Natural History, and the Hebrew University, Jerusalem), it was possible to create a constellation of related exhibitions and to merge scientific and cultural history with art. Did the crowds come?

Of course. Who could resist smiling Albert on his bicycle coming toward you on almost every light pole in the city? We communicated a great message with great civic import that dramatically enhanced the museum's profile. Now I am working in Toronto, directing the new Koffler Centre of the Arts and a Jewish history museum and library. Toronto is already a city of the twenty-first century—home to émigrés from all continents. The freshness of the immigrant experience is palpable even as significant architectural projects are redefining the urban landscape. There is an intensely independent and original art scene. My project, a campus that combines art, culture, history, heritage, health, recreation, and social services—a Jewish campus for everybody—can be a new model. The Koffler Centre of the Arts will focus on cutting-edge contemporary arts in all media. Its audience will be anyone who is interested in having a dialogue across cultural boundaries.

So many years and miles away from I. M. Pei's acute-angled, polished edge, I am more convinced than ever that museums, with their collections, changing exhibitions, and public programs will succeed only if they are nimble communicators and conveners providing safe, inspiring, and neutral ground, inviting and welcoming everyone—and loving their critics. Let's be bold and make headlines. Just spell our names correctly.

Lori Starr is executive director of the Koffler Centre of the Arts and vice president for culture for the United Jewish Appeal Federation for Greater Toronto. Before moving to Toronto, Starr was executive vice president of the Skirball Museum and Cultural Center. Previously she was in charge of public relations at the Getty Trust.

TEXTS AND CONTEXTS IN MUSEOLOGY

Javier Arnaldo

Translated by Francisca González Arias and Nigel Williams

 To say that works of art are texts of visual language is not exactly true, but it is a useful comparison when referring to the specific terms their reading requires. To comment on a work of art, it is often necessary to look at it in an appropriate context. In 1995, three years after the Thyssen-Bornemisza Museum was inaugurated in Madrid, Tomàs Llorens, then chief curator, started the series of special exhibitions called Contexts of the Permanent Collection. This is an exhibition format that has continued uninterruptedly in the museum's calendar until the present and will continue in the future. There have been twenty-two exhibitions of this kind in the museum since then. The fact that what was presented as an innovative formula in 1995 has become an established fact is well worth bearing in mind.

Contexts of the Permanent Collection are similar to other exhibition formulas in use in various world museums today. They are relatively small shows of between ten and fifteen pieces that are suggested for the study of another work from the museum's collection. The exhibition presents the selected work together with other directly related works that facilitate its interpretation on a level with its immediate context. The whole group not only offers an opportunity for gaining more in-depth knowledge of essential aspects of the work in question, but also facilitates an understanding of features it has in common with others. However, it would be rash to conclude that a common, methodical aim derives from the format and function of these exhibitions. Rather, each "context" show arises from inquiries as special as the works themselves and from revisions in which any of a variety of iconographic, technical, philological, stylistic, or indeed any other issues are prevalent. In other words, the contexts to which the texts are submitted are intentionally faithful to the latter, but could respond to different aspects of their reality. Furthermore, the continuing story of these exhibitions has been marked, as we shall see, by changes in their location within the museum that have determined their relation to the public.

The first exhibition, curated by Tomàs Llorens himself in 1995, had as its theme Picasso's *Harlequin with a Mirror,* one of the museum's major works, which, together with *The Pipes of Pan* from the Picasso Museum in Paris and a group of eleven drawings, recreated Picasso's artistic horizons in the summer of 1923. The stylistic aspects of the painter's work at the end of his classicist period were the focus of the exhibition. As a result of this show, exhibitions were subsequently organized around El Greco's *Annunciation,* Michael Andrews's *Lights,* and other ancient and modern works from the collection. Among the artists represented were Pechstein, Kokoschka, Gerard David, Memling, Corot, Dalí, Rauschenberg, Raphael, Saenredam, and Otto Dix. In each of the projects the interpretative emphasis focused on specific issues based on the curator's criteria. In this way, two to three annual exhibitions with their corresponding catalogues have contributed to the development of a supplementary critical framework for the collection. There have been times when projects were shared with other museums, as is the case of the exhibition of Tintoretto's *Paradise,* which was also presented at the Louvre and in the Doge's Palace in Venice. The dialogue thus established in this way is proof of the interest in this exhibition formula among museums that share investigative goals.

In contrast to the major thematic or monographic exhibitions that the Thyssen-Bornemisza Museum also organizes on a regular basis, admission to the "context" exhibitions is free. At the beginning they were situated in a space within the area of the permanent collection as a temporary complementary feature in accordance with their purpose. But complaints from visitors who said that admission to the exhibition was not free if they had to pay to see the museum led to a study of the possibility of preparing a space with a separate entrance so that free admission could indeed exist. Since 2003 this specific service for visitors to the "context" exhibitions has been in force, although not always in the same room. There is no doubt that free admission, whose advisability might be questioned for other reasons, has succeeded in attracting a larger number of visitors to these shows, which have slowly overcome the stigma of minority events and become an attraction in themselves for visitors in general. The accessibility that comes with free admission has helped to consolidate with the public an exhibition program that is important to the acknowledgment of content as confirmation of the validity of the goals the museum has set itself.

In this respect it is interesting to make a few observations on the relation to the public in mainly qualitative terms. With an average of fifty thousand visitors, the "context" exhibitions can be considered a popular, though not spectacular, success. I do not believe anything would be gained with a more detailed analysis of figures, as what should be considered is the museological function these shows perform. It should be noted that with the original location of these exhibitions they were intended to enhance the visit to the permanent collection. Let us reflect then on the qualitative analysis of such events with regard to those they were aimed at—the public, whose trust museums are duty-bound to gain through the high quality of their work.

It goes without saying that an exhibition series like the Contexts exhibition offers the public an exceptional opportunity to draw closer to artworks in the permanent care of the museum and thus reinforces the permanent with the temporary. The best way I can think of to describe this is as a dynamic of resistance to its own profile. From the museological point of view, it seems to me a very healthy pursuit that is worth fostering beyond the virtues inherent in "context" exhibitions. Museums, as spaces of conservation and exhibition of artworks, are always concentrations of vulnerable material. And by this I am not talking about physical safety. From the very moment when a spectator enters a museum, attitude crises are triggered, its galleries become a setting for things unforeseen by the senses and for the vulnerability of the emotions. In this respect the museum projects itself onto its visitors with a power to rule emotion that updates the expression of its material in the here and now, in the present, of sensory observation, as with music at a concert. The inertial force of every artistic manifestation of the past seeks a place in the novelty of the present. As I said, that is why museums must take care that their activities devote themselves to making the stable eloquent in the temporary. Otherwise, the museum would be working in such a way as to favor a watering-down of its own content in a magma of interchangeable emotions and gratuitous inferences. It is well known that museologies and an overeagerness to produce temporary exhibition programs with an effect different from that of their own collections favor, though not without success, a lack of differentiation and a sensationalizing of the event that negate the specific message in the exhibits. If a museum thinks that being a space for the conservation of art collections is not enough and wishes to take charge of administering the aesthetics of the new, it should meet that challenge, having judged it a legitimate one, with wisdom and discretion. And the prime recipe for control is faithfulness to the text it is interpreting and consistency in the context in which it stages its temporary exhibitions.

Javier Arnaldo is curator and head of the Research and Advanced Studies Department at the Thyssen-Bornemisza Museum in Madrid, Spain. He is also full professor of art history at the Universidad Complutense, Madrid. Professor Arnaldo has curated many groundbreaking exhibitions, including Musical Analogies, Kandinsky and His Contemporaries (2003) and Brücke, the Birth of German Expressionism (2005).

COMMUNICATING THROUGH DESIGN AND DISPLAY: THE NEW AMERICAN WING AT THE MUSEUM OF FINE ARTS, BOSTON

Elliot Bostwick Davis

 The new American Wing at the Museum of Fine Arts, Boston, will exhibit the collections of the art of the Americas, which encompasses the arts of North, Central, and South America. The Art of the Americas Department is responsible for designing and implementing the curatorial program for the American Wing, in close collaboration with designers, museum educators, and curators from other departments, especially those of prints, drawings, and photographs; textiles and fashion arts; and musical instruments, whose collections will be integrated into the new galleries. Designed by Lord Norman Foster and Partners and scheduled to open in the fall of 2010, the American Wing comprises sixty thousand square feet of gallery space and adds over two hundred thousand square feet to the original Guy Lowell building on Huntington Avenue.

The curatorial team, in planning the American Wing, was not given a tabula rasa. The site dictated the general configuration of four levels of galleries that could be dispersed within a large rectangular core; two of the levels contain additional space in square pavilions, which, added to the main core, resembled the shape of the letter T. On the vistas into the various galleries and the pavilions from the core, we situated key works of art to signify the themes of the various galleries. After studying a range of models, it became clear we were on our own to create a new approach combining the most successful features derived from earlier solutions to museum display. I am a long-standing admirer of the work of Paul Klee and the galleries Alfred Barr designed for the Museum of Modern Art, where I first came to know Klee's work in the 1987 retrospective there. I like to think of the galleries in the new American Wing offering visitors "highways" and "byways" by which to experience American art, much as one could explore Klee's approach to his work in *Highroad and Byroads* (1929, Museum Ludwig, Cologne).

Visitor surveys conducted by the Department of Museum Learning and Public Programs underscored an expectation that surprised me yet ultimately informed our decision about how to arrange the four levels. When museum-goers arrived at our present building, they believed that the history of art would unfold before them through successive galleries that established a broad time line beginning with ancient Egypt and extending through contemporary art. When balancing these findings with various factors involving ceiling heights and the ability to connect the new American Wing with the existing building, we ultimately felt it was essential to broaden the definition of American art as expressed by our mandate to represent the art of the Americas. Thus the oldest collections in our care served as the philosophic foundation for the art that would follow. As visitors traverse the four floors of the American Wing from the foundation to the top level, they travel through time as they rise vertically through space from the prehistoric era of Native American art and masterworks dating from the Olmec period of the ancient Americas through to the end of the twentieth century.

Within each of the main floors, a regular arrangement of galleries informs another aspect of our philosophy for displaying the collections. In the center of each level are generally two (although on two levels either one or three) larger-scale galleries that run along the center of the core. I like to think of these central galleries functioning as the spine of the collections and the narratives within the largest galleries sketched with a broad brush to capture the imagination visually and aesthetically. There we feature major strengths of our holdings (colonial Boston, John Singer Sargent), areas of the collection that we would like to emphasize (art of the ancient Americas and Native American art), and areas that continue to be defined (twentieth-century art). Surrounding that central spine are additional galleries running along the north and south sides that build off of the central spine and essentially augment the broad narratives with greater breadth, depth, and nuance. Anchoring the corners are four nearly square galleries of approximately 1,100 square feet, and in between each corner gallery is a more intimate gallery of approximately 750 square feet. Although the American Wing includes ten period rooms, eight are situated within the pavilions, where they are adjacent to galleries that display related objects in a way that we believe will enhance the interpretation and experience of the period room installations. In the late 1920s, when many museums in the northeast installed American period rooms, they were at the core of the presentation of American decorative arts. In this American Wing of 2010, they appear in the context of smaller-scale pavilions, where they serve as full scale "vignettes" for further discovery and appreciation for the important role period rooms play in the historiography of American art museums.

Moving up through the central core galleries, visitors encounter three millennia of the art of the Americas. On the court level, galleries for ancient American and Native American art form the central spine. The first of two galleries for ancient American art features our important Maya ceramic collection, and the second gallery displays gold from Central and South America, our superb Andean textiles, and thematic installations such as the range of musical instruments used throughout the ancient Americas. The final gallery of the central spine on this level presents Native American art from the prehistoric era to the present representing a range of cultures and media. On level one, the central spine exhibits paintings, furniture, silver, textiles, and prints of colonial Boston, as discussed earlier, and is followed by a gallery dedicated to the neoclassical style with special emphasis upon the efforts of the new nation to establish a history and iconography based upon exemplary revolutionary leaders such as George Washington as portrayed in Thomas Sully's monumental painting, *The Passage of the Delaware* (1819), and decorative arts incorporating stylistic motifs harkening back to the republics of ancient Greece and Rome. Just above on level two, one gallery showcases Sargent and his masterpiece, *The Daughters of Edward D. Boit* (1882), along with oils, watercolors, and studies for the Sargent murals in the museum's upper rotunda of the Huntington Avenue building. Continuing through the spine, the second large gallery for nineteenth-century painting and sculpture is hung in the salon style of the first Museum of Fine Arts building located on Copley Square and other grand picture galleries in Europe. This gallery highlights American artists on the grand tour in Europe, where they saw and copied the Old Masters firsthand and had an opportunity to paint the landscapes of Italy, Germany, France, and England. Finally, on the top floor, which is illuminated from above by natural light, the twentieth-century collections appear within one long gallery that is separated into interlocking spaces by alternating partitions that may be adjusted as the collection evolves. Similar to Jackson Pollock's solution for the unrealized *Ideal Museum* (1949)—without the mirrors—the resulting effect allows intimacy and prominence to themes within the present holdings. The first third of the gallery presents the foundation of early Modernists in the Lane Collection, while the arrangement of the partitions further encourages visitors to explore the interdependence and relationships between Surrealism and Abstract

Expressionism or artists working with the grid and color from Stuart Davis through Color Field painting and Pop Art.

Moving off of the core galleries, there are a variety of display strategies employed in the wing. In several instances, the larger square galleries and the smaller, more intimate galleries are dedicated to the strengths of our holdings by individual artists, makers, or schools. For example, we have reintroduced display techniques that were used at the time the works of art were created. For the gallery devoted to painting and decorative arts of the 1940s and 1950s, two major themes are emphasized. One side of the gallery is largely inspired by geometric abstraction with works by the American Abstract artists and furniture by leading figures, Charles and Ray Eames, shown within a display case that was inspired by a wall unit designed by the Eames. The resulting grid and pattern of open and closed elements punctuated by primary colors allows for a flexible system in which smaller decorative arts of the period may be rotated easily as the collection is further refined. As a counterpart, a flanking display case presents decorative arts and paintings responding to biomorphic abstraction and surrealism. Department store displays that combined furniture, decorative arts, paintings, and sculpture inform one side of the case. On the opposite side, a curved wall for exhibiting works on paper on a rotating basis derives from a similarly curved wall installed by Frederick Kiesler in the Surrealist Gallery, Art of This Century in New York City (1942).

Just as the Art of the Americas Department embraces the art of many peoples, cultures, periods, styles, and media, so we hope that visitors to the new American Wing derive a greater sense of wonder and joy in exploring the breadth of American art represented at the Museum of Fine Arts, Boston. In the process of designing the American Wing galleries, we have worked from top to bottom, from bottom to top, and from various entry points from the new Visitor Center, as well as the Ancient and European galleries. There are multiple ways to enter the collections on all levels, and we hope the new American Wing galleries serve our visitors well as they discover their own favorite paths along the highways and byways, our ways of communicating new ways of thinking about our great collections from the Americas.

An authority on nineteenth-century prints and drawings, Elliot Bostwick Davis received her PhD in art history and archaeology from Columbia University. Davis came to the Museum of Fine Arts, Boston, in 2001 from the Metropolitan Museum of Art of New York. In her position as Chair of the MFA's Art of the Americas Department, Elliot Bostwick Davis oversees the museum's extensive collection of American art.

Conclusion

MUSEUMSPACE

Selma Holo and Mari-Tere Álvarez

Over seventy years ago Kurt Lewin developed his influential field theory, positing that a field is formed by "the totality of coexisting facts which are conceived of as mutually interdependent." Kurt Lewin understood both the social and psychological "fields" as dynamic "lifespaces" that interacted with human consciousness and affected individual and group behavior. Obvious as this theory might seem today, now that it has been absorbed into so many aspects of modern thought, it was revolutionary at the time it was developed. Looking at Lewin's theory once again, this time from the point of view of museums, it might be useful to think of each of our own institutions as a field of its own, a dynamic "museumspace," the personality of which is created by the tension that inevitably exists among many sometimes compatible, more often competing facts, and, in the case of this book, values.

To be absolutely clear, the set of sustainable values we have laid out in *Beyond the Turnstile* make up only some of those values that exist in our universe. Furthermore, the variety of essays riffing on each value offers just a few reflections on how these values might jumpstart discussions in your own museum. For the reality and the perception of any "museumspace" to be positive, those values that we have proposed (the public trust, the primacy of the collections, relevance for its communities, intellectual and social inclusion, creativity and innovation, a clear relationship to globalization, the preservation of old alliances and the making of new ones, the offering of authentic experiences unique to museums, the generation and dissemination of knowledge, and an effective and affective commitment to communication) must be, to appropriate Lewin, "conceived of as mutually interdependent" (See M. K. Smith, in his 2001 article, "Groups, experiential learning and action research," which describes the essence of Lewin's theory well). Indeed, it will only be when the values we deem sustainable are conceived of as existing in mutual interdependence with the demands of the turnstile that the conversation about how our museums can succeed in achieving their best aspirations will be able to move forward.

Every member of the staff of a museum contributes to maintaining its health by virtue of his or her commitment to fulfilling a particular role in the "museumspace." But at the same time, every member of the staff needs to understand that his or her role does not exist in isolation: the avid curator of collections who is not aware of the obligation to the public trust could bring a museum down; the creation of an exhibition program that is irrelevant to the interests of the community or does not generate or disseminate knowledge will ultimately lose its significance to that community; a communications department that promotes empty marketing but does not spread the word about the heart and soul of the museum will ultimately damage its credibility; a visionary and ambitious globalization program that makes no effort to create new alliances to support it might destroy a budget; a globalized museum program that ignores its roots is doomed; a university or college museum that forgets that it is a part of a larger mission might lose its protection. And so on.

But, even though everyone on the staff should be aware of the matrix of which they form a part, it is the leadership, in the form of the director in partnership with the museum board, a ministry, or other governing bodies, that has ultimate responsibility for weaving together all of these powerful values so that they will characterize the desired "museumspace" to all of its constituencies and stakeholders. The leadership has to successfully make the case that the totality of the museum occupies a special and entirely unique (Lewinian) "imagined state" that is indispensable to its community and critical to its larger sphere of influence. Whether the museum has a staff of hundreds or a few, it is only with that kind of principled, coherent, transparent, and outspoken leadership that it will be understood to be more than just the sum of its parts.

We would add, in conclusion, that success in "making the case" for these sustainable values will also provide a more convincing foundation for success in fund-raising or even, in hard times such as our own, budget-maintenance efforts. No museum wants to fight for or beg for funding when it is already failing. Rather, museum leaders need to be conducting an ongoing argument for continued support because the museum provides a *good* for society. This is the good that makes its visitors experience their lives as better and richer than they would be if the museum did not exist *for* them. If we work to make the case for the set of sustainable values as coexisting with "turnstile values," our funders and those who are our overseers will be better able and more willing to partner with us in our efforts—and less likely to abandon us. They will know us better and, I am certain, they will work more enthusiastically to offer or seek the support—moral and financial—that our museums need to become truly sustainable.

Acknowledgments

This book would not have been possible without the ongoing support of the University of Southern California College of Letters, Arts and Sciences, in particular, Dr. Joseph Aoun, dean at the beginning of the project, and later Dr. Howard Gillman, dean during the years of the book's preparation. We would also like to acknowledge the support and collaboration of the Universidad Autónoma de Mexico (UNAM), our partners in this project.

And we want to extend an extra special word of thanks to Marco Barrera Bassols who rescued the project innumerable times. Marco's unstinting generosity of spirit never failed us, whether we were searching out authors or their texts. Thank you, Marco. And we extend our appreciation to the Mexican Association of Museum Professionals (AMPROM), which intends to shepherd *Beyond the Turnstile* into the Spanish language. We look forward to that happening.

Benjamin Cutter's technical editing at the end of the process was indispensable. We also appreciate Susana Bautista's work transcribing and editing the IMI lectures at the Getty and the Los Angeles County Museum of Art so that they could appear in this book. Francisca González Arias has been our constant and devoted translator from the Spanish. And our thanks are extended to Professor Roberto Diaz for bringing her to us.

We are deeply grateful to the Ahmanson Foundation, the American Embassy in Mexico, and Mexicana Airlines. Their financial support was critical to the book's completion. AltaMira Press and its extraordinary publishing and editing staff has made this book a concrete reality.

Beyond the Turnstile and the sustainable values it makes the case for would not have come into being without all the work and workshops of the International Museum Institute. This book is the culmination of participation from around the globe, including representatives from the United States of America, Mexico, Canada, Venezuela, New Zealand, Australia, Abu Dhabi, Spain, France, England, Turkey, and Iraq. Nor would it have come into being had not everyone accepted that we would be taking a transdisciplinary museum perspective—art, history, biology, science, gardens, and cultural history museums were represented—that we would be including large and small museums alike, and that we were welcoming to the conversation a cross-section of all those who have a stake in museums: the visitor, conservator, director, curator, critic, academic, trustee, donor, and grant-giver, along with our private boards or government-based ministries or funders.

We both know that without the ongoing, daily, ordinary and extraordinary support of our husbands, we would never have had the fortitude to bring this book project together. Fred Croton and Javier Irribaren are our mainstays. Thank you, gracias!

We would like to mention here the following people, in alphabetical order by country and name, who have helped shaped the Institute's workshops and the resulting book in numerous ways: by the contribution of their essays, their presentations at workshops, the donation of their art, their financial support, their advice, or inestimable encouragement. Some, like Michael Goran and Michael Brand, have collaborated with us institutionally. They all have our gratitude for their essays, their participation in our workshops and conferences, or their advice and good counsel.

SH
MA

THE EDITORIAL COMMITTEE

Mariana Amatullo
Marco Barrera Bassols
Faya Causey
Miguel Fernández Félix
Ramiro Martínez
Graciela de la Torre
Tim B. Wride

Abu Dhabi

Charles Merewether

Australia

Des Griffin

Canada

Lori Starr

England

James Walvin

France

Bernard Müller

Iraq

Donny George Youkhanna

Mexico

Alejandro de Ávila Blomberg
Plinio Avila
Marco Barrera Bassols
Bertha Cea
Graciela Cervantes de Ortiz
Jack Corbett
Karen Cordero
Alfredo Cruz
Gerardo Estrada Rodríguez
Eduardo Gamboa
María Isabel Grañén Porrúa
Alfredo Harp Helú
Claudina López Moralez
Elena Matute
Carlos Monsiváis
Susana Pliego
Nelly M. Robles García
Arturo Souto
Francisco Toledo
Jesús Sanchez Uribe
Lilio Weber
Quetzalli Gallery, Oaxaca

New Zealand

Vanda Vitali

Nicaragua

Ernesto Cardinal

Spain

Plácido Arango
Javier Arnaldo

Leticia Azcue Brea
Santiago Palomero
Jorge Wagensberg

Turkey

Ilber Ortayli

United States

Lita Albuquerque
Kay Allen
Maxwell L. Anderson
Joseph Aoun
Anthony Appiah
Malcolm Baker
Elazar Barkan
Susana Bautista
Marla Berns
David Bomford
Michael Brand
Elliot Davis
James Elkins
Jim Ellis
Shelly Errington
Steven Evans
James Folsom
Tom Freudenheim
Karen Symms Gallagher
Ralph Gatchal
Edward Goldman
Michael Govan
John Gray
Larry Gross
Ashton Hawkins
Fredrik Hiebert
Linda Komaroff
Leonard Krishtalka
Aleca Le Blanc
Mary Lenihan
Gregorio Luke
Clare Lyons
Gary Matthews Jr.

Kevin McCarthy
Phil Nowlen
Jane Pisano
Carrie Przybilla
Steven Seidel
Jon L. Seydl
Alan Shestack
Cherise Smith
Jonathan Spaulding
Gary Vikan
Tim Whalen
Jay Wiegel
Ari Wiseman
David Wilson

Venezuela

Guillermo Barrios

All images courtesy of Quetzalli Gallery. Special thanks to the Gallery and its owners, C.P. Graciela Cervantes de Ortiz and Arq. Claudina Lòpez Morales for their generous permission to publish the images and details of the images herein.

The art in this book is by Francisco Toledo from his *INSECTARIO* 1995–1996, published by the Galería Quetzalli and El Museo de Arte Contemporàneo de Oaxaca (MACO). The photographs of the images used in this book are by Jesús Sanchez Uribe.

Francisco Toledo is considered by many to be Mexico's greatest painter. He has been very influential among contemporary Mexican artists. Toledo has had many international exhibitions including in France, the United States, and recently, a major retrospective at Whitechapel in London. He has been the major force in reclaiming Oaxaca, Mexico, as a "city of the arts." Francisco Toledo's generosity in allowing us to use his art in whole and in detail is unparalleled.

Index